History and Financial Crisis

One striking weakness of our financial architecture, which helped bring on and perhaps deepen the Panic of 2008, is an inadequate appreciation of the past. *History and Financial Crisis: Lessons from the 20th Century* is an attempt to broaden the range of historical sources used by policy makers to understand and treat financial crises. Many recent discussions of the 2008 panic and the economic turmoil have found the situation to either be unprecedented or greatly similar to that of 1931. However, this book's wide range of expert contributors suggest that the economic crisis of 2008 cannot be categorised in this way.

This book was originally published as a special issue of *Business History*, and includes a new and comprehensive concluding chapter on the use and abuse of financial history

Christopher Kobrak is Professor of Finance at ESCP Europe, Paris and of Business and Financial History at Rotman School of Management, University of Toronto. An International Fellow at the Centre for Corporate Reputation, Oxford University, he serves on the editorial boards of several business history journals. A CPA and former business practitioner, his publications include *Banking on Global Markets: Deutsche Bank and the United States, 1870 to the Present* and *European Business, Dictatorship and Political Risk, 1920-1945* (edited with Per Hansen), as well as journal articles on a wide range of business and financial topics.

Mira Wilkins is Professor of Economics at Florida International University, Miami, USA. She has published numerous books and articles on the history of multinational enterprise and of foreign investment in general. She is currently undertaking research for the third volume of her history of foreign investment in the United States, covering 1945 to the present.

History and Financial Crisis

Lessons from the 20th Century

Edited by
Christopher Kobrak and Mira Wilkins

Routledge
Taylor & Francis Group

LONDON AND NEW YORK

First published 2013
by Routledge
2 Park Square, Milton Park, Abingdon, Oxon, OX14 4RN

Simultaneously published in the USA and Canada
by Routledge
711 Third Avenue, New York, NY 10017

Routledge is an imprint of the Taylor & Francis Group, an informa business

© 2013 Taylor & Francis

This book is a reproduction of the *Business History*, volume 53, issue 2. The Publisher requests to those authors who may be citing this book to state, also, the bibliographical details of the special issue on which the book was based.

British Library Cataloguing in Publication Data
A catalogue record for this book is available from the British Library

ISBN13: 978-0-415-62297-4

Typeset in Times New Roman
by Taylor & Francis Books

Publisher's Note
The publisher would like to make readers aware that the chapters in this book may be referred to as articles as they are identical to the articles published in the special issue. The publisher accepts responsibility for any inconsistencies that may have arisen in the course of preparing this volume for print.

Printed and bound in the United States of America by Publishers Graphics, LLC on sustainably sourced paper.

Contents

Citation Information

The following chapters were originally published in the journal *Business History*, volume 53, issue 2 (April 2011). When citing this material, please use the original page numbering for each article, as follows:

Chapter 1
The '2008 Crisis' in an economic history perspective: Looking at the twentieth century
Christopher Kobrak and Mira Wilkins
Business History, volume 53, issue 2 (April 2011) pp. 175-192

Chapter 2
Financial crisis, contagion, and the British banking system between the world wars
Mark Billings and Forrest Capie
Business History, volume 53, issue 2 (April 2011) pp. 193-215

Chapter 3
New perspectives on the 1931 banking crisis in Germany and Central Europe
Christopher Kopper
Business History, volume 53, issue 2 (April 2011) pp. 216-229

Chapter 4
Banks and Swedish financial crises in the 1920s and 1930s
Mikael Lönnborg, Anders Ögren and Michael Rafferty
Business History, volume 53, issue 2 (April 2011) pp. 230-248

Chapter 5
Canada and the United States: Different roots, different routes to financial sector regulation
Donald J.S. Brean, Lawrence Kryzanowski and Gordon S. Roberts
Business History, volume 53, issue 2 (April 2011) pp. 249-269

Chapter 6
The effect of banking crises on deposit growth: State-level evidence from 1900 to 1930
Carlos D. Ramirez
Business History, volume 53, issue 2 (April 2011) pp. 270-287

Notes on Contributors

Mark Billings is Senior Lecturer in Accounting and Business History at the University of Exeter Business School, UK. He is a chartered accountant and has previously worked in banking and business. His research interests are in accounting, business and financial history and financial reporting.

Donald J.S. Brean is Professor of Finance and Economics at the Rotman School of Management, University of Toronto, Co-director of the G20 Research Group and immediate past Directeur, Centre d'Études de la France et du Monde Francophone. His research focuses on international finance and economic integration. He is the co-author of *International financial management: Canadian perspectives* (2nd ed., 2008).

Forrest Capie is Emeritus Professor of Economic History, Cass Business School, London. He is a former editor of the *Economic History Review* and has published widely on banking, financial and monetary history. His latest book is *The Bank of England, 1950s to 1979* (Cambridge: Cambridge University Press, 2010).

Christopher Kobrak is Professor of Finance at ESCP Europe, Paris and of Business and Financial History at Rotman School of Management, University of Toronto. An International Fellow at the Centre for Corporate Reputation, Oxford University, he serves on the editorial boards of several business history journals. A CPA and former business practitioner, his publications include *Banking on Global Markets: Deutsche Bank and the United States, 1870 to the Present* and *European Business, Dictatorship and Political Risk, 1920-1945* (edited with Per Hansen), as well as journal articles on a wide range of business and financial topics.

Christopher Kopper is Professor of History at Universität Bielefeld, Germany. He received his PhD in Modern History from Ruhr-Universität Bochum in 1992. He is the author of several books on the history of banking and finance in twentieth-century Germany.

Lawrence Kryzanowski is Concordia University Research Chair in Finance. He has published widely in the fields of finance and economics, and is on the editorial board of a number of journals. He is actively engaged as an expert witness and consultant for various governmental and corporate entities and individuals.

Mikael Lönnborg is Associate Professor at the BI Norwegian Business School, Department of Innovation and Economic Organisation, Centre for Business History

(SNH), Oslo, Norway and Södertörn University, Department of Business Studies, Stockholm, Sweden. His most recent publication is the anthology *Business History in Sweden*, (Hedemora: Gidlunds, 2011), co-edited with Paulina Rytkönen.

Anders Ögren is Associate Professor at Uppsala Centre for Business History (UCBH), Department of Economic History at Uppsala University, Sweden and also teaching at SciencesPo in Paris, France. His main research is within financial and monetary history and history of economic thought. More recent books are in 2012 *The Gold Standard Peripheries. Monetary policy, adjustment and flexibility in a global setting* (Ed. with Lars-Fredrik Øksendal), and in 2010 *The Swedish Financial Revolution* (Ed.), both at London: Palgrave MacMillan.

Michael Rafferty is Research Fellow in the School of Business at the University of Sydney, Australia. He is currently an Australian Research Council Future Fellow 2012-2016. Recent publications, together with Dick Bryan, are 'Financial derivatives and the theory of money', *Economy and Society*, 36(1), 134–158 and *Capitalism with derivatives: A political economy of financial derivatives, capital and class* (London: Palgrave Macmillan, 2006).

Carlos D. Ramirez is Associate Professor of Economics at George Mason University and a Visiting Fellow at the FDIC's Centre for Financial Research. He received his MA in 1991 and PhD in 1993 in economics from Harvard University. His major fields of research are banking and banking regulation, financial economic history, corporate finance, as well as international macroeconomics and political economics.

Gordon S. Roberts is CIBC Professor of Financial Services at the Schulich School of Business, York University. Well published in the research areas of banking and fixed income securities, he has served on a number of editorial boards and conducts an active consulting practice in financial and utility regulation.

Mira Wilkins is Professor of Economics at Florida International University, Miami, USA. She has published numerous books and articles on the history of multi-national enterprise and of foreign investment in general. She is currently undertaking research for the third volume of her history of foreign investment in the United States, covering 1945 to the present.

The '2008 Crisis' in an economic history perspective: Looking at the twentieth century

Christopher Kobrak[a] and Mira Wilkins[b]

[a]ESCP Europe, Paris, France; [b]Department of Economics, Florida International University, Miami, FL, USA

This introduction sets the articles in this special issue into their historical context and explores some of the definitional problems associated with discussions of financial and economic crises. It highlights some of the unifying themes and wider lessons of the papers found in the issue and makes the case for greater historical understanding of crises while outlining the limits of historical analogy.

We step and do not step into the same rivers; we are and are not. (Heraclitus, *Fragments*, quoted in Randall, 1970, p. 71)

Hegel bemerkt irgendwo, daß alle großen weltgeschichtlichen Tatsachen und Personen sich sozusagen zweimal ereignen. Er hat vergessen hinzuzufügen: das eine Mal als Tragödie, das andere Mal als Farce. [Hegel observes somewhere that all world historical events and persons occur twice. He forgot to add: once as tragedy, the second time as farce.] (Marx, 1869/1974, p. 226)

A matter of words

With all the tomes and articles already published on the '2008 Crisis', the reader might rightly ask the question: why a special issue about learning from history? The impetus for this issue of *Business History* was our belief that history, despite many excellent studies noted below, has paradoxically played too small and too large a role in some popular and academic discussions about the recent market turmoil.[1] We feel that the papers assembled here add new and cogent insights to the recent flood of literature, much of which draws on history, sadly sometimes by rejecting any historical parallels or in some cases by relying on just one narrowly defined precedent. We are convinced that policy makers, business practitioners, regulators, and academics still have much more to learn from history and hope that this special issue will serve to broaden our knowledge and understanding of how our financial world resembles and is distinct from past periods.

Indeed, without more historical distance and insight, merely labelling the 'financial crisis' that stimulated the recent surge of literature entails certain judgements about its nature that we probably cannot now hope to know. Should we call this the '2008 Crisis', as we have in the title, implying that it was a mere short-term banking crisis lasting a year, or the 'recent crisis', implying that it is finished, or the 'current crisis', implying that we are still in it? Historical analysis reminds us that those living through events rarely have sufficient perspective to judge the historical import and duration of what they are experiencing. They simply lack sufficient clairvoyance to know what is going to follow and are often swept up by the 'spirit' of the times.

'Our crisis' – to use a much less charged term – was probably born in early 2008 out of the earlier bursting of a property bubble, which had been nurtured by fragile financial devices.[2] At the time of this writing (September 2010), we have already witnessed capital market calamities, heightened perception of counterparty risk, a nearly worldwide downturn in production and higher unemployment, and wide-spread government efforts to bolster liquidity and confidence. Despite many calming signs, the recovery has been marked by a great deal of uncertainty, a strong sense of not knowing whether the hopeful indicators signal the beginning of the end or the eye of the hurricane. But in many popular accounts, there are no shortages of historical parallels between this crisis and others, many of which encourage only a bleak outlook. Extreme rhetoric, such as 'the worst crisis since the Great Depression' or, as one author put it in his title, 'the failure of capitalism and the descent into depression', is frequently heard without much regard for how and why the causes, cures, dimensions, and timing of other crises might resemble or differ from this one, or, for that matter, how some crises of the second half of the twentieth century witnessed deeper downturns and higher unemployment levels, at least in the United States, than this one (see Posner, 2009).[3] While some pundits claim that this crisis has no precedent, others see it as repeat of (or preface to) what occurred in 1929–33, comparable to the 'crisis of 1933' or to the entire 1930s, and, accordingly, must be met with precisely the measures central banks and governments failed to apply then. In any case, a lot of the prescriptions for remedies to the current situation use historical analogy or conversely historical exceptionalism based on *classifications* of and *extrapolations* from current events for which there is only limited intellectual justification.

With this in mind, we beg the readers' indulgence should we slip into terminology that is not intended to imply answers to the above largely unanswerable questions about how our current circumstances will evolve. For the purposes of this paper, we will use the terms '2008 Crisis', 'recent crisis', 'current crisis' and even just 'our crisis' interchangeably without implying anything about its causes or duration.

Our call for papers (September 2009) was for a Special Issue 'On History and the Economic Crisis' and indicated that the issue would focus on the lessons that can be derived from historical analysis on the nature and timing of economic crises. Soon we realised that our original terminology was problematic. The very breadth of responses indicated how much is contained under the rubric 'economic crisis', a fact that highlighted the need for further clarification about what counts as a crisis, economic or otherwise. Understandably, many of the authors here also felt compelled to tackle this issue.

Although our call for papers used the term 'economic crisis', nearly all of the submissions focused on 'financial crises' that were connected to broader economic breakdowns. The two terms are distinct, but in terms of our discussion, seem unavoidably linked. This led the two authors of this introduction to a fruitful, but by no means conclusive, debate on the relationship of financial and economic crises. Given the importance of these two terms to economics and economic history, the absence of a strong consensus or at least a range of options about definitions seems a little odd. Although some of our authors to their credit explore this tricky area, most papers and books dealing with the current or past crises give little or no thought to defining the terms. Even the *Oxford dictionary of economics* gives no definition of 'crisis, economic or financial', merely explanations of balance-of-payments, debt and oil crises (Black, 2002).

Charles P. Kindleberger used the term 'financial crises' in the subtitle of his classic *Manias, panics, and crashes*. But he recognised that there was a fundamental issue about the relationship between 'financial' and 'economic' crises. Although financial breakdowns may arise when other markets weaken – labour or housing, for example – or when the prices of securities lose any kind of meaningful relationship with the real assets they represent, the term 'economic crisis' has tended to be more associated with severe drops in indicators such as employment and Gross Domestic Product, which may themselves be spill-over effects from financial or other events. Kindleberger was clearly not interested in cyclical economic downturns, but he knew that 'turbulent financial prices' evolved into crises as they threatened broader economic indicators. For him the terms 'financial and economic crises' were separate but intertwined. Like our own crisis, so many previous ones began with a downturn in some asset class or some broad based economic indictors, which in turn affected others and then seemed to spiral out of control. In the first edition of his volume on *Manias, panics, and crashes*, published in 1978, Kindleberger was very specific on his subject matter, emphasising the linkage between 'financial and economic crisis':

> Financial crises are associated with the peaks of business cycles. We are not interested in the business cycle as such, the rhythm of economic expansion and contraction, but only in the financial crisis that is the culmination of a period of expansion and leads to the downturn. If there be business cycles without financial crises, they lie out of our interest. On the other hand, financial crises that prove so manageable as to have no effects on the economic system will also be neglected. The financial crisis we shall consider here are major both in size and in effect and, as a rule, international in scope. (Kindleberger, 1978, p. 3)

In later editions, Kindleberger confessed his failing to define 'financial crises', asserting that this key term, like many others, may be beyond some sort of Socratic precise and generally agreed clarification (Kindleberger, 2000, pp. 3–4).[4] While there is much to be said for his view, others do not share it. Kindleberger himself brings in the views of two distinguished scholars. He quotes Raymond Goldsmith, who wrote that a financial crisis was 'a sharp, brief, ultracyclical deterioration of all or most of a group of financial indicators – short-term interest rates, asset (stock, real estate, land) prices, commercial insolvencies and failure of financial institutions', specifically excluding foreign-exchange difficulties as a necessary feature. Kindleberger contrasts Goldsmith with Michael Bordo, who listed 10 elements of financial crisis, including, as two of our authors do, reduction in money supply. Interestingly, Bordo includes perceptions such as a change in expectations and fear of financial institution insolvency (Kindleberger, 2000, pp. 3–4).

Although Kindleberger may have been right to avoid a precise definition – perhaps recognising that what is perceived as a financial crisis at any time might be a function of the economic and social context in which 'financial turbulence' occurs – for some discussions a definition may be absolutely necessary. It plays a crucial role in Mark Billings and Forrest Capie's argument in this volume, for example. According to them, Britain avoided a financial crisis in the early 1930s. They take as their starting point Anna Jacobson Schwartz's definition of a 'real financial crisis' as one that poses a threat to the money stock, thereby threatening the whole payment system. Other authors, including several of our contributors, prefer to refer to specific kinds of crises, such as banking, avoiding the more generic term, but for many reasons even this is not so simple, as several authors in this issue and elsewhere have pointed out.

Like Kindleberger, we are inclined to think of financial crises in terms of 'manias and panics'. This means for us situations in which financial and real assets radically depart from fundamental values, fluctuate wildly, and have been supplemented or sustained by a blind faith that recent historical movements – both positive and negative – will continue indefinitely. This notion then includes both an economic and a psychological component, which are terribly difficult to recognise even with historical distance.

This line of thinking has led over the past few decades to some of the most fruitful developments in financial theory. But although much of modern finance's attempts to integrate sentiment into our understanding of markets relies to a large extent and crucially on historical insights, behavioural finance's insights are still far from complete and economic history's input in characterising market 'abnormalities' and untangling myths is still hardly acknowledged (Forbes, 2009).[5] Some financial theorists view bubbles as periods when we undervalue risk and panics conversely as periods where it is overvalued. But to date no one has come up with a convincing benchmark for a universally valid risk premium – or even some vague methods of how one might calculate it for future investment – and perhaps more importantly some general notion of what creates and constitutes bubbles and panics. Duration, degree and depiction of irrational emotions play a role in whether risk is being reasonably assessed or not at any given time, but how much and in what way they affect or are a part of market sentiment during bubbles or panics is less clear. Is the element of panic crucial, or the level of danger of future panic, or the extent of the collapse? Perhaps the severity of the downturn has less to do with the economic crisis (or the sense of crisis) than the amount of perceived uncertainty or surprise associated with circumstances.

A similar line of questioning applies to labelling crises. Not only is there a broad range of types and causes for 'economic and financial crises', but degree is a factor in differentiating a normal downturn in a regular business cycle from a crisis. How sharp a drop in employment and economic growth must occur before we call a reversal of economic circumstances a crisis? How long does it have to last? For this we had better turn to historical enquiry, at least as a starting point for evaluating and understanding perceptions of severity.

As Mark Billings and Forrest Capie as well as other authors in this collection point out, perhaps globalisation may tend to magnify a sense of despair. The more localised a financial or economic crisis remains, or perhaps the less people know of the despair of others, the easier it may be to maintain hope. As Carlos Ramirez argues here, individual American states did a lot to avoid the worst effects of financial panics by containing their impact. World contagion may reinforce a sense of panic in the same way as pandemics may be scarier than local outbreaks of disease.

We have provided no absolute definition of either financial or economic crises here – merely something about the importance and difficulty of defining and distinguishing them. Although most of the papers in this issue deal with what is better called a financial crisis rather than an economic crisis, the real question is why do some very serious financial crises turn into broad economic crises and others not. Some of the papers here stress the importance of financial regulation; all in one way or another acknowledge the importance of path determinacy in explaining the breadth and depth of crises. As testimony to the importance of financial markets, finding a major economic downturn that did not arise or become more virulent because of turmoil in the world of securities, bank lending, and foreign exchange seems well-nigh impossible. This collection of articles, however, deals with how and why some severe disruptions in financial markets and banking arose and, in turn, affected (or did not affect) broader economic indicators in the twentieth century.

Historical contexts and lessons

We hope that our selections for this issue – with a little historical distance from the beginning of a crisis that in many ways is still with us – will help us learn from the past. But historical lessons are tricky. As economic historians we should understand this. Although Kindleberger, one of the greatest economic (and financial) historians, tried to synthesise the two, he recognised at the outset that 'History is particular; economics is general' (Kindleberger, 1978, p. 14, and repeated in each subsequent edition). It is a methodological tension that he understood well could be both productive or debilitating; part of our intention is that these essays make some contribution to reconciling the two by showing how good economic history integrates the general with the particular, showing how historians might address broad economic questions and exposing economists to the complex historical data necessary for good theory.

All the essays included in this issue highlight what is commonplace and unique in their subjects. At times, this detail of historical narrative is frustrating for those looking for a higher level of generalisation with which to build theory. The lessons imparted by history tend to be cautionary tales or rather exercises in expanding the imagination rather than precise policy roadmaps. Although the *American heritage dictionary* defines 'lessons' as 'an experience or observation that imparts beneficial knowledge or wisdom (or what is learned in such a manner)', our positivist age tends to favour knowledge that helps predict and control. Historical lessons contribute more to deepening our understanding of what is true, right, and lasting, in short, wisdom that is much less systematically and scientifically defended (Morris, 1969, pp. 750, 1469).

The Nobel Prize-winning economist and columnist, Paul Krugman, has pointed out correctly that this crisis is not without precedent. True, in one sense, but we should also not be beguiled into thinking that the study of the past alone offers us sufficient information to know when and how hard a crisis will hit, and, more importantly, enough information to programme a GPS system (Krugman, 2008). While a better understanding of history might have helped policy makers, as Krugman rightly also acknowledges, studying the past rather provides a broader vision of possible outcomes with which to navigate between hysteria and complacency (see, for example, Krugman, 2009).[6] Even a cursory review of the past suggests that the range of sensible counter-measures and outcomes for this economic downturn is far broader than most commentators imagine. In any case, probing the past is probably the only effective way to escape the noise of daily hand wringing and spurious comparisons, which characterises much of the press and popular literature.

One of the lessons of history, then, is that our own perceptions and prescriptions for common sense and good judgement are deeply embedded in the economic spirit of our times. Part of the wisdom we can attain from history is a sense of how the questions we ask of and the answers we frame from historical analysis are themselves shaped or conditioned (not determined) by our times. For nearly 30 years preceding 2007, for example, many policy makers and social scientists gained confidence that they could prevent financial crises from turning into broader economic ones.

Some of Kindleberger's financial crises (documented in the later editions of the book) could hardly be called economic crises, a problem that seems to haunt particularly the fifth edition of *Manias, panics and crashes*, published in 2005. The first edition of Kindleberger's classic account of manias, panics, and crashes was published in 1978 and written in the context of the demise of Bretton Woods and the memories of the Great Depression. Each new edition has had to deal with and integrate the new and evolving financial architecture of the post-Bretton Woods period and has been updated in light of the new economic experiences and theory. In the last two decades of the twentieth century, however, crises seemed to have become milder and more controllable, reinforcing the faith held by many that panics were events of the past.

The effects of financial or other market price distortions of the 1982–2001 period had little or no immediately palpable negative effect on the overall economy. One by one, circumstances or events came and went without a worldwide calamity following: the Latin American debt crisis, the mid-1980s dollar rate readjustment, the 1987 stock market crash, the savings and loan crisis, the bursting of the Japanese real estate bubble, several emerging market crises, as will be discussed, the Long-term Capital Management (LTCM) failure, the bursting of the dot.com bubble, Enron and 9/11. For nearly 20 years financial markets facilitated the US's twin (domestic and foreign) deficits with no crash. Most of the world seemed to have embraced liberal capitalism. Small wonder that investors and regulators came to believe that historical patterns had been broken, justifying much lower risk premiums. Although Kindleberger's fourth and fifth editions incorporated most of the events discussed above, the fifth edition did not update the Appendix, with its 'Stylized outline of financial crises, 1618–1998'. Thus, in the 2005 edition, not only was the bailout of LTCM excluded but so was the dot.com bubble from the Appendix. This fifth edition of *Manias, panics and crashes*, co-authored with Robert Aliber, which appeared after Kindleberger's July 2003 death, was released during the high tide of optimism about our ability, with a little help from social scientists and politicians, to rely on seemingly 'failsafe' market mechanisms to contain human economic frailties (Kindleberger & Aliber, 2005). We now know that many of the very measures designed to protect society from economic pain had hidden, long-term costs (Rajan, 2010, pp. 21–45).

One of the liabilities of focusing on financial crises that are linked to broader breakdowns or that reflect only our most pressing concerns is that some of the scariest financial events float off our radar screen. The collapse and successful bailout of LTCM provides a sad, but instructive example for this phenomenon. That event, along with the US savings and loan problems and the meltdown of the emerging market bubble at the end of the last century share many elements of our current crisis. Although in some sense the focus of the crisis was one American institution, these crises were in many respects global. Ignited by turbulence in emerging markets, LTCM's downfall came to a head in the context of new types of global transactions and institutions, part of whose competitive advantage lay in circumventing national regulatory control. The resolution of the LTCM crisis required the participation of traditional banks from all over the world.

Founded in 1996 by some of the best minds in finance, Long-term Capital Management was an institution many believed could not fail. Like the Titanic before it, hubris was a fatal flaw. With two Nobel Prize Laureates who had themselves developed the pricing mechanism used all over the world for valuing options as well as by the best traders on Wall Street, LTCM sought to exploit pricing differences, even very small ones, between markets. Like other hedge funds, providing abnormal returns to investors, it relied on its ability to keep its trading strategies secret, and to reduce taxes and other transaction costs. Recording transactions in offshore entities (in places such as the Cayman Islands) helped with both. Its first years were very successful, but as imitators copied its methods, profits fell. Management took on more debt and became more aggressive about applying the firm's impressive mathematical modelling to more and more markets, some of which were later found to be unsuited for their formulas. As the Russian and Asian financial crises unfolded, LTCM's losses mounted, eating away at its thin capitalisation. The Federal Reserve got wind of the problem. Much like J.P. Morgan nearly 100 years earlier, they called in the big banks and brokerage houses which had lent funds to LTCM in the hopes of attracting more of its lucrative transactions (Lowenstein, 2000).

The 1998 bailout allowed the company to unwind its positions over time, reducing the ultimate losses for everyone, and relieving the world of a huge threat to the financial system. LTCM had become not only too big but also too complicated to fail, even though its balance sheet contained less than 25% of the derivative instruments held by just one major bank, Citibank, 10 years later. By 2008 derivative trading had grown to nearly $500 trillion (as measured by the notional value of contracts), much in the form of hugely complicated over-the-counter (OTC) instruments without normal market controls and often traded by unregulated and opaque institutions, which themselves had difficulty pricing their own positions, in what some characterise as financial 'black pools' (Erturk, Froud, Johal, Leaver, & Williams, 2008, pp. 7–8).

That most people hit by and worried about the current economic state of the world have never heard of LTCM – even those for whom the term sub-prime mortgage is an everyday expression – is in some sense testimony to regulatory and banker prowess in working out the problem, but sadly, the success had another unintended effect. It lulled both regulators' and bankers' perception about the risks of dealing with extremely complex hedging products and strategies aggressively promoted by private, often offshore entities, whose financial viability was extremely hard to assess. Bankers and regulators seemed to reinforce each other's faith that market mechanisms coupled with an occasional governmental tweak were sufficient to tame animal passions of financial engineers and any genies they conjured out of bottles.

As mentioned, recent editions of Kindleberger's classic on financial crises discuss LTCM management, but the collapse of this new form of institution, a kind of hybrid bank-hedge fund, is not to be found in the book's Appendix. It does include the emerging market crisis of 1998, suggesting that Kindleberger and his co-author may have had some difficulty in evaluating the place of these new institutions, instruments and the risks they posed in his schema. Given his original intent, however, the exclusion may have been completely deliberate. As Kindleberger explained even in the first edition of *Manias, panics, and crashes* and noted earlier: 'financial crises that prove so manageable as to have no effects on the economic system will ... be neglected' (Kindleberger, 1978, p. 3).

The events of 2008 put the relationships between financial and economic crises once more into the spotlight, and with it the importance of many recent financial innovations. In this vein, it seemed useful to expand Kindleberger's oft-cited Appendix including LTCM (for 1998) and providing key features of the crises of 2001 and 2008–09 (Table 1). While some aspects of the decade after 1998 do not fit neatly into Kindleberger's schema, others do very nicely. Of course, it is premature to take very seriously a stylised rendition of 2008–09. We date the 2008–09 crisis a little differently, but as noted for some commentators, that crisis was the result of sustained monetary expansion and bubble dating back to at least the early 1990s, if not longer.

Crises take shape in the context of particular historical contexts, and attitudes about what financial and political actors should do. The history of bubbles and panics is intertwined with the question of whether and when governments, alone or together, should intervene. This very line of enquiry is at odds with some key points of post-Bretton Woods financial economics. Kindleberger's question and some of his answers about defining and controlling crises must be set against the dominant Keynesian thinking of the post-World War II quarter-century, just as much as more

Table 1. Stylised outline of financial crises, 1998–2008, following Kindleberger.

Year	1998	2001	2008–09
Countries (cities): related to crisis	New York: US and Western Europe	United States: Europe	New York and London: Worldwide, especially United States, United Kingdom, and parts of continental Europe
Preceding speculation in	Emerging markets, derivative instruments	Equities, especially dot.com and energy trading	Housing, derivatives, private collateralised and government debt
Monetary expansion from	1992	1998*	2001*
Speculative peak	1997	2000	2006
Crisis (crash, panic)	1998	2001	2008
Lender of last resort	Federal Reserve, multinational banks and brokerage houses	Federal Reserve	Federal Reserve, European Central Bank, International Monetary Fund

Note: *The dating of the beginning of the monetary expansion is somewhat controversial. Looking at the period from 1992 through 2006 as one period of nearly continuous monetary expansion has some merit.

recent reluctance to tamper with markets must be seen against the successes of those markets in the last two decades of the twentieth century and the dominant trends in economic thinking. While some historians tend to believe that through history we might learn if and when financial regulators should step in to mitigate bubbles or the effects of their bursting, modern financial economics has led in the opposite direction. The events of the past few years have posed many intellectual problems for mainstream financial economists, especially those who tend to rely on what is called the Efficient Market Hypothesis (EMH) and mathematical modelling, while downplaying the importance of institutions and *ipso facto* their histories (MacKenzie, 2006).

But for those economists schooled in the various forms, especially the weak and semi-strong varieties, of the EMH, the very idea of bubbles and panics is almost unintelligible.[7] If the market has integrated all relevant information into market values, how can we second-guess it by calling some upswings bubbles and some downswings panics? The Catch-22 of modern economics is that if a reliable way of knowing that we were in a bubble or even in a panic, an overreaction to market fundamentals, were known, that information would be integrated into market prices, bursting the bubble or alleviating the panic. While clearly the Fed and Treasury have responsibility to provide liquidity when markets block, the Nobel Laureate Robert Lucas raised the question, implied by the EMH, on what basis should any central bank or government official take pre-emptive measures to counteract potential threats, when they are only potential and not real (Lucas, 2009, p. 63). Financial economists have understandably been criticised for not realising that the fall of housing and mortgage backed securities prices would lead to a financial meltdown. But how do we know, when they are happening, that an upturn is a bubble? Moreover, not all bursting of bubbles lead to spin-off calamities. Why did this one and not the dot.com bubble end the euphoria? Realistically, too, as will be discussed, there are many historical warnings for policy makers indicating that their measures may have many unforeseen consequences and that even some of the best intended palliative antidotes can be worse than the disease they are suppose to cure.

Nevertheless, some economic historians believe that they can untie this Gordian Knot. The quest to find a typology or universal cause of financial crises and then economic crises – and with it, of course, a cure or, at least, some hope of dealing with them – is a long one indeed. The quest has a political and an intellectual component, both of which tend to push the search toward very clear actionable diagnoses and remedies. Despite Kindleberger's many cautionary remarks about the nature of history and defining crises, many scholars and popular writers – perhaps including Kindleberger himself – have tried to first categorise and then generalise about crises. It should be kept in mind that defining bubbles, even with historical hindsight, can be tricky. We all would probably agree and some of us wrote that capital markets had gone crazy circa 2000, but when Alan Greenspan made his famous 'irrational exuberance' remark in 1996 the Dow was just over 6000 and probably not terribly overvalued. Indeed, technological changes and market discipline justified greater faith in equities – in the 1990s and early twenty-first century.[8]

Understandably, the present crisis has brought out a new collection of books that promise the Holy Grail of economic history[9] – a universal explanation and cure for crises. One of the most often cited and plausible explanations of both bubbles and their ensuing crashes (crises) is the prevalence of debt financing, but the desire to generalise can lead to trite formulations. Take, for example, a key sentence from the preface of one of the best new books on the subject: 'If there is one common theme to the vast range of crises we consider in this book, it is that *excessive* (the stress is ours) debt accumulation, whether it be by government, banks, corporations, or consumers, often poses greater systemic risks than it seems during a boom' (Reinhart & Rogoff, 2009, preface, p. xxv). While some may interpret Reinhart and Rogoff as meaning that 'excessive debt' is a necessary but not sufficient condition for booms to turn ugly, they beg the key question: how much debt is too much?

Any basic finance book – since the 1930s – teaches that debt increases risk. Finance texts also teach, however, that there are many forms of debt, each with its own and varying degrees of risks, which can best be evaluated in the context of how and why the borrowing is being done. For example, companies, countries, and individuals who borrow short-term for long-term projects and in currencies other than the ones that they control take on more risk than those that do not. Taking on debt for economically value adding projects may increase risk but it can also enhance the value of the project. As an article in the *Financial Times* reminded us, much depends on how we spend the funds, whether on projects that really increase future productivity or just sustain current consumption (El-Eriam, 2010). Some of the serious financial crises of the past, moreover, had little to do with the accumulation of debt; for example, the collapse of the Bretton Woods arrangements.

The issue itself

This special issue was intended to address these topics. We welcomed articles covering a wide geographic area that dealt with specific crises in history from which lessons could be learned, that debunked false analogies, recounted journalistic and other popular portrayals of crises as they were unfolding, discussed typologies of crises, including their dating and origin, and also papers that dealt generally with the subject of drawing policy lessons from history. Based on the submissions, we had to limit our initially broad endeavour.

We have several regrets. Our original plan was to include papers covering the last few centuries. In reviewing the many promising proposals, this much wider temporal scope yielded a special issue without sufficient thematic unity. While the decision to select papers related only to the twentieth century has given the special issue more unity, it has also contributed to leaving us with papers more heavily weighted on the early 1930s than we had hoped. But given that the 'current crisis' has been called the 'Second Great Contraction' – with the first being that of the 1930s (Reinhart & Rogoff, 2009) – it should not be surprising that the Depression plays a central role in this collection of essays.

The literature about crises prompted by recent events understandably keeps coming back to the 1929 New York Stock Market Crash, the 1930–32 US downturn, defaults in central Europe, and breakdown of the foreign exchange system. The dramatic rise and sustained high levels of unemployment during the decade of the 1930s alone made this period a pivotal reference point for historical inquiry into economic crises. Not only do many policy makers derive their views of what to do in financial crises from the failures of the 1930s, their reactions to the crisis will be measured against their success or failure in avoiding a repetition of its calamities, against which the shocks of the prior as well as the subsequent 80 years pale by comparison.

We were disappointed by the geographic distribution. Although the selected contributions contain some regional breadth and some country comparisons, we unfortunately received no proposals dealing with Asia – particularly Japan's problems in the 1990s – and Russia. And, we were sorry not to be able to include a paper on Latin American financial crises. We received surprisingly little on the United States. Only two of the papers presented here deal at all with the United States, one of the two, just by way of comparison to the Canadian experience. Through much of the past 150 years, the United States has been at the epicentre of most worldwide financial crises, no matter what their cause, duration, and effect. In some sense, however, American banking and capital markets are players in all the stories of this issue; in the twentieth century, American finance carried weight when present, and perhaps even more when absent. But the recent shakiness of European finances serves as a useful reminder that financial or other crises are rarely limited in time and space. Indeed, as important as the US economy is, perhaps a salient feature of the 2008–10 period, compared with the 1930s, for example, may be the similarities of country problems and reactions caused by the convergence of worldwide banking regulation.

Our disappointments aside, the issue includes five pieces, though differing in style and manner of argumentation, that deepen our understanding of financial crises. Some of the papers include new primary source materials; others are based on new databases and statistical analyses; and still others revisit older debates with new discussions of previously published work.

As implied by the above, much of what follows in this issue is built around two intertwined themes, regulation and globalisation. For much of the twentieth century, globalisation created a set of financial opportunities and challenges, and regulation a national response to them, a distinction that some may think the last 30 years has blurred. Some of the stories here deal with how well national regulation worked and others how it could exacerbate or even create problems, a useful lesson for those who believe that more regulation in and of itself is beneficial or, conversely, that increased fluidity of capital across borders is universally bad, good, or irrepressible.

We begin with Mark Billings and Forrest Capie's contribution for several reasons. Their essay forms a bridge between the 1930s and our recent crisis. Although by 1930 Britain had lost much of its financial clout, then and now, it was one of the 'capitals of capital' (Cassis, 2006), linked to the rest of the world by a complex network of financial agreements. Despite the breakdown of international payments, key British banks weathered the crisis admirably, avoiding many of the problems German and American banks suffered, and thereby a good many of the economic consequences suffered by the leading debtor and creditor nations. They remind us of how stable the British banking system was, despite the effects of World War I and the return to the gold standard, which leads to a fruitful discussion of the benefits of stability versus innovation. Arguing that the crisis was merely a foreign exchange issue, they deliver a nuanced account of the advantages and disadvantages of British banking, and the limits of globalisation in the 1930s that serves as a useful contrast to the present period. By highlighting foreign exchange problems – the role of the gold standard – faced by the United Kingdom in the 1930s, Billings and Capie's story, for example, emphasises the benefits of flexible foreign exchange rates in the adjustment process during our recent shocks.

No discussion of the financial crises would be complete without revisiting central Europe during the 1930s. Not only were the United States and Germany the two developed countries hit the hardest by the financial and economic crises, in Germany the political ramifications of the crises unleashed the horrors of World War II.

Building on his earlier work on the economics and politics of German banking in the 1930s, Christopher Kopper recounts the specifics of German banking regulation. Although Germany had a worldwide reputation for good regulation and sound banks prior to World War I, the powers given to the Reichsbank were not up to many of the demands placed on it after the war. A system that had relied on bankers' prudence and sense of social responsibility with light Reichsbank surveillance broke down for many reasons. In contrast to the view widely held by economists, Kopper argues that the monetary straightjacket which Germany wore was only a part of Germany's financial dilemma. After World War I German banks had less power, and perhaps also less inclination, to resist populist pressures and client demands for additional financing than many of their foreign investors in particular supposed.

One of the most powerful lessons in the issue is provided by Mikael Lönnborg, Anders Ögren, and Michael Rafferty in their essay about two Swedish crises occurring roughly a decade from one another. The first crisis involves the immediate destabilising effects, at least those prior to 1925, of World War I. Like many countries following the war, Sweden suffered sharp falls in national product and increases in unemployment, which were accompanied by declines in liquidity and financial valuations. But the crisis had its origins in structural capacity imbalances resulting from worldwide over-investment during World War I. The second was brought on by the collapse during the early 1930s of Ivar Kreuger's financial empire. Though based in Sweden, it was highly dependent on financing from many international centres and vulnerable to their vicissitudes. Not only did the crises have different origins, they entailed different degrees of connectedness with the world. They argue that whereas in the 1920s Sweden suffered more than most other developed countries, in the 1930s it suffered less. As in most countries and most times, buoyant economic conditions fed 'irrational exuberance' with debt. But as these authors contend, the severity of the first crisis led to stricter bank regulation and more cautious bank policies that helped shelter the country from the demise of the archetypical financial adventurer.

Collectively, the articles dealing with Europe paint a varied picture of national crises during the inter-war years, whose causes and development seem both close and distant to our own experience. Whereas the rigours of a fixed foreign exchange system no longer apply among the major currencies, they do within the euro and dollar zones. Fraud, heavy dependencies on foreign borrowing, much of which is relatively mobile and used to fund consumption, and the difficulty of adapting regulation to quickly changing, new and complicated economic circumstances are all still major parts of our financial environment.

From Europe then we move our attention to essays dealing with North America. For most of the past 100 years the vast size of the US economy in general and its financial markets in particular has ensured that most of US strengths and weaknesses have had a global reach. In their history of Canadian banking regulation, Donald Brean, Lawrence Kryzanowski, and Gordon Roberts contrast many of the failures of US banking regulation and their contribution to making the American (US) Depression the second steepest in the developed world (after Germany) with the prudence and political wisdom of Canadian regulators. Although national regulation is a leitmotif in all the pieces, in their comparison of the American and Canadian banking system, Brean, Kryzanowski, and Roberts delve into comparative path dependencies. These authors emphasise the benefits of Canadian traditions in stabilising that country's financial system. As they remind us, for all its economic strengths America has a rather chequered (to be generous) history of regulating financial markets and a low capacity for controlling populist sentiment, two causally connected features of the American landscape. Although Canada and the United States share many economic exchanges and cultural characteristics, Americans were slow to accept the advantages of centralising many elements of banking regulation. The fragmentation that dominated the American system left it more vulnerable to shocks than the Canadian and other systems. Like the Billings and Capie paper, the Canadian paper also raises the question of trade-offs between stability and innovation. While Canada has effectively reduced the impact of financial crises, the nation also lost many of the innovations that helped other markets become more vibrant centres of capital. Like Germany and France, for example, Canadian banks had to go to New York and London if they wanted to become serious players in world financial markets.

Carlos Ramirez's piece serves to balance the above Canadian view of how the fragmentation of the American banking system contributed to its weakness. If you will, we chose to end on an optimistic note. Like so many interesting stories about the United States, Ramirez shows how effective local regulation and responses can be, often leading the way to national progressive reform. Government responses, even state or local ones, can shape the aftermaths to a crisis' nadir. Using a newly constructed database of bank failures during the first 30 years of the twentieth century, he found that bank runs were effectively avoided in eight states which adopted deposit insurance. Analyses of bank failures during the 1980s and 1990s yield similar results, indicating that deposit insurance is a very effective tool in sheltering systems from panic in the case of rampant bank failures. His work suggests that many government responses to the recent crisis instituted under severe political pressures to ameliorate the effects of the financial turmoil may not have had as much effect as some of the long-standing protections, such as deposit insurance. As he also warns, government protection is not a panacea. It often comes with a very high price tag, which society has to bear.

Conclusion

We will have succeeded with this special issue if it helps us understand what we do not know, how both historical narrative and economic policy are forged and limited by their historical context. As bubbles build and burst, almost by definition, perspective is needed and all too often is lacking. Hubris and panic seem to be just two sides of an 'ill-balanced coin of the realm' before and during most financial crises. But distinguishing them from rational optimism and pessimism, especially as we are living with heated emotions and can only guess at an uncertain future, seems to be a quintessential human predicament.

Some of the essays here allude to this all-too-human dimension of history. For all the importance of institutions, we should not forget the importance of the people who build and work with them. As Marx observed well over 150 years ago, people make their own history, but 'in conditions' bequeathed to them by an historical process, for him largely economically determined (Marx, 1869/1974). Good historical narrative recognises the tension between 'path dependencies', accident, and individual foibles. Policy makers and bankers are not immune to human weakness. Like generals fighting the last war, sometimes they get stuck in old paradigms, as a recent book on the 'Lords of Finance' in the 1920s and 1930s points out (Ahamed, 2009). They lacked sufficient historical perspective to distinguish the commonplace and the uniqueness of their own situation. While understanding history is no guarantee against being trapped in the present, it is a good start.

But no matter how well it is done, historical study unfortunately can be both an ally and a hindrance in creating wisdom without a proper sense of its limits. As Nietzsche observed over 100 years ago, an over-reliance on history can breed a sense of determinism, overconfidence or its opposite, despair (Nietzsche 1873/1996). The run-up to and playing out of the recent crisis witnessed its share of both. Consider the hubris of many economists. Ben Bernanke is a well-known and careful student of the crisis of the 1930s. His devotion to its study appears to have influenced his handling of problems before and after panic hit in autumn 2008. According to one plausible source, when asked in the summer of 2008 about the likelihood of the 1930s' or 1990s' crises repeating themselves, Bernanke confidently replied that 'We have learned so much from the Great Depression and Japan, that we won't have either' (quoted in Sorkin, 2009, p. 221). Perhaps he is right or perhaps he was exuding some required central banker confidence, but perhaps also our fate will be that of so many other generations – to forge some new and unpleasant reality. One could argue that the very nature of panic implies unnerving new circumstances for which we cannot plan. Indeed, his very early policy decisions may have altered events in such a way as to make comparison with the 1930s Depression and the crisis in Japan in the 1990s less fruitful.

History does repeat itself, but which story? There are so many, and one of the enduring lessons is that despair or euphoria based on historical analogy is as common as it is dangerous. This in no way implies that economic historians are unable to highlight interesting patterns associated with financial crises, such as the added risk arising out of large increases in debt, especially foreign debt, financing. Rather it merely suggests that economic historians should recognise the complementary perspectives of both their parent disciplines – economics and history – namely, that there is both repetition and uniqueness in events. We may learn through history how to treat financial diseases with economic policies, but the precise dosing and timing of medicines need to differ with each occurrence.

Not only do crises have many causes, forms, and rhythms, as discussed in detail, there always seem to be spill-over effects, which exacerbate or change a crisis, making categorising crises hard to achieve. Although foreign exchange issues, for example, were not at the heart of the current crisis, private banks with huge amounts of foreign lending, including intra-firm transactions, found themselves unable to cover billions in foreign exchange positions. They turned to central banks in their currency zone, who in turn had to rely on foreign exchange swaps from other central banks to provide the necessary forward cover (Moessner & Allen, 2010). Almost all crises are in some way connected with irrational or corrupt behaviour. Some begin with their revelation; others reveal them relatively quickly. Some crises begin with exogenous shocks, like a war or natural disaster, and have dramatic beginnings and sometimes endings. Many, like the booms that often precede them, take on a life of their own, with one piece of bad news after another eliciting a crowd response, richly deserving the appellation panic. One of the recent discussions of the crisis has taken to calling it, with much justification, the Great Panic of 2008 (Wessel, 2009), a state of mind that may aptly describe both the initial cause and the later approaches to curing the ailment.

And the crises have many different outcomes, generally surprising ones for those living through them. For example, in contrast to conventional wisdom about crises, for many reasons not all lead to a collapse in demand and prices, a fact highlighted by several of the essays, most notably Billings and Capie and by implication Ramirez as well as Brean, Kryzanowski, and Roberts. History is rich with conflicting examples. With increasing government spending and deficits, the end of Bretton Woods, for example, demand and inflation grew. Growth was not strong in comparison to the previous decades, and inflation as well as free-floating foreign exchange rates produced dangerous economic volatility. But flexible (for some chaotic) macroeconomic conditions also may have contributed eventually to adjusting economies and cushioning against a politically unacceptable collapse of growth, in ways those who cut their financial teeth on fixed exchange rate system could hardly imagine in advance. On the other hand, one does not have to look far for examples of crises that lead to very slow or no growth and price deflation – Germany after 1873, the world after 1931, Japan in the 1990s, quickly come to mind. That our current problems might have aspects in common with all these earlier ones should have immense policy implications.

Even though dissecting the various kinds of crisis and their outcomes seems like such a natural starting point for policy makers, one wonders why there is so little sober analysis before jumping at costly remedies. Here too history provides insights. Finding a bubble, including the last housing one, unaided by specific government initiatives is hard. Moreover, it is not only speculators who instil fear in populations. History is full of extreme examples of politicians trying to sweep problems under the carpet or couching their comments so as to increase rather than lower insecurity. In a rush to be seen doing something big or to avoid appearing apathetic to human misery on their watch, policy makers seem to prefer to do too much rather than be accused of doing too little. It is often these very government measures that broaden and lengthen crises. Our introduction and the collection of papers herein should help to illustrate that some financial events occur at times of more general political and economic weakness, and that policy reactions can turn what might have been a minor market correction into a more general panic with longer-term general economic consequences.

Looking at historical contexts broadly should help us avoid violent ideological swings. Completely dismissing the pre-2008 financial architecture and theory, as some would have it, may be intellectually too simplistic. To be sure, there was too much risk taking – or, better put, too little understanding of the systemic risks being taken – but the very free flow of funds from those with capital to those in need over the past decades has brought untold political and economic benefits to much of the world (Rajan, 2010, pp. 1–20). Some aspects of the Panic of 2008 suggest that our insights about the workings of the economy are still as imperfect as the institutions and individuals whose activities were at the centre of the crisis, but as of this writing regulators seem to have learned enough to avoid the worst of the 1930s crisis, hopefully without too many unforeseen negative consequences.

As many of the articles in this issue remind us, although much of economics is very international, politics, for good or ill, remains very national, especially during crises. Even in the face of a 'worldwide financial meltdown', national differences, for real and sometimes imagined reasons, still count. How willing are national governments to tolerate some loss of sovereignty to deal with new financial realities and how willing are their constituencies, many of whom benefited from much of the financial innovation that contributed to the crisis, to live with the uncertainty that nearly always accompanies meaningful change? The track record of governments during the 1930s was not good (James, 2001). The experience of that period is that 'globalisation' is a fragile phenomenon. Despite its many benefits, for many it is the root cause of a host of social as well as economic problems. As many of the essays point out, prior reforms and sound banking regulation can help avoid many of the most unwanted consequences of contagion.

Today reform seems to require even greater international consensus than in the 1930s. Economic adversity makes that consensus harder to forge, a political fact that is nothing new for historians and economists, but our era has its own twist. In the post-Reagan/Thatcher world economic theory and regulation took a decidedly internationalist but non-interventionist turn, creating huge transnational financial and other private institutions, and leaving governments relatively free in a wide swath of countries to take political steps designed to ward off unwanted national social and economic outcomes. Many aspects of those measures have a global impact – not all negative – but they can only be evaluated and controlled internationally. Righting the problems associated with financial turmoil is not just a cross-border economic but also a political question. In this, we cannot forget that adjusting to new political circumstances is not easy for politicians to swallow for themselves, or to sell to their constituencies and powerful economic actors, especially when the adaptation entails a loss of control or a potential threat to economic privileges. Effective reform may require a whole new consensus built around international norms of acceptable financial behaviour and a transfer of national sovereignty to uncompromising international regulators to deal with supranational issues.

Acknowledgements

We would like to thank the editors of *Business History* for their support and guidance, John Wilson, Steven Toms, and Andrew Popp (book review editor). Moreover, this special issue would not have been possible without the help of an impressive group of scholars: Leslie Hannah, Richard Sylla, Martin Jes Iversen, Tom Kärrlander, Harold James, Michael Bordo, Duncan Ross, Per Hansen, and Aldo Musacchio.

Notes

1. There is a long list of academic papers, books and websites (among them, not cited later in this paper: Almunia, Bénétrix, Eichengreen, O'Rourke, & Rua, 2010; Bordo, 2009; Bordo & James, 2009; Cohan, 2010; Gorton, 2010a, 2010b; Greenspan, 2010; Haldane, 2009; McDonald & Robinson, 2009; Nelson, 2008; Schlenkhoff, 2009; Schularick & Taylor, 2009; White, 2009; as well as Paulson, 2010).
2. An argument could be made that the panic really started earlier as falling real estate prices began in 2007 to disrupt the securitised debt and credit default transactions (Gorton, 2010b).
3. Posner provides a wonderful example of the tendency to draw on one historical example and assume the worst. Even though US unemployment stood at just over 7% and the United States had witnessed only four quarters of downturn (3.8% decline in fourth quarter GDP in 2008 from a year earlier) when he wrote in early 2009 (figures he himself quotes), he repeatedly refers to the 'crisis' as a depression. Apart from a short discussion on how much we should have learned from the Long-term Capital Management bailout in 1998, a point about which we agree wholeheartedly, his book is about what we should learn from the Great Depression, ignoring the many other financial crises of the nineteenth and twentieth centuries.
4. The second edition was published in 1989, the third in 1996, the fourth in 2000.
5. Forbes spends a good deal of time discussion historical bubbles and their import for finance, but he thanks 'psychologists' for their insights, not economic historians.

6. In his (2009) updated version of his 1999 study, Krugman quite rightly highlights several lessons from the past that were ignored and takes economists like Robert Lucas and Ben Bernanke to task for their naïve belief that 'the central problem of depression-prevention has been solved, for all practical purposes' (2009, p. 9). But his chronicle of past market failures, in the first 1999 edition and the revised 2009 one, reads as if the current malaise was unavoidable rather than a consequence of policy leaders ignoring very visible warning signs. More importantly, even though he argues for some very sensible reforms of the whole financial system, at the time of writing, his pessimism about the need for more bailouts in the United States seems unjustified, embarrassingly so considering the excessively high profits and bonuses at many banks.

7. For a good discussion of the strengths and weaknesses of the Efficient Market Hypothesis and its importance to modern finance, see Ball (1999). Much of the original work in this area goes back to a series of seminal pieces E.F. Fama in the 1960s and 70s. See, for example, Fama (1970).

8. On the difficulty of even categorising well-known historical bubbles, see Garber (2001).

9. See the excellently researched book by Reinhart and Rogoff (2009). The authors' tongue-in-cheek title highlights their rival argument that a high level of debt is the universal cause of countries suffering financial crisis. Just when economists think that 'this time is different', they are proved to be wrong.

References

Ahamed, L. (2009). *Lords of finance: The bankers who broke the world*. New York: Penguin.

Almunia, M., Bénétrix, A., Eichengreen, B., O'Rourke, K.H., & Rua, G. (2010). From Great Depression to great credit crisis: Similarities, differences and lessons. *Economic Policy*, 25(62), 219–265.

Ball, R. (1999). The theory of stock market efficiency: Accomplishments and limitations. In Donald H. Chew, Jr. (Ed.), *The new corporate finance: Where theory meets practice* (pp. 35–48). Boston: Irwin-McGraw Hill.

Black, J. (2002). *Oxford dictionary of economics*. Oxford: Oxford University Press.

Bordo, M.D. (2009, December). *An historical perspective on the crisis of 2007–2008* (NBER Working Paper no. w14569). Cambridge, MA: NBER.

Bordo, M.D., & James, H. (2009, December). *The Great Depression analogy* (NBER Working Paper). Cambridge, MA: NBER.

Cassis, Y. (2006). *Capitals of capital: A history of international financial centres, 1780–2005*. Cambridge: Cambridge University Press.

Cohan, W.D. (2010). *House of cards*. New York: Random House.

El-Eriam, M. (2010, June 25). Beyond the false growth austerity debate. *Financial Times*.

Erturk, I., Froud, J., Johal, S., Leaver, A., & Williams, K. (2008). *Financialization at work: Key texts and commentary*. London: Routledge.

Fama, E.F. (1970). Efficient capital markets: A review of theory and empirical work. *Journal of Finance*, 25, 383–417.

Forbes, W. (2009). *Behavioural finance*. Chichester: Wiley & Sons.

Garber, P.M. (2001). *Famous first bubbles: The fundamentals of early manias.* Cambridge, MA: MIT Press.

Gorton, G.B. (2010a, February). *Questions and answers about the financial crisis* (NBER Working Paper no. 15787). Cambridge, MA: NBER.

Gorton, G.B. (2010b). *Slapped by the invisible hand: The panic of 2007.* Oxford: Oxford University Press.

Greenspan, A. (2010, March 9). *The crisis* (Working Paper). Retrieved March 20, 2010, from http://www.brookings.edu/~/media/files/.../ES/.../spring2010_greenspan.pdf

Haldane, A.G. (2009, November). *Banking on the state* (Working Paper). Retrieved December 22, 2009, from http://www.biz.org/review/ro9111e.pds

James, H. (2001). *The end of globalization.* Cambridge, MA: Harvard University Press.

Kindleberger, C.P. (1978). *Manias, panics, and crashes: A history of financial crises.* New York: Basic Books.

Kindleberger, C.P. (2000). *Manias, panics, and crashes: A history of financial crises* (4th ed.). Foreword P. Bernstein. New York: Wiley & Sons.

Kindleberger, C.P., & Aliber, R. (2005). *Manias, panics and crashes: A history of financial crises.* 5th ed. New foreword R. Solow. New York: Wiley & Sons.

Krugman, P. (1999, 2009). *The return of depression economics and the crisis of 2008.* New York: Norton.

Krugman, P. (2008, October 28). Lest we forget. *New York Times.*

Lowenstein, R. (2000). *When genius failed: The rise and fall of long-term capital management.* New York: Random House.

Lucas, R. (2009, August 8). Economic focus: In defence of the dismal science. *The Economist.*

MacKenzie, D. (2006). *An engine, not a camera: How financial models shape markets.* Cambridge, MA: MIT Press.

Marx, K. (1869/1974). Der achtzehnte Brumaire des Louis Bonaparte. In *Karl Marx and Friedrich Engels: Ausgewählte Schriften in Zwei Bände* (Vol. I). Berlin: Dietz Verlag.

McDonald, L., & Robinson, P. (2009). *A colossal failure of common sense: The inside story of the Lehman Brothers failure.* New York: Crown Business.

Moessner, R., & Allen, W.A. (2010, May). *Central Bank co-operation and international liquidity in the financial crisis of 2008–09* (BIS Working Paper). Basel: BIS.

Morris, W. (Ed.). (1969). *The American heritage dictionary of the English language.* New York: Houghton Mifflin.

Nelson, S.R. (2008, October 17). The real Great Depression. *Chronicle of Higher Education.*

Nietzsche, F. (1996). *Vom Nutzen und Nachtheil der Historie für das Leben.* Munich: Taschenbuchverlag. (Originally published under a different title in 1873)

Paulson, H.M. (2010). *On the brink.* New York: Business Plus.

Posner, R.A. (2009). *A failure of capitalism: The crisis of '08 and the descent into depression.* Cambridge, MA: Harvard University Press.

Rajan, R.G. (2010). *Fault lines: How hidden fractures still threaten the world economy.* Princeton, NJ: Princeton University Press.

Randall, J.H., Jr. (1970). *Plato: Dramatist of the life of reason.* New York: Columbia University Press.

Reinhart, C.M., & Rogoff, K.S. (2009). *This time is different: Eight centuries of financial folly.* Princeton, NJ: Princeton University Press.

Schlenkhoff, G. (2009). *Can great depression theories explain the Great Recession?* (Working Paper). Munich: MPRA.

Schularick, M., & Taylor, A.M. (2009, November). *Credit booms gone bust: Monetary policy, leverage cycles and financial crises, 1870–2008* (NBER Working Paper no. 15512). Cambridge, MA: NBER.

Sorkin, A.R. (2009). *Too big to fail.* New York: Viking.

Wessel, D. (2009). *In Fed we trust: Ben Bernanke's war on the great panic.* New York: Crown Business.

White, E. (2009, December). *Lessons from the great American real estate boom of the 1920s* (NBER Working Paper no. w15573). Cambridge, MA: NBER.

Financial crisis, contagion, and the British banking system between the world wars

Mark Billings[a] and Forrest Capie[b]

[a]Nottingham University Business School, Nottingham, UK; [b]Cass Business School, London, UK

In a globalised world, when financial crisis strikes, can countries which are well-integrated into the world financial system escape? Recent experience suggests not. In the early 1930s, Britain's openness at the centre of the world financial system left it vulnerable, particularly to the central European financial crisis. Yet there was no financial crisis in Britain in 1931, rather an exchange-rate crisis, and sterling left the exchange-rate regime of the gold exchange standard. The most important financial institutions, the joint-stock commercial banks, the central part of the payments system, remained robust and contributed to the stability of the British economy.

[F]inancial crises ricochet from one country to another ... Domestic lenders of last resort have been established to enhance the stability of the financial system although not necessarily of individual financial banks. (Kindleberger & Aliber, 2005, pp. 124 and 292)

Introduction

The current crisis has given new impetus to research on globalisation, the gold standard, financial crises and contagion in the 1930s. In this article we re-examine the question of financial crisis in Britain in 1931, considering how the financial system might have been at risk. We focus on the banking system, and argue that the major British commercial banks were sound, in contrast to certain merchant banks. For a financial crisis to develop the links between these sectors would need to have been sufficiently strong to threaten the commercial banking system in a way that would have endangered the payments system. But even if this had arisen, the Bank of England ('the Bank') was a mature lender of last resort (LLR), a role it had more or less perfected in the course of the nineteenth century.

We first consider the nature of globalisation and financial crises, and whether there was a 'financial crisis' in Britain in 1931. The next section briefly reviews Britain's interwar economic performance, outlines the Bank's role as LLR and the operation and some criticisms of British commercial banks, and considers the possible spread of 'contagion' to Britain from central Europe. We then review a range of evidence on the main commercial banks in the 1930s, including new material from archival sources. In the final section we discuss and contrast the nature of banking problems in other major countries to those in Britain and draw conclusions.

Globalisation, crisis and British banking

Globalisation, the increasing integration of markets and economies around the world, sees greater flows of goods, services, capital, and even labour. The economic theory that predicts convergence in trade and factor prices also predicts resistance to the increased openness since the process will produce winners and losers. The outcome depends upon the relative strengths of these groupings and on the prevailing institutional environment. Not surprisingly there are crisis points.

The current era is sometimes described as one of unprecedented globalisation. An earlier era of globalisation, with its origins in the eighteenth century and its real beginnings in the nineteenth century, is variously argued to have ended with World War I or with the dislocations of the late 1920s and 1930s. The justifiably highly acclaimed analysis of the distinguished historian Harold James (2001) argued that the globalisation which began to accelerate around 1870 ended in the years between the two world wars. Many maintain that the end had come with the outbreak of war in 1914, but support for James can be found in, for example, Rajan and Zingales (2003), whose measures of financial development appear to have started falling in the 1930s or 1940s, not recovering to similar levels until 1990.

World War I was hugely disruptive for trade and capital flows, trade policy, migration, international monetary arrangements and much else. The postwar Treaty of Versailles, which imposed punitive reparation payments on Germany, and squabbling among the allies over the repayment of debts accumulated in the war were damaging to international relations. James argued that globalisation continued until the financial systems of the world crumbled in the Great Depression years between 1929 and 1932. He then suggested that at the end of the twentieth century weak financial systems appeared similar to those of the 1930s and therefore signalled likely doom.

It is vitally important to learn the correct lessons from the past as the current experience of globalisation experiences understandable strains. The essence of the James thesis is that globalisation was brought to a halt as governments struggled to influence their domestic economies in the 1920s and 1930s because 'financial and banking systems were volatile and vulnerable to panic' (James, 2001, p. 31). We agree with James on the weaknesses in central European finance, but suggest a caveat to an important part of the thesis on 'the vulnerability of the British financial system' (James, 2001, p. 69).

Defining 'financial crisis'

Taxonomies of 'crises' abound (Kindleberger & Aliber, 2005, p. 34). We consider that Schwartz (1986) provides the most satisfactory definition of a 'real financial crisis' as circumstances when the money stock is under threat, i.e. only when there is a threat to the payments system. A collapse in the money stock in the face of sticky wages and prices leads to a collapse in real output, for which reason growth in the money stock should be preserved. The failure of a large financial institution, or perhaps a major company or municipality, represents a 'pseudo-crisis', which may create problems for shareholders and taxpayers but not threaten the financial system.

The money supply is determined by the actions of the monetary authorities, the banks, and the non-bank public. The latter two hold currency and deposits in certain proportions. When the public fear banking difficulties they move out of bank deposits into currency, and the banks raise their cash reserves to accommodate that demand. Banks in fractional reserve systems take deposits, and make loans, and thereby multiply the stock of money. When banks fail, or take steps to reduce their assets, they reduce the money stock, abrupt falls in which will damage the real economy when wages and prices are sticky. The monetary authorities need to know how to act in these circumstances, and to do so quickly. In the face of a need for liquidity, they must inject the appropriate amount of monetary base into the system to keep the money supply growing at its normal rate given the different ratios now prevailing.

Financial crisis in Britain in 1931?

At the beginning of the 1930s, against the background of growing international economic and political tensions, the British economy and some financial institutions experienced various problems. These included currency crisis and abandonment of the gold standard, payment difficulties of international borrowers, especially those in Germany and other central European countries, and struggling domestic borrowers in traditional industries. The idea of a financial crisis in Britain in 1931 first entered the economic history literature with an article which confused the different elements of crises and labelled them 'financial crisis' (Williams, 1963). It is still sometimes asserted that there was such a crisis, no doubt partly because financial crises were experienced in many other countries. We contend there was no 'financial' or 'banking' crisis in Britain in 1931, a view shared by others (for example, Grossman, 1994; Jonker & van Zanden, 1995; Kindleberger & Aliber, 2005; Reinhart & Rogoff, 2009).

The problems of the 1930s affected the different types of British banking institution to different degrees. Some merchant banks and British-owned banks operating overseas ('British overseas banks') were particularly hard-hit, but the principal commercial banks, the joint-stock clearing banks, proved to be sound. This group of institutions, small in number but of key importance, were the country's largest financial institutions and the core of the payments system. Their performance in the twentieth century has been subject to many criticisms, many of these unjustified or exaggerated. Underlying the debate on their role is an implicit trade-off between stability and risk-taking. We argue that at a time when many of the developed world's banks were in difficulty these banks were in a position of relative strength. This contributed greatly to the stability of Britain's financial system and its economy, still a leading economy in the interwar period, with an important, albeit weakened, currency.

Britain and its banking system

The interwar British economy

The picture often presented of interwar Britain is one of unremitting gloom – deflation, exchange-rate shame, the General Strike, unemployment, the Jarrow

March, and other such features. Space precludes a comprehensive assessment, but in aggregate the British economy performed well in the interwar period (Crafts, 2003; Eichengreen, 2003). After the World War I boom, GDP per capita fell, but reached its 1913 level again in the mid-1920s. The next peak in 1929 was followed by recession, but Britain suffered no Great Depression. Output fell significantly in just one year (1931) and was static in two others between 1929 and 1932, with an overall fall in GDP per capita of around 7.5% from the peak. GDP per capita then rose by more than 22% from its 1931 level in the strongest ever upswing in British economic history between 1932 and 1937 (Feinstein, 1976, Table 17). The 1930s was the decade of ring-roads and 'interwar semis', a huge construction boom and growth in 'new industries'.

Unemployment rose sharply from around 1 million in the 1920s to peak at around 3 million, then fell quite quickly as economic growth rose sharply in the 1930s, although significant regional variations remained (Hatton, 2003, p. 350, Table 13.1). This unemployment is explained best in terms of rising real wages, the consequence of falling prices, fixed labour contracts, and changes in the benefit system, which encouraged the supply of labour and dampened the demand for it (Beenstock, Capie, & Griffiths, 1984). The principal explanation for the good performance after 1932 was the abandonment of the gold standard, generally experienced by countries which abandoned it (Bernanke & James, 1991), and the resulting freedom to use monetary policy flexibly, with low interest rates from 1932. This all took place in the face of collapsing international trade to which the British economy was more exposed than most.

Capie, Mills, and Wood (1986) showed that there was no 'real financial crisis' in 1931, although sterling suffered an exchange-rate crisis as the pound was forced off the gold standard and the exchange rate declined precipitately in the closing months of that year. The restoration of the gold standard in 1925 had been unsatisfactory in terms of the various rates adopted by different countries in the following few years. The pound was overvalued and pressure mounted on sterling through the summer of 1931, in large part due to the decline in the capital account of the balance of payments and weak government finances, which led to political crisis and the formation of the National Government (Eichengreen, 1992, pp. 279–285; Williamson, 1992). Reserves were insufficient to sustain the fixed rate without the support of damagingly high interest rates, and the link with gold was broken in September after it became clear that the parity could not be defended.

The Bank of England's lender of last resort role and the commercial banks

The risk of financial crisis, which would endanger the commercial banks and the payments system, could be averted by appropriate LLR action. In Britain, the Bank was a mature LLR, a role slowly learned in a favourable legislative period and near-to-ideal institutional setting in the course of the nineteenth century (Capie, 2002). When banks learned that they could always access liquidity they were less inclined to panic, as the Bank could inject liquidity as soon as its carefully attuned antennae detected fears of illiquidity. The operation of the discount houses as a buffer between banks and the Bank allowed anonymity to prevail and prevented special pleading, very much in line with the mood of that time in keeping special interests at a distance. The gold standard was a complicating factor, as the monetary base was determined via the balance of payments. The solution would be to suspend the gold standard when there was the risk of a financial crisis, and supply all the cash needed to satisfy demand. This could be done only where the supplying institution had strong credibility, as the Bank achieved in the nineteenth century, when there was almost complete trust in the system and appreciation of its workings. These arrangements contributed to the remarkable stability of the British financial system from the 1870s to the late twentieth century. There was no 'real financial crisis' after 1866, although the Bank provided liquidity as LLR on occasions when fear made an appearance. The British system remained stable even when other countries suffered financial crises, such as in 1873 or 1907. So in 1929–31 the banking system understood how the Bank would behave if panic began to appear – the Bank could supply the markets with all the liquidity needed at an appropriate rate of interest.

The commercial banking system evolved into a highly concentrated one as the Bank's role became more clearly defined and understood. By 1920 the five largest banks dominated. The 'Big Five' were all London-based, held about 80% of all deposits and had around 10,000 branches. They had learned prudence, were well diversified across the country geographically and across all sectors of the economy, and had shifted to more liquid asset structures (Collins & Baker, 2001, 2003), which allowed capital ratios to fall. This system has been subject to long-standing criticisms that the banks were too conservative and failed to: lend to new, small and deserving businesses or to risky ventures; provide long-term capital to support industry; promote industrial restructuring; and charge competitive lending rates or pay competitive deposit rates. Additionally the banks are argued to have held excessive amounts of government debt, demanded unreasonable security from borrowers, and used their 'cartel' to enjoy a quiet and comfortable life.

The banks could claim that their role in the provision of finance was expected to be a limited one, but criticisms have persisted, partly due to the banks' failure to contradict them. For example, the banks were so keen to preserve their reputation for sound finance that in their evidence to the 1931 Macmillan Committee they accepted that they did not lend on anything other than a short-term basis, for anything other than working capital. Many studies have shown these criticisms and the contrasts often made to other countries, particularly in continental Europe, to be exaggerated (for fuller discussion of these issues, see, for example, Ackrill & Hannah, 2001, pp. 93–95; Baker & Collins, 2010; Collins, 1998; Newton, 2003; Ross, 1996).

Central European problems in 1931 and the German Standstill

If there was no financial crisis in Britain in 1931, was the banking system nevertheless at risk? James (2001, pp. 71–72) argues that it was threatened by the exposures of those British merchant banks closely linked to continental Europe to the severe liquidity and solvency problems which developed rapidly there in the first half of 1931, a theme recently revisited by Accominotti (2009). The May 1931 insolvency of Credit Anstalt, Austria's largest bank but poorly managed in the 1920s, quickly shifted attention to the closely connected German universal banks. One of the six large banks, the Darmstädter- und Nationalbank (Danat), failed due to its large exposure to the textile company Nordwolle. The Berlin Great Banks operated on very low cash and reserve ratios, and their total assets and liquidity declined further in June and July 1931 as panic spread and depositors, including those from overseas on whom they relied heavily, withdrew their funds (Eichengreen, 1992, pp. 261–279; Kindleberger, 1986, pp. 144–159; Kindleberger & Aliber, 2005, pp. 258–262). The Reichsbank, with limited experience as a central bank, failed to behave as the LLR, and to lend freely to the market, although given the practices of the universal banking system and the size of the leading banks it was difficult for it to act (Capie et al., 1986).

The German banks' difficulties and the country's international payment position, against the wider background of World War I reparations and political, economic and social problems, led to a partial moratorium covering much of its international debt. The six-month September 1931 German Credit Agreement ('the German Standstill'), renewed annually from 1932, formalised the position of short-term debt, much of which arose from trade finance. Approximately £54 million was initially due to British creditors, around one-third of this to the clearing banks. The smaller merchant banks accounted for most of the remainder, and were therefore proportionately much more heavily exposed (Accominotti, 2009). The international debts of Austria and Hungary were subject to similar arrangements, although British exposures to these were a small fraction of the German Standstill exposures – Austria £1.2 million and Hungary £5.5 million at the end of 1931 (Westminster, 1932–38).

German business was a mainstay for the merchant banks with European origins – 'family enterprises linked to much of the rest of the world by "separate" family firms in other countries' (Kobrak, 2009, p. 53). These firms included Kleinworts and Schroders, which had the largest German Standstill exposures – respectively three times the partners' capital (Diaper, 1986, p. 68), and approximately 1.3 times partners' capital and bad debt reserves (Roberts, 1992, p. 264). Others with large exposures included Lazards (Forbes, 2000, p. 40), but not all were so heavily exposed – Morgan Grenfell, for example, had largely avoided private German business (Burk, 1989, p. 85). The Bank, with the Treasury's approval, took the lead role in ensuring British banks remained engaged in the Standstill. It exercised 'moral suasion', asking commercial banks to provide sufficient support to their merchant bank customers to allow them to continue in business (Roberts, 1992, pp. 252–253, 266).

Seen by some as economic appeasement, but by others as pragmatism or resigned realism, the Standstill arrangements represented a compromise between political and financial interests – a means to maintain credit lines to Britain's largest trading partner, to facilitate trade, and sustain economic relations and encourage economic stability in Germany, thereby protecting the creditors' interests against the collapse in international trade and rising protectionism and political tensions (Forbes, 1987, 2000). The result was that British bankers appeared less aggressive than many German Standstill creditors in reducing their exposures. By 1939 credit lines extended by British-based creditors had increased from 24% to 57% of the overall totals outstanding under the Standstill, which had fallen considerably (Forbes, 2000, p. 193, Tables 7 and 8). But, generally, British bankers accepted the Standstill reluctantly, fearing that the alternatives, such as a complete moratorium, the use of clearing arrangements, or extracting themselves with considerable losses, were worse (Forbes, 1987, p. 586; Kynaston, 1999, pp. 434–435). Ultimate repayment came only after the 1952 Lancaster House conference secured a comprehensive settlement of Germany's pre-World War II debts, including long-term debts, much of which were owed to US creditors.

The resilience of British commercial banks in the 1930s

What evidence is there to support our contention that Britain's major commercial or clearing banks demonstrated resilience during the 1930s? Data from secondary sources combined with new archival material provide a reasonably clear picture, but variations in the operations of different banks and the inevitable vagaries in the survival of archival data mean that the same information is not available for all institutions.

Clearing banks' support for the Bank

The large clearing banks neither needed nor received support from the Bank. Table 1 summarises a number of support operations of various types in the period, the existence and details of which have usually only become known subsequently. The Bank often played a leading role, and virtually all these operations related to merchant banks or British overseas banks. The notable exception was Williams Deacon's, the small Manchester-based clearing bank with a heavy concentration of lending to the cotton industry. Its takeover by the Royal Bank of Scotland was engineered by the Bank, which met those losses which arose prior to the takeover. The Bank bore the bulk of losses from the identified operations, which totalled around £8 million (a little over £400 million at end-2009 prices) from Anglo International, Anglo-South American Bank (ASAB), Huths, and Williams Deacon's. The clearing banks also incurred some losses. Their involvement in such operations was not new; they had, for example, joined together under the leadership of the Midland Bank and the Bank to support the Yorkshire Penny Bank in 1911 (Holmes & Green, 1986, pp. 143–147).

The clearing banks also assisted the Bank's efforts to support sterling. Barclays entered into an exchange with the Bank, receiving British government Treasury bills for commercial bills, which the Bank then used as security for its August 1931 loan of £25 million from the Bank of France (Tuke & Gillman, 1972, p. 31). At the request of the Bank the banks also participated in a scheme in the forward foreign exchange market, and at one of the smaller clearing banks 'the General Manager reported that forward [US] dollars and [French] francs had been sold for account of the Bank of England to the extent of £1,700,000' (Martins, 1920–39, 22 September 1931). This operation involved about £20 million of forward sales (Sayers, 1976, pp. 408–409), not insubstantial compared to the Bank's gold and foreign exchange holdings of £141 million at 30 December 1931 (Sayers, 1976, Vol. 3, Appendix 37, p. 355), or total UK reserves at the same date, including Treasury holdings, of £210 million (Howson, 1980, p. 80, Table 3).

Capital flight from Britain and bank deposits

We noted earlier the reliance of German banks on short-term international deposits. Short-term foreign capital was withdrawn from London during the 1931 exchange-rate crisis (see, for example, James, 1992, pp. 602–603; Williams, 1963, pp. 525–528). Some of this capital flight represented withdrawal of bank deposits, but it is also believed that foreign holdings of securities were liquidated. Estimates of capital outflows are problematic, with contradictory accounts, both as to the identity of the sellers of sterling and the amounts involved. Although detailed

Table 1. Support operations in British banking, 1927–39.

	Date	Amount of support (£000s)	Amount of loss (£000s)	Support provided/loss suffered by	Source
Anglo International Bank	1927–43	1000	1600	BoE	Jones, 1993, pp. 230–231
Anglo-South American Bank[1]	1931–36	5000–8500	4568, of which BoE 2351	BoE and Big Five excluding Lloyds	Jones, 1993, pp. 240–242; Sayers, 1976, pp. 263–267
			800	Westminster	Westminster (1928–60)
			c. 500	Barclays	Holmes & Green, 1986, p. 186
			c. 500	Midland	
Banca Italo-Britannica/ British-Italian Corporation	1929–30	5100	3861 to 5347	Lloyds, National Provincial, Westminster	Jones, 1993, pp. 231–234
			1080	Lloyds	Winton, 1980b; Winton, 1982, pp. 57–59
British Overseas Bank[2]	1938	250	250	BoE	Sayers, 1976, pp. 261–262
		1000	300	BoE	Jones, 1993, pp. 243–244
		750		National Provincial	
		250		Union Bank of Scotland	
			c. 400	Williams Deacon's	Williams Deacon's, 1971, p. 161
Cox & Co.[3]	1929	900 BoE guarantees	267	BoE	Jones, 1993, p. 240; Sayers, 1976, p. 242
Glyn, Mills[4]	1939	–	–	–	
Hambros (A)	1932	100	–	BoE	Kynaston, 1999, p. 359; Sayers, 1976, p. 531
Higginson & Co. (A)	1932	340	–	BoE	Kynaston, 1999, p. 360; Sayers, 1976, p. 531

(continued)

Table 1. (*Continued*).

	Date	Amount of support (£000s)	Amount of loss (£000s)	Support provided/loss suffered by	Source
F. Huth & Co. (A)[2]	Early 1930s	–	1000	BoE	Jones, 1993, pp. 243–244; Sayers, 1976, p. 270
Kleinwort, Sons & Co. (A)	1931	3250 (repaid by Sept. 1932)	–	Westminster	Diaper, 1986, p. 69
Lazard (A): fraud in Brussels office	1939 / July 1931	1000 (repaid 1940) / 3500 (repaid over seven years)	– / 6000	Westminster / BoE	Diaper, 1986, p. 71 / Kynaston, 1999, p. 228; Sayers, 1976, pp. 530–531
Lazard (A): 'problems in Paris'	1932	2000	–	Lazard / In equal shares: BoE and National Provincial	Kynaston, 1999, p. 360
Lloyds and National Provincial Foreign Bank	1931–39	1500 guarantees/payments to recapitalise	–	Lloyds, National Provincial	Jones, 1993, p. 143; LNPFB (1933–37)
J. Henry Schröder & Co. (A)	1936 / 1939	1000 (repaid) / 1000	– / –	Westminster	Roberts, 1992, p. 266
Williams Deacon's[5]	1929–38	4000 maximum	3212	BoE	Sayers, 1976, p. 258

Notes: 'Support' usually took the form of loans. For comparison, when the City of Glasgow Bank failed in 1878, the shortfall to the shareholders with unlimited liability was £5.2 million (Collins, 1989, p. 504), equivalent to £9.1 million at 1931 prices and £471 million at end-2009 prices. £1 million in 1931 is equivalent to approximately £52 million at end-2009.

Big Five=Barclays, Lloyds, Midland, National Provincial and Westminster banks.

BoE=Bank of England.

A=member of the Accepting Houses' Committee of merchant banks.

[1]=merged with Bank of London and South America in 1936.

[2]=F. Huth & Co. taken over by British Overseas Bank in 1936.

[3]=taken over by Lloyds 1929.

[4]=taken over by Royal Bank of Scotland in 1939.

[5]=taken over by Royal Bank of Scotland in 1930; losses to BoE reflect losses on pre-takeover lending by Williams Deacon's.

data on foreign depositors' funds at the clearing banks are not available to reconcile the various accounts, the available data do indicate that major British banks were much less reliant on international deposits, did not suffer withdrawals on the same scale, and remained much more liquid.

The clearing banks' aggregate deposits fell by around £125 million in calendar year 1931, but by only 4% from June to September (Capie & Webber, 1985, pp. 437, 444, Table III(4)). Deposits of the Big Five, with stronger London bias to their business, fell more sharply than those of the smaller clearing banks and the Scottish banks (Table 2). Deposits of the merchant banks were small in relative terms, but 'the acceptance houses had £105 millions of deposits, nearly all of foreign origin' at the end of 1930 and lost about 40% of these (Truptil, 1936, p. 314). Deposits in the British overseas banks, typically with distinct geographical biases to their activities, did not generally decline more than those of the clearing banks. The exception was ASAB, whose deposits contracted sharply, reflecting the fears for its future which forced the Bank to organise a major and long-running support operation (see above).

New archival data for weekly deposit balances throughout 1931 for two clearing banks, one large (Westminster) and one small (District), suggest that variations during the year were not particularly wide (Table 3), although Westminster's deposit balances touched their minimum immediately after gold standard suspension. In Table 4 we report monthly averages of aggregate deposits for the clearing banks in 1931 and in the five years before and after. The range of variation in 1931 was wider than in some years, and the levels of deposits in September and October 1931 a little lower than typical for these months, but the overall data do not indicate major deposit losses around the time of exit from the gold standard.

Limited archival evidence from Westminster Bank implies that withdrawals of deposits placed by foreign customers with the clearing banks would have represented only a small proportion of short-term capital outflows in 1931:

> When five years ago, England [sic] went off gold, we had approximately £20 millions of sterling balances from customers domiciled abroad ... by September 1934, such balances were reduced to £17¼ millions ... now the Foreign Sterling Balances are at the record figure of £31½ millions ... This Bank habitually holds more than one fifth of the Foreign Balances deposited with the eleven Clearing Banks. (Westminster, 1930–39, 'Report of Chief General Manager' to Board meeting of 29 September 1936)

Foreign currency deposits at the Westminster were small. US dollar deposits and loans were roughly equal at approximately $11 million at 31 October 1927. When German payments were suspended there was a mismatch, very small in relation to the overall balance sheet, with approximately $14 million in deposits and $5 million in loans at 13 July 1931, reduced to $10.5 million and $3 million respectively by 7 September 1931 (Westminster, 1931–34).

Asset structures

The clearing banks' aggregate balance sheets for 1930 and 1931 suggest that their deployments of assets were not notably different from earlier decades (see Table 5), although higher proportions of the 'bills discounted' and 'investments' categories were represented by British government debt. In the 'crisis year' of 1931, the clearing banks remained sufficiently liquid to maintain normal business.

Table 2. Banks' deposits at financial year-end dates, 1930–32.

	Deposits (£m)	Index of deposits, 1930=100		
	1930	1930	1931	1932
Big Five clearing banks				
Barclays	347.9	100	96	109
Lloyds	364.6	100	92	105
Midland	399.6	100	90	105
National Provincial	291.5	100	90	100
Westminster	291.6	100	93	102
Other main commercial banks				
District	52.4	100	96	108
Martins	78.6	100	97	109
Williams Deacon's	32.0	100	91	106
Scottish banks				
Bank of Scotland	32.3	100	101	96
Clydesdale	30.2	100	93	106
Royal Bank of Scotland	50.4	100	98	111
British overseas banks				
Anglo-South American	49.8	100	82	51
Bank of Australasia	34.2	100	107	111
Bank of London and South America	39.4	100	87	105
Barclays DCO	62.7	100	109	114
Chartered	40.8	100	95	107
Hongkong	50.6	100	110	115
Merchant banks				
Baring Brothers & Co.	17.6	100	100	99
Erlangers	4.1	100	30	41
Hambros	18.4	100	58	58
S. Japhet & Co.	6.2	100	37	32
J. Henry Schröder & Co. ('Schroders')	8.8	100	50	38
Aggregate data				
UK banks	2396.0	100	93	105
Joint stock banks of England and Wales	1976.8	100	92	104
London clearing banks	1903.4	100	92	104
London clearing banks, average of monthly statements	1801.0	100	98	99

Notes: 'Deposits' represents 'Deposit and other accounts' at financial year-end dates, except for 'average of monthly statements' for London clearing banks. The financial year-end date is 31 December for all banks except: Anglo-South American (31 October); Bank of Australasia (30 June); Barclays DCO and Bank of London and South America (30 September); Hambros (31 March in following year); Hongkong (31 August); Royal Bank of Scotland (11 October 1930, 10 October 1931, 8 October 1932).

Sources: Authors' calculations. Bank of Scotland: Saville (1996, p. 962, Table A8); British overseas banks: Jones (1993, Appendix 5); Clydesdale Bank: Munn (1988, p. 340); merchant banks except Schroders: Truptil (1936, pp. 336–337, 339, Appendices III and V); Schroders: Roberts (1992, p. 530, Appendix IV (i)); other banks: published annual reports; aggregate data: Sheppard (1971, pp. 116–119, Tables (A) 1.1, 1.2, pp. 130–133, Tables (A) 1.8, 1.9, pp. 138–139, Table (A) 1.13).

Despite rumours in May 1931 in the New York market that it was in difficulty (James, 2001, p. 71), archival data show that Barclays continued to make large advances to a wide range of customers before and after the German Standstill and abandonment of the gold standard (Barclays, 1930–32). A similar picture of 'business as normal' can be found in the approvals given by Lloyds' Board of Directors (Lloyds, 1931). The major change in the clearing banks' asset structures

Table 3.   Fluctuations in weekly deposits, District and Westminster banks, 1931.

	District	Westminster
Annual average	100	100
Minimum	95.67	95.02
Maximum	108.16	109.92
Standard deviation	2.79	3.41
Date of minimum	8 April 1931	24 September 1931
Date of maximum	21 January 1931	1 January 1931

Note: Data are summarised for 'Deposits and other accounts'.
Sources: Authors' calculations from weekly balance sheet data, District Bank (1920–68) and Westminster (1920–43).

occurred in 1932 – advances fell in absolute and relative terms, offset by the rise in investments, which consisted almost wholly of British government securities (see Table 5). At every year-end from 1932 to 1939 investments represented between 31% and 33% of total assets and advances ranged from 33% to 37%.

Profitability and capital

Previous studies such as Grossman (1994) and Jonker and van Zanden (1995) relied on published data for the profits and capital of British banks. In this period the banks were not obliged to publish their 'true' positions, which they obscured by various means, the most important of which was 'hidden reserves'. The banks used these to smooth fluctuations in performance over the business cycle to help present a picture of strength and stability (Billings & Capie, 2009). In a recession, when profits were relatively low, they would draw from hidden reserves to report higher profits and at the peak, when profits were relatively high, they would add to hidden reserves, reporting lower profits.

Returns on capital measured using 'true' profits and capital figures were rather more volatile than those the banks published, but, on average, did not deviate dramatically from their reported positions (Capie & Billings, 2001, pp. 380–381, Tables 2 and 3). Overall the 1930s were less profitable than the 1920s and later decades, except for the Midland Bank, and it was a very rare event for any clearing bank to make a loss on a 'true' basis. Predictably, advances were the most profitable asset category (Capie & Billings, 2004). Investments were also profitable, and the policy of 'cheap money' from 1932 provided some banks with a useful cushion of unrealised profits on investments (Billings & Capie, 2007, p. 151, Table 7). Published financial statements consistently understated the strength of clearing banks' capital positions due to significant hidden reserves (Billings & Capie, 2007, pp. 150–151, Table 6). Calculations based on archival data indicate that 'true' capital ratios deteriorated to some extent through the 1930s, with variations from bank to bank (Table 6). But declines were not sharp, and arguably, given the fall in advances, lower capital ratios were appropriate.

Bad debts

Archival sources yield new data on the clearing banks' experiences of bad debts during the interwar period. Three measures are presented in Table 7 where data

Table 4. Fluctuation in aggregate deposits of London clearing banks, 1926–36.

	1926	1927	1928	1929	1930	1931	1932	1933	1934	1935	1936	Mean
January	100.6	101.1	101.0	102.6	100.2	106.4	95.9	101.6	102.1	99.2	97.7	100.8
February	98.7	98.7	98.2	100.8	97.3	103.4	92.8	100.3	100.3	97.8	95.8	98.5
March	97.6	97.5	96.8	98.7	95.5	100.2	93.8	98.6	97.3	96.2	95.1	97.0
April	97.8	98.0	97.8	98.9	97.2	98.6	94.1	98.9	98.5	97.1	97.2	97.6
May	97.7	98.5	97.7	98.3	98.8	98.7	95.1	99.6	98.8	98.1	98.6	98.2
June	100.2	100.5	100.1	100.4	101.4	101.2	98.8	101.3	99.4	100.2	100.6	100.4
July	101.1	100.4	101.1	100.9	101.7	101.6	101.0	101.1	99.4	101.0	101.3	101.0
August	100.4	99.6	100.1	99.8	100.2	99.1	101.0	100.3	98.7	100.7	101.4	100.1
September	99.7	99.5	100.2	99.5	100.0	97.2	104.4	100.3	98.8	101.3	101.9	100.3
October	101.3	102.0	101.3	100.1	101.5	97.9	106.0	99.9	100.5	101.9	102.9	101.4
November	101.2	101.1	101.3	99.4	102.1	96.9	106.3	98.8	101.6	102.0	103.2	101.3
December	103.7	103.1	104.4	100.6	104.2	98.7	111.0	99.4	104.8	104.6	104.5	103.5
Minimum	97.6	97.5	96.8	98.3	95.5	96.9	92.8	98.6	97.3	96.2	95.1	96.6
Maximum	103.7	103.1	104.4	102.6	104.2	106.4	111.0	101.6	104.8	104.6	104.5	104.6
Standard deviation	1.8	1.7	2.1	1.2	2.5	2.8	5.9	1.0	2.0	2.4	3.1	2.4

Note: Annual average in each year=100.
Source: Authors' calculations from Capie and Webber (1985, Table III(4), p. 444).

Table 5. Composition of joint-stock banks' aggregate balance sheets: percentages represented by main asset categories, 1860–1913, 1920–39.

	Cash and near-cash	Bills discounted	Investments	Advances
Decade				
1860–69	13	31	11	45
1870–79	16	26	12	46
1880–89	21	25	17	37
1890–99	21	17	21	41
1900–09	24	11	18	46
1910–13	26	13	16	45
1920–29	21	13	20	44
1930–39	21	11	30	36
Year				
1930	22	14	19	43
1931	21	12	21	44
1932	20	16	28	34

Sources: Collins and Baker (2001, p. 183, Table 2 (1860–1913 decadal averages)); authors' calculations from Sheppard (1971, pp. 116–117, Table (A) 1.1 (1920–29 and 1930–39 decadal averages, and years 1930–32)).

Table 6. 'True' capital as percentage of total assets, 1930–39.

	Barclays	Lloyds	Martins	Midland	National Provincial	Westminster	Mean
1930	8.7	n/a	n/a	8.1	7.8	9.7	8.8
1931	9.1	n/a	n/a	9.1	8.2	9.7	8.6
1932	7.8	7.4	10.9	7.6	7.1	8.9	8.5
1933	7.9	7.7	11.7	8.3	7.2	9.0	8.7
1934	7.9	7.9	11.5	8.3	7.3	9.4	8.7
1935	7.4	7.7	10.9	7.9	n/a	9.3	8.5
1936	7.2	7.9	10.9	7.5	n/a	8.5	8.3
1937	7.4	7.4	10.6	7.8	7.7	8.5	8.3
1938	7.1	7.6	10.1	8.4	8.2	9.1	8.0
1939	6.7	7.0	n/a	8.2	7.6	7.8	7.2

Note: n/a=not available.
Sources: Authors' calculations from published annual reports and the following archival sources: Barclays (1909–39); Martins (1920–39); Midland (1920–39, 1923–69); National Provincial (1911–25, 1926–34, 1937–40); Westminster (1911–50); Winton (1980a).

permit: total bad debt provisions, being the total amount set aside against bad debts at the year-end as a percentage of year-end advances; the annual bad debt charge, being the *net* new provisions for bad debts as a percentage of year-end advances (negative figures indicate that provisions no longer required exceeded new provisions); and the annual bad debt write-offs, the total amount of bad debts written off in the year as a percentage of year-end advances. Total provisions are almost invariably a multiple of the annual charge or write-offs, as banks usually maintain for some time provisions against those debts which they consider might 'go bad', before actually writing off the unrecovered debts. Bad debt provisions are not treated as part of capital in the capital ratios we report in Table 6, so over-provision for bad debts, whether simply misjudgement of the possibility of loss, or deliberate

Table 7. Bad debt experience, 1920–39.

	1920–29 average	1930–39 average	1930	1931	1932	1933	1934	1935	1936	1937	1938	1939
total bad debt provisions												
Barclays	1.7	3.1	2.7	2.9	3.9	4.0	4.0	3.9	3.1	2.8	2.7	1.5
Martins	3.6	6.6	5.0	5.0	9.7	11.5	7.9	7.4	5.3	4.8	3.9	5.1
Midland	2.7	4.0	3.7	4.0	n/a	4.5	4.6	4.2	3.9	3.7	3.9	3.6
National Provincial	3.2	4.0	3.5	4.3	4.9	5.5	5.7	n/a	n/a	3.0	2.6	2.1
Westminster	n/a	n/a	n/a	n/a	n/a	n/a	n/a	n/a	n/a	n/a	n/a	5.2
bad debt charge												
Barclays	0.5	0.3	0.6	0.6	0.7	0.3	0.3	0.2	0.0	0.1	0.1	0.5
Lloyds	0.3	0.2	0.4	0.5	0.6	0.1	0.0	0.1	0.1	0.0	0.0	0.1
Martins	0.4	0.8	0.6	0.6	2.2	1.7	1.7	0.4	0.0	-0.2	-0.2	1.0
Midland	0.6	0.5	0.3	0.3	0.4	0.6	1.4	0.7	0.5	0.4	0.2	0.3
National Provincial	0.4	0.8	1.4	1.1	0.3	0.6	0.7	n/a	n/a	n/a	n/a	n/a
Westminster	0.6	0.5	1.0	0.9	0.6	0.4	0.0	0.0	0.0	0.9	0.6	0.9
bad debt write-offs												
Barclays	0.5	0.6	0.4	0.8	1.1	0.2	0.2	0.3	0.7	0.2	0.2	1.8
National Provincial	0.1	0.8	0.6	0.8	1.0	0.7	0.7	n/a	n/a	n/a	n/a	n/a
Westminster	n/a	0.5	n/a	0.4	0.3	1.2	0.5	0.3	0.1	0.4	0.8	0.3

Notes: See text for definitions of the three measures of bad debt experience.
n/a=not available.
Sources: As Table 6, plus National Provincial (1900–36); Westminster (1928–60).

over-provision out of a sense of prudence, could be considered additional capital (see Ackrill & Hannah, 2001, pp. 448–450, for discussion of issues in the measurement of bad debts).

Overall, the data do not suggest a marked deterioration in bad debt experience from the 1920s to the 1930s, and reflect levels of bad debt which would be considered low by international comparisons. Although total provisions expressed as a percentage of advances were worse in the 1930s, falls in advances exaggerate this apparent deterioration. New provisions for bad debts were generally lower in the 1930s than in the 1920s, and actual write-offs similar for Barclays, the only bank for which full records of write-offs in both decades survive. The reported data include provisions and write-offs for German Standstill debt, and the unusually high 1939 write-off for Barclays reflects its write-off of Standstill debt.

The clearing banks, in common with the merchant and British overseas banks, were not a homogenous group, and the diversity of operations within the sector can be considered a stabilising factor. Barclays, with significant operations in its international subsidiary, Barclays DCO, showed different bad debt experience in its domestic and international operations (Ackrill & Hannah, 2001, p. 451), suggesting some benefit from diversification. The Midland and Lloyds banks provide additional examples.

The Midland's exposures to British trade and industry were greater than those of other banks, and by 1930 it already had 'a particularly heavy concentration [of doubtful or bad debts] in the textile industry, coal, iron and steel, and in stockbroking and the commodity trades' (Holmes & Green, 1986, pp. 179, 189). Its exposure to the Royal Mail Shipping Group, through its Belfast Bank subsidiary, was £3.4 million, roughly equivalent to its initial German Standstill exposure (Holmes & Green, 1986, p. 185). But the Midland suffered few problems from international business, having pursued a different strategy from the other Big Five banks. It had no subsidiary or branch operations outside Britain, but its London-based overseas branch, with an extensive correspondent network, was consistently profitable (Holmes & Green, 1986, p. 165).

In contrast, Lloyds' exposure to heavy industry was relatively low. For example, advances to collieries in July 1931 amounted to only £1.43 million, less than 0.4% of assets (Lloyds, 1931, Board Minutes, 28 July 1931). But Lloyds had relatively large indirect exposures to South America and Europe through subsidiaries or associates which it was forced to support. It owned 57% of the Bank of London and South America (BOLSA) in the early 1930s, diluted to below 50% after BOLSA's 1936 merger with ASAB, and declined to participate in the support operation for ASAB due to its interest in BOLSA (Jones, 1993, pp. 140, 241). Lloyds' 10%, £100,000, shareholding in British-Italian Corporation generated a loss of more than 10 times its original investment (Jones, 1993, pp. 231–234; Table 4). An equal partner in Lloyds and National Provincial Foreign Bank, with its head office in Paris and most of its operations in France, Lloyds shared in providing support of £1.5 million by the outbreak of World War II, representing approximately 10% of the joint venture's total assets at November 1935 (LNPFB, 1933–37).

The clearing banks pursued various approaches to manage their Standstill debts by: bringing non-Standstill German exposures within Standstill arrangements; taking steps to minimise currency losses from exchange-rate volatility after breakdown of the gold standard; and bringing exposures of their international subsidiaries within parent bank arrangements. Some banks realised losses to reduce

Standstill exposures, but others allowed the Standstill to take its course and, being well capitalised, could afford to do so. Archival data show that the exposures of Lloyds and National Provincial banks to Standstill debt were lower than those of the other large clearing banks, and the declines in their exposures between 1931 and 1939 reflected greater willingness to accept losses in reducing these (see Table 8).

Discussion and conclusion

Controversies continue over the causes of banking failure and financial crises in the 1930s. We do not set out in this article to explain experience in countries other than Britain in the interwar years, but it is appropriate to reflect on the various factors put forward to explain variations in experience from country to country. These include differences between universal and specialised banking systems, but 'neither "bank-oriented" nor "market-oriented" financial systems escaped the crisis; and it is not easy to say which system proved the more resilient' (Tilly, 1998, p. 23). It is, however, clear that universal banking could produce bad outcomes as, for example, in Italy, where 'connected lending' resulted in poor lending decisions and weak monitoring (Battilossi, 2009).

The question of branch versus unit banking may be another important factor. Branching is generally thought to offer benefits such as greater diversification, resilience to shocks, and ease of co-ordination (Calomiris, 2010). In Britain and Canada, large branch networks were a stabilising factor (Bordo, Rockoff, & Redish, 1994; Grossman, 1994). But evidence on branch banking elsewhere, including in Germany and the US, is not clear-cut, with the effects of branching on competition and risk-taking behaviour difficult to disentangle (Carlson, 2004; Schnabel, 2009).

Many have argued that central bank policies were inadequate, with the German Reichsbank and the US Federal Reserve ('the Fed') notable examples. Richardson (2007, pp. 643–644) summarises the contrasting views on the Fed's role in the Great Depression. Its failure to inject sufficient high-powered money to offset the reduction in the money stock may have allowed the normal US business cycle to turn into the Great Depression (Bordo, Choudhri, & Schwartz, 2002; Friedman & Schwartz, 1963). James is unconvinced: 'the Friedman and Schwartz account is inadequate … their argument is somewhat slippery as to causality' (James, 2001, pp. 76–77). One possible answer is the vulnerability of banks that cleared cheques via correspondents to the collapse of correspondent networks. With widespread unit banking, clearing houses played a prominent role and provided a route by which contagion could be spread, which the Fed failed to offset (Richardson, 2007). Richardson and Van Horn (2009) demonstrate that failures of banks in New York City, the centre of the US money market, resulted from increased regulatory scrutiny rather than contagion from European problems. Calomiris (2010) also rejects the judgement that panic or international contagion contributed to significant bank failures in the US, but is critical of the view that the Fed failed, drawing attention to sector-specific and regional shocks, magnified by the extent of unit banking.

Overall, we suggest that structural weaknesses found in banking systems elsewhere, such as the absence of an effective LLR, poor governance, the dependence of the main commercial banks on overseas deposits, and the prevalence of unit banking, were absent from Britain. Other factors present in Britain, such as strong liquidity and capital positions, were missing elsewhere. These features were reinforced by the crucial decision to depart from the gold standard, which protected the real

Table 8. Standstill exposures, 1931 and 1939.

	German Standstill 1931 £000s	German Standstill 1939 £000s	Hungarian Standstill 1931 £000s	Austrian Standstill 1931 £000s	Source
Clearing banks					
Barclays	4232	3300	92[1]	45[1]	Barclays, 1931–33, 1933–36; Tuke & Gillman, 1972, p. 39
Lloyds	1988	438	n/a	n/a	Lloyds, 1940–53
Martins	n/a	242	n/a	n/a	Martins, 1920–39, Board Minutes, 7 November 1939
Midland	3300	2750	69	112	Holmes & Green, 1986, pp. 186–187; Midland, 1931–38, 1932–36
National Provincial	1280	nil	n/a	n/a	Lloyds, 1940–53, described as 'unofficial figures'
Westminster	2779	3034[2]	177	200[3]	Westminster, 1930–39, 1932–38, 1956–58
Williams Deacon's	58	n/a	n/a	n/a	Williams Deacon's, 1915–51
Clearing banks' international subsidiaries					
Barclays DCO	575	390[3]	n/a	n/a	Barclays DCO, 1931, 1938–43
Barclays Bank France	560	203	n/a	n/a	Barclays, 1946–54; Barclays France, 1928–68
Lloyds and National Provincial Foreign Bank*	n/a	800[5]	n/a	n/a	LNPFB, 1938
Westminster Foreign Bank	1021	nil[2]	n/a	n/a	Westminster, 1930–39

Notes: The 1931 figures are for the closest date available to the inception of the Standstill. The 1939 figures are for the closest date available to the outbreak of war. There are minor inconsistencies between the latter figures and those found on a Foreign Office file (Foreign Office, 1946–47).
n/a = not available.
1 = at May 1932.
2 = Westminster Foreign Bank's exposures were taken over by its parent, Westminster, in 1935.
3 = at August 1938.
4 = Lloyds and National Provincial banks each owned 50%.
5 = deposits held with German banks at end-1937.

economy from undue suffering, allowing Britain to enjoy its strongest ever upswing from 1932 to 1937, after a recession (not depression) in 1929–32. Britain's escape from the non-monetary effects identified by Bernanke (1983) helped to ensure that the banking system did not suffer cripplingly high levels of bad debt. To follow the taxonomy of Reinhart and Rogoff (2009), Britain suffered a currency crisis, but avoided the banking, debt and inflation crises which often accompany this.

The financial system experienced contagion, notably from capital flight by overseas investors during the 1931 exchange-rate crisis, although evidence on the nature and extent of this is unsatisfactory. But evidence of a 'run' on British banks is lacking, the system emerged intact, and we argue was not under serious threat, thereby contributing to the financial and monetary stability which underpin macroeconomic stability. This argument is not new, but the new archival data we present enhance the range and quality of evidence available, and therefore provide more comprehensive support for this view than has been recognised previously.

The increased concentration arising from the amalgamation process which created the Big Five clearing banks had produced powerful and resilient institutions, able to absorb the external shocks of abandonment of the gold standard and the Standstill, at a time when severe banking problems were found in many other countries. The Big Five proved sound: they were strongly capitalised and none needed to raise new capital in the 1930s; they had large branch networks and strong earning power; there were no mergers between them or with other banks; and their diversified and liquid balance sheets contrasted, for example, with their German counterparts. These were not universal banks and their much-criticised conservatism and prudence, albeit overstated, helped them to avoid the fate of banks elsewhere, and to ensure that this concentrated banking structure delivered stability.

The British banks which experienced serious problems in the 1930s were those which were smaller and more specialised than the large clearing banks and whose business was relatively undiversified: small clearing banks with large exposures to the Lancashire cotton industry; merchant banks, whose main business was the financing of international trade, much of it Anglo-German; and some British overseas banks, particularly those with heavy dependence on Latin America. Several merchant banks experienced both liquidity and solvency problems, the result of substantial Standstill debt, high leverage, and heavy reliance on foreign deposits. They were effectively insolvent, kept afloat by a mixture of owners' capital, funding from the large clearing banks and the Bank, mergers, and changes to market practice.

The Bank used its full range of powers and persuasion in its active, discreet, and highly discriminatory, support of individual institutions. It often co-opted the large clearing banks into support operations, and the existence of this small group of strong, 'well-behaved' institutions greatly assisted it. Overall, the results were consolidation around the periphery of the clearing banks, but with more fundamental change among the merchant banks and discount houses. The collapse of individual institutions, while not a threat to the British financial system as a whole, would have disrupted the London discount market, still the world's major money market. This would have damaged the status of the City of London as a financial centre, and also British trade, already under pressure from rising trade barriers and falling economic activity in many countries. Thus the Bank acted in its traditional way, but it did not make a conscious choice to support particular institutions at the expense of abandoning the gold standard. Circumstances meant that the exchange rate was no longer sustainable, but liquidity could be provided to the system.

In the late 2000s a crisis hit a highly concentrated British domestic banking system, which was threatened by contagion from international problems. There are notable contrasts to the 1930s, when the major commercial banks had adequate capital resources and liquidity, whereas in the 2000s the largest institutions were less well diversified than they appeared and had abandoned robust liquidity and capital positions for alternative models. Market concentration in the banking sector may be undesirable from the perspectives of competition and the provision of finance. But within such a system in the 1930s, large, well-diversified, and prudent banks, supported by active central banking and the flexibility of a floating exchange rate regime, were able to avoid panic, escaped the need for 'fire sales' of problem assets, could sustain their capital positions, and were able and willing to support the Bank's efforts to protect the banking system. For smaller, weaker banks, the existence and effective operation of formal or informal mechanisms ensured that their problems could be managed within this system. This all took place within an institutional framework in which there was less transparency than today and detailed rules-based regulation was absent.

Acknowledgements

We thank the archivists, past and present, of the major banks: Maria Sienkiewicz, Nicholas Webb and Jessie Campbell (Barclays); Karen Sampson and John Booker (Lloyds Banking Group); Edwin Green, Tina Staples and Julia Banks (HSBC); Philip Winterbottom and Susan Patterson (Royal Bank of Scotland); and Fiona Maccoll (formerly of National Westminster). We are also grateful to Chris Kobrak, Mira Wilkins, and two anonymous reviewers for helpful comments.

References

The archival sources used in this article were as follows:
Barclays Bank PLC, Group Archives, Manchester (BGA).
HSBC Holdings plc, Group Archives, London (HSBCGA).
Lloyds Banking Group plc, Archives, London (LBGA).
The National Archives, Kew, London (NA).
The Royal Bank of Scotland Group plc, Group Archives, Edinburgh (RBSGA).

Accominotti, O. (2009). *London merchant banks, the central European panic and the sterling crisis of 1931.* Unpublished manuscript, Sciences Po, Paris and University of California, Berkeley.
Ackrill, M., & Hannah, L. (2001). *Barclays: The business of banking 1690–1996.* Cambridge: Cambridge University Press.
Baker, M., & Collins, M. (2010). English commercial banks and organizational inertia: The financing of SMEs, 1944–1960. *Enterprise and Society, 11,* 65–97.
Barclays Bank Limited (Barclays). (1909–39). *Unpublished accounts.* W.F. Tuke, General Manager (3/336). BGA.
Barclays. (1930–32). *Records of advances made, Mr. Murrell's section* (140/65). BGA.
Barclays. (1931–33). *Report on Germany's foreign indebtedness; Report on Germany's financial situation in the early 1930s; German public debtors supplemental agreement 1933* (200/10). BGA.
Barclays. (1933–36). *Figures, no.8 German Standstill Agreement returns* (1262/58). BGA.

Barclays. (1946–54). *Barclays Bank (France), Paris German Standstill figures* (1262/66). BGA.

Barclays Bank (Dominion, Colonial & Overseas) Limited (Barclays DCO). (1931). *Circulars re German Standstill Agreement* (11/1831). BGA.

Barclays Bank (France) Limited (Barclays France). (1928–68). *Accounting papers* (3/1534). BGA.

Barclays DCO. (1938–43). *Minutes, London Committee No. 02* (80/665). BGA.

Battilossi, S. (2009). Did governance fail universal banks? Moral hazard, risk taking, and banking crises in interwar Italy. *Economic History Review* [Special issue], *62*, 101–134.

Beenstock, M., Capie, F.H., & Griffiths, B. (1984). *Economic recovery in the United Kingdom in the 1930s* (Panel Paper 23). London: Bank of England.

Bernanke, B.S. (1983). Nonmonetary effects of the financial crisis in the propagation of the Great Depression. *American Economic Review, 73*, 257–276.

Bernanke, B.S., & James, H. (1991). The gold standard, deflation and financial crisis in the Great Depression: An international comparison. In R.G. Hubbard (Ed.), *Financial markets and financial crises* (pp. 33–68). Chicago, IL: University of Chicago Press.

Billings, M., & Capie, F.H. (2007). Capital in British banking 1920–1970. *Business History, 49*, 139–162.

Billings, M., & Capie, F.H. (2009). Transparency and financial reporting in mid-twentieth century British banking. *Accounting Forum, 33*, 38–53.

Bordo, M.D., Choudhri, E.U., & Schwartz, A.J. (2002). Was expansionary monetary policy feasible during the Great Contraction? An examination of the gold standard constraint. *Explorations in Economic History, 39*, 1–28.

Bordo, M.D., Rockoff, H., & Redish, A. (1994). The U.S. banking system from a Northern exposure: Stability versus efficiency. *Journal of Economic History, 54*, 325–341.

Burk, K. (1989). *Morgan Grenfell 1838–1988: The biography of a merchant bank*. Oxford: Oxford University Press.

Calomiris, C.W. (2010). Bank failures in theory and history: The Great Depression and other 'contagious' events. In A. Berger, P. Molyneux, & J. Wilson (Eds.), *The Oxford handbook of banking* (pp. 692–710). Oxford: Oxford University Press.

Capie, F.H. (2002). The emergence of the Bank of England as a mature central bank. In D. Winch & P.K. O'Brien (Eds.), *The political economy of British historical experience, 1688–1914* (pp. 295–315). Oxford: Oxford University Press.

Capie, F.H., & Billings, M. (2001). Profitability in English banking in the twentieth century. *European Review of Economic History, 5*, 367–401.

Capie, F.H., & Billings, M. (2004). Evidence on competition in English commercial banking 1920–70. *Financial History Review, 11*, 69–103.

Capie, F.H., Mills, T.C., & Wood, G.E. (1986). What happened in 1931? In F.H. Capie & G.E. Wood (Eds.), *Financial crises and the world banking system* (pp. 120–148). Basingstoke: Macmillan.

Capie, F.H., & Webber, A. (1985). *A monetary history of the United Kingdom, 1870–1982: Volume 1: Data, sources, methods*. London: George Allen & Unwin.

Carlson, M. (2004). Are branch banks better survivors? Evidence from the Depression era. *Economic Inquiry, 42*, 111–126.

Collins, M. (1989). The banking crisis of 1878. *Economic History Review, 42*, 504–527.

Collins, M. (1998). English bank development within a European context, 1870–1939. *Economic History Review, 51*, 1–24.

Collins, M., & Baker, M. (2001). English commercial bank liquidity, 1860–1913. *Accounting, Business & Financial History, 11*, 171–191.

Collins, M., & Baker, M. (2003). *Commercial banks and industrial finance in England and Wales, 1860–1913*. Oxford: Oxford University Press.

Crafts, N. (2003). Long-run growth. In R. Floud & P. Johnson (Eds.), *The Cambridge economic history of modern Britain. Vol. 2: Economic maturity, 1860–1939* (pp. 1–24). Cambridge: Cambridge University Press.

Diaper, S.J. (1986). Merchant banking in the inter-war period: The case of Kleinwort, Sons & Co. *Business History, 28*, 55–76.

District Bank. (1920–68). *Accountant's statistics book of Manchester and Liverpool District Banking Co Limited* (DIS/102). RBSGA.

Eichengreen, B. (1992). *Golden fetters: The gold standard and the Great Depression, 1919–1939*. Oxford: Oxford University Press.

Eichengreen, B. (2003). The British economy between the wars. In R. Floud & P. Johnson (Eds.), *The Cambridge economic history of modern Britain. Vol. 2: Economic maturity, 1860–1939* (pp. 314–343). Cambridge: Cambridge University Press.

Feinstein, C.H. (1976). *Structural tables of national income, expenditure and output of the United Kingdom 1855–1965*. Cambridge: Cambridge University Press.

Forbes, N. (1987). London banks, the German Standstill Agreements, and 'economic appeasement' in the 1930s. *Economic History Review, 40*, 571–587.

Forbes, N. (2000). *Doing business with the Nazis: Britain's economic and financial relations with Germany, 1931–1939*. London: Frank Cass.

Foreign Office. (1946–47). *Standstill claims of British banks* (FO 944/394). NA.

Friedman, M., & Schwartz, A.J. (1963). *A monetary history of the United States 1867–1960*. Princeton, NJ: Princeton University Press.

Grossman, R.S. (1994). The shoe that didn't drop: Explaining banking stability during the Great Depression. *Journal of Economic History, 54*, 654–682.

Hatton, T.J. (2003). Unemployment and the labour market, 1870–1939. In R. Floud & P. Johnson (Eds.), *The Cambridge economic history of modern Britain. Vol. 2: Economic maturity, 1860–1939* (pp. 344–373). Cambridge: Cambridge University Press.

Holmes, A.R., & Green, E. (1986). *Midland: 150 Years of banking business*. London: B.T. Batsford.

Howson, S. (1980). The management of sterling 1932–39. *Journal of Economic History, 40*, 53–60.

James, H. (1992). Financial flows across frontiers during the interwar depression. *Economic History Review, 45*, 594–613.

James, H. (2001). *The end of globalization: Lessons from the Great Depression*. Cambridge, MA: Harvard University Press.

Jones, G. (1993). *British multinational banking 1830–1990*. Oxford: Oxford University Press.

Jonker, J., & van Zanden, J.L. (1995). Method in the madness? Banking crises between the wars, an international comparison. In C.H. Feinstein (Ed.), *Banking, currency and finance in Europe between the wars* (pp. 76–93). Oxford: Clarendon Press.

Kindleberger, C.P. (1986). *The world in depression, 1929–1939* (2nd ed.). Berkeley: University of California Press.

Kindleberger, C.P., & Aliber, R.Z. (2005). *Manias, panics and crashes: A history of financial crises* (5th ed.). Hoboken, NJ: John Wiley.

Kobrak, C. (2009). Family finance: Value creation and the democratization of cross-border governance. *Enterprise and Society, 10*, 38–89.

Kynaston, D. (1999). *The City of London. Vol. 3: Illusions of gold 1914–1945*. London: Chatto & Windus.

Lloyds. (1940–53). *German Standstill Agreement* (HO/GM/OFF/28/2). LBGA.

Lloyds Bank Limited (Lloyds). (1931). *Main board minutes* (HO/D/BOA/MIN/36 & 37). LBGA.

Lloyds and National Provincial Foreign Bank (LNPFB). (1933–37). *Balance sheets and guarantees position of Lloyds and National Provincial Foreign Bank Limited* (LBI/14). RBSGA.

LNPFB. (1938). *German Standstill Agreement profit and loss and balance sheet figures* (F/7/B/22). LBGA.

Martins Bank Limited (Martins). (1920–39). *Board minutes* (38/569–579). BGA.

Midland. (1923–69). *Working papers, Contingent Fund* (227/3). HSBCGA.

Midland. (1931–38). *Notes and correspondence between Overseas Branch and Austrian Credit Anstalt Committee, with analyses of accounts* (O252/075). HSBCGA.

Midland. (1932–36). *Agreements on Hungarian debt standstill and Pengo Transfer Agreement between National Bank of Hungary, Hungarian debtors, and committee representing British and American banks* (O252/082). HSBCGA.

Midland Bank Limited (Midland). (1920–39). *Accounts volumes (described as 'black books')* (0532). HSBCGA.

Munn, C.W. (1988). *Clydesdale Bank: The first 150 years*. London: William Collins.

National Provincial. (1911–25). *Supplementary ledger* (NAT/1005/6). RBSGA.

National Provincial. (1926–34). *Supplementary ledger* (NAT/1005/7). RBSGA.

National Provincial. (1937–40). *General abstracts of accounts of head office, branches and city office (NAT/1005/10)*. RBSGA.

National Provincial Bank of England Limited (National Provincial). (1900–36). *Bad debt ledger* (NAT/1000). RBSGA.

Newton, L. (2003). Government, the banks and industry in inter-war Britain. In T. Gourvish (Ed.), *Business and politics in Europe, 1900–1970: Essays in honour of Alice Teichova* (pp. 145–168). Cambridge: Cambridge University Press.

Rajan, R.G., & Zingales, L. (2003). The great reversals: The politics of financial development in the twentieth century. *Journal of Financial Economics, 69*, 5–50.

Reinhart, C.M., & Rogoff, K.S. (2009). *This time is different: Eight centuries of financial folly*. Princeton, NJ: Princeton University Press.

Richardson, G. (2007). The check is in the mail: Correspondent clearing and the collapse of the banking system, 1930 to 1933. *Journal of Economic History, 67*, 643–671.

Richardson, G., & van Horn, P. (2009). Intensified regulatory scrutiny and bank distress in New York City during the Great Depression. *Journal of Economic History, 69*, 446–465.

Roberts, R. (1992). *Schroders: Merchants & bankers*. Basingstoke: Macmillan.

Ross, D.M. (1996). Commercial banking in a market-oriented financial system: Britain between the wars. *Economic History Review, 44*, 314–335.

Saville, R. (1996). *Bank of Scotland, a history, 1695–1944*. Edinburgh: Edinburgh University Press.

Sayers, R.S. (1976). *The Bank of England 1891–1944*. Cambridge: Cambridge University Press.

Schnabel, I. (2009). The role of liquidity and implicit guarantees in the German twin crisis of 1931. *Journal of International Money and Finance, 28*, 1–25.

Schwartz, A.J. (1986). Real and pseudo-financial crises. In F.H. Capie & G.E. Wood (Eds.), *Financial crises and the world banking system* (pp. 11–31). Basingstoke: Macmillan.

Sheppard, D.K. (1971). *The growth and role of UK financial institutions 1880–1962*. London: Methuen.

Tilly, R. (1998). Universal banking in historical perspective. *Journal of Institutional and Theoretical Economics, 154*, 7–32.

Truptil, R.J. (1936). *British banks and the London money market*. London: Jonathan Cape.

Tuke, A.W., & Gillman, R.J.H. (1972). *Barclays Bank Limited 1926–1969*. London: Barclays Bank.

Westminster. (1920–43). *Weekly statements of London County Westminster and Parr's Bank Limited* (WES/561). RBSGA.

Westminster. (1928–60). *'Annual Return of Accommodation', 1957–1960. Also includes summary of advances, provisions and recoveries, and provisions and interest in suspense written off, 1928–1959*. A.D. Chesterfield, Chief General Manager (ADCCGM) (WES/1177/96). RBSGA.

Westminster. (1930–39). *Germany – Committee's reports on Bank's commitments*. Charles Lidbury, Chief General Manager (CLCGM) (WES/1174/187). RBSGA.

Westminster. (1931–34). *Germany*. CLCGM (WES/1174/249). RBSGA.

Westminster. (1932–38). *Austria – general*. CLCGM (WES/1174/120). RBSGA.

Westminster. (1956–58). *German Standstill debts*. ADCCGM (WES/1177/102). RBSGA.

Westminster Bank Limited (Westminster). (1911–50). *Statistics of the Chief Accountant for preparation of the annual accounts* (WES/1319/2). RBSGA.

Williams, D. (1963). London and the 1931 financial crisis. *Economic History Review, 15*, 513–528.

Williams Deacon's. (1971). *Williams Deacon's 1771–1970*. Manchester: Williams Deacon's.

Williams Deacon's Bank Limited (Williams Deacon's). (1915–51). *Head office memoranda files: Foreign business* (WD/50/6). RBSGA.

Williamson, P. (1992). *National crisis and national government: British politics, the economy and empire, 1926–1932*. Cambridge: Cambridge University Press.

Winton, J.R. (undated, c. 1980a). *Capital, reserves, and dividends*. Winton research files (no call number). LBGA.

Winton, J.R. (undated, c. 1980b). *Investments*. Winton research files (no call number). LBGA.

Winton, J.R. (1982). *Lloyds Bank 1918–1969*. Oxford: Oxford University Press.

New perspectives on the 1931 banking crisis in Germany and Central Europe

Christopher Kopper

Department of History, Universität Bielefeld, Bielefeld, Germany

Until today, most research on the Great Depression has focused on the failures of monetary and currency policies. A new look at the Great Depression challenges the dominant research opinion that the credit contraction was the main cause for the aggravated depression. The big German banks did not reduce the amount of credit and defaulted because of their high write-offs on big loans. The write-offs occurred as a consequence of the insufficient monitoring of debtors. The relation between the banks and their debtors was highly asymmetric and was characterised by the opportunistic behaviour of debtors.

Due to the complete helplessness of the government and the lack of any camaraderie in the banking sector, the banks were totally at the mercy of foreign pressures in summer 1931. (Hjalmar Schacht at the Institut für Weltwirtschaft, Universität Kiel, 26 January 1934)

Introduction

The banking crisis of 1931 was Central Europe's most severe banking crisis in the twentieth century. Recently, the financial crisis of 2008 triggered memories of the Great Depression. The experiences of the 1930s served as a negative example of how a financial crisis might have evolved if central banks and governments had failed to learn the right lessons from history. Prior to 2008 historians had debated the question of whether the crisis of 1931 should be primarily considered a banking crash (Born, 1968, 1983; James, 1984) or rather be treated as a currency crisis (Balderston, 1994; Ferguson & Temin, 2003; Hardach, 1976). Since the first hypothesis, which characterised the crisis as a failure of banks and the banking system, was developed before the second hypothesis, macroeconomic historians tended to view the banking crisis explanation as outdated.

The classical theory of the financial crash as a failure of banks and banking was based on a microeconomic research perspective. Their diligent focus on the course of events and the structures of balance sheets led business historians to the inevitable conclusion that the causes of the crisis have to be identified with the structural deficits of commercial banking and the blunders of bankers and borrowers (Feldman, 1994, 1995). But the microeconomic perspective was not free of shortcomings. Some of these publications were too narrative, lacked analytical stringency and neglected the structural causes of the banks' failure in favour of an intriguing but too personalised history of great (and not so great) bankers and monetary policy makers.

Because of their different methodological approach and the use of more or less sophisticated quantitative methods, macroeconomic historians came to the opposite conclusions. Economic historians viewed the banking crisis as a consequence of a deficient currency system and a failure of central banking policies. In 2004, the economist and economic historian Isabel Schnabel tried to bridge the epistemological gap between economic and business historians by using a set of data which had so far been overlooked by economic historians because of their focus on aggregate currency statistics: the monthly balance sheets of the big German banks in 1931 and their quarterly reports of foreign debts. Based on these statistics, Schnabel elaborates a more balanced conclusion. The external shock of foreign withdrawals from Germany's big banks and the internal shock through major failing bank debtors were not connected at the beginning of the banking crisis, but became more and more intertwined in the course of the crisis until the bank collapse of July 1931. Still, Schnabel puts the bigger part of the blame on the German central bank (Reichsbank) and its failure to flush the banking system with fresh liquidity to prevent a confidence crisis among bank creditors and the inevitable run to the bank counters. Unlike other economic historians, she does not downplay the risky liquidity holding preference of the big banks and recognises their 'moral hazard problem of excessive risk-taking ..., risky loan policies and small equity covers' (Schnabel, 2004, pp. 861ff, 865ff).

This conclusion by Schnabel is a recent achievement of quantitative economic history, but is not new to the community of business historians. Business historians such as Gerald Feldman have always stressed the moral hazard problem of German banking in the late 1920s and early 1930s, embodied by the leading German banker Jakob Goldschmidt. Goldschmidt, the chairman and dominant executive of Darmstädter und Nationalbank (Danat-Bank), did not stand out because of the size of his bank. Among the big German banks, Danat-Bank ranked only fourth in terms of capital and reserves, but second in balance size (Untersuchungsausschuss, 1934). By 1931 the controversial parvenu Goldschmidt had earned substantial fame – and some notoriety – as a skilful risk-taking investment banker and avid schemer of mergers and acquisitions in the German financial community and drew substantial envy and resentment as an alleged megalomaniac (Feldman, 1994, 1995). Historians writing history as the history of individuals – and not so much of corporate, market and economic structures – framed the climax of the banking crisis in June and July 1931 as a showdown between the failing maverick Goldschmidt and his more conservative adversaries at Deutsche Bank who allegedly denied him a helping hand and caused the domino pieces to fall. Some historians adopted the contemporary equation about the tense relations between Goldschmidt and Deutsche Bank executive chairman Oscar Wassermann as a conflict between David and Saul (Feldman, 1994, 1995), a comparison which loaded the history of the financial crisis with – literally – biblical dimensions. A contemporary expert even evoked a motive of the popular Nibelungen saga and charged Wassermann of having stabbed Goldschmidt in the back (Argentarius, 1931).

A systematic and comprehensive approach to the causes of the banking crisis has to include the methodologies from business and from economic history. This paper will focus on several structural aspects that have only been examined by a few historians of the banking crisis: the institutional setting of banking policy, debtor–creditor relations and the exact causes of the tremendous equity losses in the German and Austrian banking system in 1931.

The regulatory context

Only a few publications paid close attention to the malfunction – or rather absence – of public banking control in the 1920s and early 1930s. The only German public institution with some powers to regulate banking was the central bank, the Reichsbank. Unlike the Federal Reserve Bank, the Reichsbank demonstrated its determination not to allow the growth of a speculation bubble. Reichsbank governor Hjalmar Schacht publicly declared in May 1927 that he would not accept unrestricted borrowing for the purchase of stock and planned to restrict the re-discounting facilities of banks. At this time, the German stock market was in a similar situation to the US stock market in summer 1929: stock quotes had doubled within a few months and the ratio between stock quotes and corporate revenues had grown out of proportion (Ritschl, 2002). The banks fuelled the speculative frenzy by tripling their overall loans for the purchase of stock within just one year (Abramowski, 1991).[1] The purpose of Schacht's manoeuvre was to prevent the banks from financing stock speculation on a bullish market. Schacht forced the air out of the growing bubble and prevented the stock speculation bubble from further inflating and bursting. In the months after May 1927, the Berlin stock index dropped by 25% and returned to a normal level. Despite the criticism of contemporary economic historians such as Hans-Joachim Voth (2001), Schacht's intervention against speculation burdened investors with substantial losses of equity, but prevented them from incurring even higher losses if the bubble had continued to inflate. The gross capital stock and the gross investment rate demonstrate that the equity losses of 1927 were far too low to trigger a depression through under-investment and/or under-capitalisation.

The Reichsbank had the tools to regulate the price and the quantity of bank lending by setting the discount rate and the amount of re-discounted bills. In addition, the Reichsbank received monthly balance statements from the major banks and quarterly reports about a potentially crucial portion of their foreign liabilities. But apart from its monetary policy powers and rights to demand monthly statements, the powers of the Reichsbank to exert control over the banks were strictly confined to the purpose and means of monetary policies. In 1908, prominent scholars of economics and finance such as Adolph Wagner and Georg Obst had spoken up in favour of a public banking control agency on the occasion of a parliamentary banking *enquete* committee (Paersch, 1933; Untersuchungsausschuss, 1934). But their suggestion of setting up a public banking agency could never be achieved against the determined veto of the German banking community. The liberal consensus within the German banking community formed a powerful veto block that policy makers could never overcome before summer 1931. Since the German banking system had not been riddled with cyclical waves of bankruptcies before

1931, policy makers had no powerful case that might have constituted an urgent necessity for public control and intervention. The senior officials in the Reichsbank and the Ministry of Economic Affairs were unaware of the potential dangers of laissez faire in banking.

The causes

The main cause of the banking crisis of 1931 was the failure of public governance – but in a different way than many economic historians have perceived. The main failure was not the monetary policy of the Reichsbank (Kaserer, 2000), but the absence of public risk control in the financial sector. Unlike in 2007–08, the German banking crisis of 1931 took place under the institutional framework of non-existent banking regulation. The monthly bank balances of the big banks informed the Reichsbank about their current liquidity status, one potential case for concern and default. But the Reichsbank only had rights to demand basic balance information, and no executive power to enforce special auditing for hidden risks. The general fall of liquidity ratios raised some concerns in the financial community, but the Reichsbank was still denied the right to set minimum rates for cash and first-order liquidity. Apart from this, the balances did not reveal any information about the current status of major loans such as credits to big industrial corporations. The 1930 balances of the big banks (Deutsche Bank, Dresdner Bank, Commerzbank and Danat-Bank) hid all significant risks that might have prompted the Reichsbank to act.

For good reasons, US historiography has focused on the negative effects of bank loans recalled from industrial debtors. Undoubtedly, the recall of loans (credit squeeze) after Black Friday contributed to the growing illiquidity of the non-banking sector in the US and had disastrous pro-cyclical macroeconomic and monetary effects. But the theory of a pro-cyclical credit contraction has never been thoroughly checked or challenged in regard to the German banking system. The level of loans from the big German banks to the non-banking sector grew steadily from 1925 to 31 December 1929 (from RM 2301 to RM 5300 million (Reichsmark)) and even rose in the first and second years of depression, reaching a peak of RM 5441 million at the end of February 1931 (Untersuchungsausschuss, 1934).

Unlike in the US, the supply of bank loans to the non-banking sector did not shrink right from the start of the Great Depression, but only after the banking crisis of July 1931. In the months before the climax of the banking crisis, the fall in loans to the non-banking sector was still rather slight. A decrease of 3.0% from 28 February to 30 June 1931 (RM 5235 m) was not a convincing indicator of a massive loan recall. German banks trying to recall loans were hampered by the problems of shrunken or frozen assets of their industrial debtors.

Contrary to Ben Bernanke's research on the non-monetary effects of the financial crisis in the US, the German banking system did not significantly contract to the disadvantage of credit debtors before and even after July 1931 (Bernanke, 2000). A significant contraction did not take place before the end of 1931 when the loans of the big banks to the non-banking sector had dropped to RM 4417 m or by 18.8% from the peak in February 1931. The significant drop from November to December 1931 (from RM 4939 to RM 4417 m) was certainly not the result of major loan recalls, but the consequence of depreciations for the banks' annual statements. Despite the criticism of mid-size enterprises that charged the big banks with unwarranted refusal of loans, the official German banking enquête in November 1933 did not confirm these allegations. The German Reichsbank proved these charges wrong and declared that nothing like this had ever become public.[2] Further evidence will demonstrate that banks were often trapped in an asymmetric principal–agent position towards their debtors and were often unable to implement credit cuts. As in the US, the rise of the real interest rate from 1930 seriously affected the position of the debtors. But because of growing bankruptcies, the banks did not benefit from higher real interest rates.

Withdrawal of foreign funds and bank health

The Reichsbank became accustomed to the high percentage of foreign deposits at the big banks that were more likely to be withdrawn in a serious crisis than domestic deposits. In June 1930, foreign deposits at the big German banks accounted for between 38% (Deutsche Bank) and 45% (Danat-Bank) of their overall deposits (Schnabel, 2004). Historians often named the high ratio of foreign deposits as the major cause for the banking crisis of 1931. Macroeconomic historians like Ferguson and Temin identified the foreign run on bank deposits in Germany as the major cause of the banks' failure in July 1931 (Ferguson and Temin, 2003). But if the ratio of foreign deposits had been the decisive factor of their vulnerability, the two biggest non-branch banks in Germany – Reichs-Kredit-Gesellschaft (RKG) and Berliner Handels-Gesellschaft (BHG) – with 51% and 69% foreign deposits respectively would have fallen first. In addition, the BHG was slightly worse off in terms of its first-order liquidity ratio of only 30% (cash + bank deposits + bills divided by short-term deposits and acceptance liabilities) compared to a 32% liquidity ratio at the big branch banks (Schnabel, 2004, p. 850).[3] But the BHG and the RKG survived the banking crisis against all the expectations of financial common sense. They did not even incur capital losses that would have required public intervention (Untersuchungsausschuss, 1934).[4]

The official monthly statements demonstrated the accelerating speed of foreign withdrawals since March 1931 and pointed the Reichsbank to the aggravating problems of liquidity within the banking sector, but did not reveal the dangerous status of the major debtors. The German accounting law (*Handelsgesetzbuch*) allowed the banks – and other enterprises – to accumulate so-called silent reserves (*stille Reserven*) through non-taxed revenues. These silent reserves could be dissolved to make up for declining revenues in recessions. Thus shareholders, bank creditors and the general public were usually tempted to expect that the annual reports – at least in good times – rather *understated* the earning power and reserves of the banks.

Even in the first depression year, 1930, the big banks still demonstrated sufficient earning power by paying dividend rates of 6% (Deutsche Bank, Dresdner Bank), 7% (Commerzbank) and even 8% (Danat-Bank) (Untersuchungsausschuss, 1934). Compared to 1929 and the years before, the big banks had to reduce their dividend rates by 4%. Already at this time, the payment of dividends was rather a disguise of their falling profitability and a short-term remedy against falling stock quotes. By maintaining its customary rate difference of 2% towards its biggest competitors (Deutsche Bank and Dresdner Bank), Danat-Bank defended its reputation as the most aggressive and most shareholder-oriented bank. But this demonstration of earning power came at the price of insufficient reserves for pension liabilities, insufficient depreciations for loans and securities and a general lack of clarity in accounting. In 1930, Deutsche Bank was the only big branch bank that listed pensions and pension liabilities separately, whereas its competitors hid their rather insufficient payments to the pension funds amongst their administrative and staff expenses. Despite the growing insolvency rates of commercial borrowers and the general drop of stock rates, the big banks were highly reluctant to adjust the nominal value of loans to the expected losses of interest and principal and to allow depreciations for the value of securities. Their overall adjustment and depreciation of only RM 42.3 million stood in gross disproportion to the listed value of securities and the amount of loans to non-banks (RM 5390 m) (Untersuchungsausschuss, 1934). Therefore, the bank asset portfolios were rather black boxes for the Reichsbank and the government.

The collapse of the German banking system became an acute danger when Danat-Bank detected the imminent bankruptcy of its biggest debtor, Nordwolle AG. On 11 May 1931, a senior manager of Danat informed his boss Goldschmidt that Nordwolle would face a loss of RM 145 million. As this loss exceeded the equity and the reserves of Nordwolle by far, the bankruptcy of Nordwolle and the consecutive default of its RM 48 m loan was a given fact. The looming Nordwolle bankruptcy spelled the worst for Danat-Bank. As Danat equity only amounted to RM 85 m (Born, 1968; Feldman, 1994) it was facing bankruptcy unless it received a substantial capital injection.

The imminent bankruptcy of Danat triggered the chain reaction that brought Germany's big joint stock banks to collapse. Business historians told the story of the banking crisis of 1931 as a chain reaction. The imminent end of Danat eroded the confidence of foreign and German bank creditors in Germany's banking system and triggered an unprecedented withdrawal of funds. Since the Reichsbank as lender of last resort had run out of liquidity in making up for the loss of foreign and domestic creditors, the banks and the government saw no alternative to a temporary closedown and a partial freeze of deposits. A more timely co-operation between the big banks, greater trust between the banks' executives and an earlier and more determined intervention by the Reichsbank would have probably prevented the partial and temporary default of the German banking system.

Most of the historiography on the financial crisis of 1931 focuses on the bankers' inability to co-operate and the Reichsbank's failure to inject sufficient liquidity into the financial sector. Unlike in 2008, the central banks in Europe and the US did not co-operate sufficiently to prevent the temporary illiquidity of the Reichsbank and the subsequent closing of banks in Germany. The relevance of these accounts is undisputed, but they tend to neglect the fact that the default of non-bank debtors was a major cause of the confidence crisis in the financial sector. The Nordwolle bankruptcy was the consequence of strained financial resources and serious mismanagement (Escher, 1988; von Reeken, 1996), aggravated by the slump in demand in the Great Depression. This means that the 1931 financial crisis was definitely rooted in the real economy, in the defaulting loans of industrial corporations and department store chains. A determined attempt to save Danat-Bank through close and trusting co-operation between the Reichsbank and the executive boards of the big banks might have prevented the climax of the liquidity crisis, but would not have helped Danat-Bank to recover from its severe capital losses. Even in a more efficient institutional environment, the recovery operation for Danat-Bank would have been similar: Danat-Bank might have survived without a merger with Dresdner Bank, but would still have required a significant injection of public capital to make up for its high capital losses.

Banks and their customers

What were the structural reasons for the high capital losses of the big banks? The big banks, and Danat in particular, broke the rules of common sense when they lent money to big enterprises. A bank with only RM 25 m equity and a paltry capital reserve of RM 60 m lending RM 48 m in total to one single debtor ran an irresponsible risk by putting all its eggs in one basket. The Nordwolle case was a perfect example of faulty or non-existent risk management. Certainly, Goldschmidt would have tried to recall his loan sooner if he had known about the dire condition of his biggest debtor. But the Nordwolle CEO gave orders to fake the balance statements in order to conceal the looming loss of RM 145 m (Escher, 1988) and the overall liabilities of RM 240 m. Finished products and raw wool were overvalued in order to hide losses. To make things worse, a Dutch brass plate company owned by Nordwolle secretly held a third of the Nordwolle nominal capital (RM 25 of 75 million) (Escher, 1988) to keep the Nordwolle stock quotes from falling. This meant that Nordwolle only had a nominal capital of RM 50 m instead of RM 75 m and was far more under-capitalised than Goldschmidt could imagine. The same brass plate company concealed high losses at Nordwolle through fake sales of wool. By inventing the sale of wool to the brass plate company at prices far above market level, Nordwolle turned losses through falling wool prices of about RM 80 m into claims against an affiliated company (Kalveram, 1950). In order to conceal its poor liquidity status, Nordwolle borrowed bills from its affiliate companies before the end of each month, used them to beef up its monthly balance statements and then sent the bills back to its affiliates after the end of the month.

But Danat-Bank was no innocent victim of a fraudulent debtor. Goldschmidt should have noticed and become suspicious when Nordwolle made no depreciations in 1929, insufficient depreciations in 1930 and listed a growing part of its maintenance expenses as investments. No Danat executive manager took offence at Nordwolle for hiding the bank debts under a general title for all creditors. Danat-Bank had no chance to detect the significant amount of debts to other banks. Thanks to his obstinacy, a senior manager of Danat-Bank finally received approval to check the Nordwolle balance in April and May 1931 (Escher, 1988) and discovered the loss. Since there was no legislation compelling the banks to limit their loans to a single debtor to a maximum percentage of their capital, legal checks and balances against a serious culmination of risks did not exist – and were not introduced until 1934.

Danat-Bank was not the only bank with inefficient loan controls. In 1930, the executive board of Deutsche Bank instructed its branch managers to monitor debtors regularly and to refrain from automatic loan prolongations. Debtors occasionally misspent bank loans for investments for the purchase of raw materials and for private consumption. A circular letter by Deutsche Bank's executive board demanded determination to ensure that loans would be repaid with priority and before the debtors distributed their profits to their shareholders (Feldman, 1994). This circular letter was clear evidence that regular and thorough loan monitoring procedures faced considerable resistance among debtors and were difficult to enforce. In the course of the Great Depression, Deutsche Bank's executive managers had to learn the hard way that its regular monitoring procedures were insufficient protection against loan fraud and faulty information about their debtors' financial status.

In October 1931, the near-bankruptcy of the big Schultheiss brewery revealed to Deutsche Bank that the Schultheiss CEO had intentionally withheld information about the loans taken from other banks. He told the company's main creditor, Deutsche Bank, that Schultheiss did not borrow money from other banks and faked its financial status in a stock prospectus (Feldman, 1994; Untersuchungsausschuss, 1934, p. 310). The Schultheiss case revealed that the presence of bankers on the supervisory boards of debtors could not protect the banks from being misinformed or even defrauded. Executive managers of Danat-Bank and Deutsche Bank sat on the Nordwolle and the Schultheiss supervisory boards, but were denied true information about the financial status of their clients. The bi-annual or tri-annual meetings of the supervisory boards did not provide timely information about the current financial status. The insufficient means of the banks to control their debtors resulted in an asymmetric relation between banks and debtors. Banks had insufficient leverage to enforce transparency and truthfulness.

How can the asymmetric relations between the banks and their big debtors be explained? The German finance market for big loans was oligopolistic, but highly competitive. For example, the joint stock companies in the iron and steel sector thwarted all attempts by the banks to establish exclusive ties between a bank and its debtor. Big corporations maintained debt accounts at several big banks in order to avoid dependence on one single bank. On the one hand, the common practice of borrowing from more than one bank helped the banks to limit their risks. But this risk limitation strategy came with the price of restricted transparency and a limited power of loan monitoring. Since the big banks tried to secure ties with a maximum number of corporations, they courted their debtors. The big corporations in the steel industry wielded sufficient power to avoid intrusive loan monitoring procedures. Usually, the steel industry held sufficient bargaining power to negotiate lower interest rates than the banks were ready to offer at first. The market for loans to the steel industry was a customers' and not a creditors' market.

Generally, the relations between the steel industry and the banks did not shift during the course of the Great Depression. Big corporations such as Krupp and the Friedrich Flick Trust were well enough endowed and well enough connected with the government to withstand a financial crisis without having to beg a bank for help. Flick took care to limit his dependence on big German banks. Instead, he preferred to finance his acquisitions through long-term securities and took big loans from private bankers like Simon Hirschland and A. Levy (Priemel, 2007; Wixforth, 1995). Even in late 1931, at a time when bankruptcy was looming over his trust, Friedrich Flick and his managers successfully rejected the attempts of the banks to demand a detailed and precise financial status. Other enterprises such as Europe's biggest steel trust – the Vereinigte Stahlwerke – denied the banks substantial collateral. In many cases, the banks had to accept insubstantial guarantees like an unspecified guarantee declaration (*Bürgschaftserklärung*) instead of real deposits on raw materials as collateral. The competition among the big banks was strong enough that debtors had the power to play one bank off against the other. Usually, bankers adopted a benevolent strategy towards debtors and avoided alienating them through extensive monitoring activities (Wixforth, 1995).

The size of debtors mattered – and mattered in a negative way. The risk of losing money through write-offs and defaulting on loans was highest for big loans and lowest for small ones. According to a statistical survey by the Reichsbank, loans of more than RM 5 m were the most likely to fail. In 1931, at the climax of the banking crisis, 13.2% of all loans above RM 5 m had to be written off. The write-off rate for loans between RM 1 and 5 m was 11.1%, whereas defaults on loans between RM 0.5 and 1 m were 10.8%. As the average default rate in 1931 amounted to 10.1%, the biggest lenders – the big banks – incurred the highest defaults and ran the highest risks (Untersuchungsausschuss, 1934). The default risk of loans grew proportionally with the size of the loans. Only 3.4% of all loans under RM 5000 and 5.0% of all loans between RM 5000 and 20,000 had to be written off. The situation for the big banks improved in 1932 when only 2.7% of all loans above RM 5 m and 5.0% of all loans between RM 1 and 5 m were written off. This was one important reason why smaller and mid-size banks fared better than the big banks. Their limited scale protected the mid-size regional banks, the local savings banks and the many small co-operative banks from making big loans, accumulating high risks and incurring big losses.

Generally, the banks were in a weaker rather than stronger position regarding their big debtors. In some cases like the relation between Deutsche Bank and Daimler-Benz, the bank maintained a more powerful position and exerted considerable pressure to enforce a painful reconstruction and rationalisation of the ailing car manufacturer. In the Daimler case, Deutsche Bank drew considerable power from the fact that Daimler seriously depended on bank loans. A member of Deutsche Bank's executive board acted as chairman of Daimler's supervisory board and had access to all relevant information about productivity, quality and product management (Feldman, 1994).

Some of the losses through defaulting on loans would have been prevented if the legal framework had obliged the banks to pursue a more prudent lending policy. The intense competition among the big banks was beneficial for the monetary supply of the German non-banking sector, but generated a problematic asymmetry between the banks and their debtors. In a depression, the benefits for the non-banking sector – such as a more liberal credit policy and competition for interest rates and better loan terms – were offset by a lack of risk control and a higher probability of bankruptcies. Corporate greed was one of the lesser evils: only two of the four big branch banks in Germany (Danat-Bank and Commerzbank) played an aggressive part in competition for shareholders. Despite some widespread assumptions in the financial community, Jakob Goldschmidt did not ruin Danat-Bank through stock speculation, but through negligence in the loan business. The exemplary stories of Nordwolle and Schultheiss demonstrate the importance of moral hazard for banking.

But unlike in 2007/08, the main offenders with a moral hazard issue were not reckless investment bankers, but the executive managers of industrial corporations. These managers put not only their own enterprises, but also the banks, in imminent danger of bankruptcy. The problem of being too big to fail applied to the big debtors rather than to the banks. Debtors such as Nordwolle and Schultheiss intentionally exploited the asymmetrical access to information to the disadvantage of their creditors. Apart from this, they relied on their assumption that a bank would rather prolong than cancel their loans if a major creditor came close to bankruptcy. Debtors assumed that the recall of a loan would drive them into illiquidity and force the bank to a total write-off, whereas a prolongation might still contain some hope for a recovery. The trial against the Nordwolle CEO was symptomatic of the low power of banks vis-à-vis their debtors and their difficulties in enforcing their rights. The Nordwolle CEO deceived Danat-Bank about his financial status, but was not sentenced for fraud (*Betrug*) and bankruptcy crimes (*Konkursverbrechen*), but only for embezzlement (*Untreue*). Instead of being sentenced for faking the balances (*Bilanzfälschung*), he was only found guilty of concealing the financial status (*Bilanzverschleierung*).

The dishonoured Danat loan to Nordwolle was just the tip of the iceberg. The overall amount of dishonoured and written off loans was never published and only known to the banks and the Reichsbank. After Danat-Bank was merged with Dresdner Bank in 1932, the executives of Dresdner Bank calculated total write-offs of RM 620 m, while the capital and the open reserves of both Dresdner Bank and Danat-Bank only amounted to RM 254 m. Danat-Bank and Dresdner Bank incurred most of their depreciation losses through failing loans reaching a total of RM 478 m. The write-offs of Deutsche Bank and Commerzbank were lower, but showed a similar pattern. Deutsche Bank incurred total depreciations of RM 482 m (about RM 361 m on loans), whereas the Commerzbank accounted write-offs of RM 247 m, including RM 157 m on loans.[5] Their total losses through loan depreciations alone reached RM 996 m, while the total equity (without silent reserves) of the three banks did not exceed RM 780 m. The quoted numbers included both open and silent write-offs and exceeded the published write-offs by far. The annual reports of the big branch banks for 1931 and 1932 listed open write-offs of RM 863 m, whereas the total number for open and silent depreciations – as listed in the reports to the Reichsbank – ran up to RM 1349 m (Untersuchungsausschuss, 1934). This means that a substantial amount of depreciations were covered by silent reserves the banks had accumulated before the Great Depression.

The conclusions from these numbers are obvious. The big banks incurred most of their losses through dishonoured loans, and not through speculation with securities. This means that the causes of the near collapse of the big banks were located in the non-banking sphere and not in the inter-banking or the securities trade. The statistics about the origins and the causes of depreciations provides additional evidence that the banking crisis of 1931 originated from the non-banking sector. Severe losses among the non-bank debtors were the main reason why a substantial amount of loans were dishonoured. Unlike in 2007/08, the losses through dishonoured loans exceeded the losses through depreciated securities by far.

The banks were not compelled to depreciate their inter-bank loans, since the Reichsbank relaxed the strict quality criteria for bills in July 1931 in order to restore the liquidity of the banks. The central bank allowed the banks to draw bills (acceptance bills) on each other and permitted the discounting of acceptance bills as a temporary surrogate for regular bills. In July 1931, the Reichsbank and the big commercial banks established the Akzept- und Garantiebank (Acceptance and Credit Bank) as a joint venture for the discounting of acceptance bills. The Akzept- und Garantiebank served as a legal bypass for the central bank and as a *second* lender of last resort, since the Reichsbank was legally prohibited from discounting acceptance bills. The implementation of a currency control and the conclusion of a *standstill* agreement between the German debtors and their foreign creditors protected the German banking system from losing additional liquidity. Otherwise, the Reichsbank would not have been able to lift the temporary restrictions of domestic withdrawals and to relax the tight credit restrictions on the banking sector.

Conclusion

Since the US and German banking systems were affected by two different evils, legislators and the executive drew different regulatory lessons from the financial crisis of the early 1930s. As the US banking system had been most severely affected by speculation on stock and losses through depreciation of securities, the Senate and the House of Representatives enacted the Glass–Steagall Act in 1933 (Meltzer, 2003). The Glass–Steagall Act enforced a strict separation between investment and commercial banking in order to prevent banks from speculating with the deposits of creditors. In Germany, the Reichsbank and the government never seriously considered this kind of institutional separation in banking and never questioned the German system of integrated commercial and investment banking (*Universalbankensystem*). The German banking system did not face the abyss because of a bursting speculative bubble, but as a consequence of imprudent lending and the morally hazardous behaviour of debtors. German policy makers never considered the creation of a Federal Deposit Insurance Corporation (FDIC) as in the US since they considered the reform of banking regulation as a sufficient safeguard against bank failures being repeated. Thanks to the very costly rescue operation for the big banks in Germany and the very low number of real bank bankruptcies (compared to the US), none of the policy makers saw the need for a deposit insurance company.

After the Nazi seizure of power, the Reichsbank evolved as the main political agent in banking. The Reichsbank achieved the dominant status as a legislator and executive agent of banking policies because of the extraordinary powers of the Reichsbank governor Hjalmar Schacht. In March 1933, right after appointing Schacht as the new Reichsbank governor, Hitler invested him with extraordinary powers to re-order the banking sector and to implement any legislation to stabilise the financial system of Germany. Schacht agreed with the executives of the big banks that the banking crisis had not been caused by structural deficiencies of the German banking system, but by the absence of regulation and control (Kopper, 1995). The first[6] and the final version of the Banking Regulation Law (*Reichsgesetz für das Kreditwesengesetz*) (Reichsgesetzblatt, 1934, pp. 1208–1214) were not drafted by the Ministry of Economic Affairs (*Reichswirtschafts-ministerium*), but in the Economics Department of the Reichsbank. The core of the Banking Regulation Law was the establishment of a federal agency for the control of the financial sector (*Aufsichtsamt für das Kreditwesen*). Above all, the purpose of this federal agency was to control the balances of banks and to set guidelines for minimum liquidity rates. For the first time, a public control body was given power to set a maximum limit for loans to a single debtor. The Reichsbank gave up the original intention to restrict the maximum loan to a single debtor to 10% of the bank's equity. The final version of the law contained a more flexible regulation and left the power to set quantitative loan limits to the *Aufsichtsamt für das Kreditwesen*. This part of the Banking Regulation Law was obviously inspired by the experiences of the banking crisis and the dangerous dependence of banks on big debtors. The Banking Regulation Law also included stipulations about loan approval and loan prolongation procedures. As a lesson from the financial crisis of 1931, the new law mandated an examination of the debtors' balance sheets before the approval of loans. Banks were legally required to report all major loans exceeding RM 1 million to the *Aufsichtsamt für das*

Kreditwesen in order to prevent any undetected accumulation of risks. Cases like the Schultheiss scandal where debtors were double-crossing their creditors should be avoided in the future.

The German *Kreditwesengesetz* (enacted in December 1934) was an important step for the modernisation of banking policies. This law was the obvious response to the absence of public monitoring and regulation of banking which caused the climax of the German banking crisis in 1931. In the 1930s, the loan and securities business had not reached a complexity that might have prevented efficient monitoring. Unlike today, public control agencies did not face the challenge of extremely complex and highly unintelligible derivative securities that take control agencies beyond their limits of expertise. The assessment problems of Collateralized Debt Obligations (CDOs) and other over-complex derivative securities were not an issue in the financial crisis of the early 1930s when international securities trade ranked far behind trade in national stock and securities. Current dangers like the import of risky and overrated mortgages – through globally traded CDOs – were hardly imaginable in domestically oriented financial markets. In the early 1930s, the danger of an imported banking crisis already existed. But the withdrawal of US and other foreign deposits from German banks in 1931 did not so much reflect the financial crisis in the US as a decline of confidence in the German banks. The German case was proof that the financial crisis mainly originated from domestic causes such as loan defaults of depression-ridden debtors, inadequate risk management by the banks, insufficient co-operation between the commercial banks and a belated and insufficient response of the central bank.

At a time of non-existent banking regulation, the national differences between highly and sparsely regulated financial markets did not affect the spread of a financial crisis. The countries affected by the financial crisis of the 1930s – such as the US, Germany and Switzerland – responded to the challenges of their national markets through nationally specific forms of regulation addressing the specific causes of their financial crisis.

Based on a diligent empirical assessment of crises of banking and balance-of-payments from the 1970s to the early 1990s, Graciela Kaminsky and Carmen Reinhart (1999) concluded that many payment crises originated in the banking sector. Although banking crises do not necessarily have to be the immediate cause of a currency and payment crisis, both crises tend to be intertwined and tend to reinforce each other in a vicious circle. the German banking crisis of 1931 proves their conclusion right: the collapse of the German banks originated in the faulty transformation of short-term foreign deposits into defaulting long-term loans, but was additionally aggravated by the depletion of foreign currency reserves after a growing loss of foreign confidence in Germany's economy and politics. But contrary to Kaminsky and Reinhart's patterns of financial crises, the German currency crisis did not follow the banking crisis, but developed at the same time. As they reached their peak in July 1931, interlocking banking-currency crisis would be the most accurate description.

Notes

1. Report of the Reichsbank governor about currency and financial affairs to the Reich government, 7 March 1927 (in Abramowski, 1998, vol. 2, pp. 577–609).
2. Bundesarchiv Berlin, Record Group Reichsfinanzministerium, no. 13682.

3. Figures for November 1930.
4. See the Reichsbank statistics about the depreciations and the equity status of the big commercial banks in 1931 and 1932 (in: Untersuchungsausschuss, 1934, part 2, pp. 222f., 228f.).
5. Bundesarchiv Berlin, Reichsbank, no. 6918. The numbers are based on confidential letters from the Dresdner Bank (15 August 1933) and the Deutsche Bank (24 August 1933) to the Reichsbank and an internal report of the Commerzbank for 1931/32 (not dated).
6. Bundesarchiv Berlin, Reichsbank, no. 6913.

References

Abramowski, G. (1998). *Die Kabinette Marx III und IV*. Vol. 2. Boppard: Boldt.
Argentatius (pseudonym for Alfred Lansburgh). (1931). Der Dolchstoss. *Die Bank 1931*, 824–831.
Balderston, T. (1994). The banks and the gold standard in the German financial crisis of 1931. *Financial History Review*, *1*, 43–68.
Bernanke, B. (2000). Nonmonetary effects of the financial crisis in the propagation of the Great Depression. In B. Bernanke, *Essays on the Great Depression* (pp. 41–69). Princeton, NJ: Princeton University Press.
Born, K.E. (1968). *Die deutsche Bankenkrise*. Munchen: Piper.
Born, K.E. (1983). Vom Beginn des Ersten Weltkriegs bis zum Ende der Weimarer Republik. In Institut fur bankhistorische Forschung (Ed.), *Deutsche Bankengeschichte* (Vol. 3, pp. 105–148). Frankfurt/Main: Fritz Knapp.
Escher, O. (1988). *Die Wirtschafts- und Finanzkrise in Bremen 1931 und der Fall Schröderbank*. Frankfurt/Main: Fritz Knapp.
Feldman, G.D. (1994). Jakob Goldschmidt. The history of the banking crisis of 1931 and the problems of manoeuvre in the Weimar Republic. In C. Buchheim (Ed.), *Zerrissene Zwischenkriegszeit* (pp. 307–327). Baden-Baden: Nomos.
Feldman, G.D. (1995). Die Deutsche Bank vom Ersten Weltkrieg bis zur Weltwirtschaftskrise 1914–1933. In L. Gall (Ed.), *Die Deutsche Bank 1870–1995* (pp. 138–314). Munchen: C.H. Beck.
Ferguson, T., & Temin, P. (2003). Made in Germany. The German currency crisis of July 1931. *Research in Economic History*, *21*, 1–53.
Hardach, G. (1976). *Weltmarktordnung und relative Stagnation. Währungspolitik in Deutschland 1924–1931*. Berlin: Duncker & Humblot.
James, H. (1984). The causes of the German banking crisis of 1931. *Economic History Review*, *38*, 68–87.
Kalveram, W. (1950). Lehren aus Irrtumern der Vergangenheit. Der Zusammenbruch der Nordwolle. *Zeitschrift für Betriebswirtschaft*, *20*, 95–104.
Kaminsky, G.L., & Reinhart, C. (1999). The twin crises. The causes of banking and balances-of-payment problem. *American Economic Review*, *89*, 473–500.
Kaserer, C. (2000). Die deutsche Bankenkrise von 1931. *Bankhistorisches Archiv*, *26*, 3–26.
Kopper, C. (1995). *Zwischen Marktwirtschaft und Dirigismus. Bankenpolitik im Dritten Reich 1933–1939*. Bonn: Bouvier.
Meltzer, A. (2003). *A history of the Federal Reserve. Vol. I (1913–1951)*. Chicago, IL: University of Chicago Press.
Paersch, F. (1933). Massnahmen des Staates hinsichtlich einer Beaufsichtigung und Reglementierung des Bankwesens. In Untersuchungsausschuss fur das Bankwesen (Ed.), *Untersuchung des Bankwesens* (Part 1, Vol. 2, pp. 33–66). Berlin: Carl Heymanns.
Priemel, K.C. (2007). *Flick*. Gottingen: Wallstein.
Ritschl, A. (2002). *Deutschlands Krise und Konjunktur 1924–1936*. Berlin: Akademie.
Schnabel, I. (2004) The German twin crisis of 1931. *Journal of Economic History*, *64*, 822–871.
Untersuchungsausschuss fur das Bankwesen. (1934). *Untersuchung des Bankwesens*. Berlin: Carl Heymanns.

Von Reeken, D. (1996). *Lahusen. Eine Bremer Unternehmerdynastie*. Bremen: Temmen.

Voth, H.-J. (2001). *With a bang, not a whimper. Pricking Germany's 'stock market bubble' in 1927 and the slide into depression* (Research paper). Barcelona: Universitat Pompeu Fabra, Department of Economics.

Wixforth, H. (1995). *Banken und Schwerindustrie in der Weimarer Republik*. Köln: Böhlau.

Ziegler, D. (2006). Der Ordnungsrahmen. In J. Bähr (Ed.), *Die Dresdner Bank in der Wirtschaft des Dritten Reiches* (pp. 43–74). München: Oldenbourg.

Banks and Swedish financial crises in the 1920s and 1930s

Mikael Lönnborg[a], Anders Ögren[b] and Michael Rafferty[c]

[a]BI Norwegian Business School, Oslo, Norway; [b]Stockholm School of Economics, Stockholm, Sweden; [c]Workplace Research Centre, University of Sydney, Sydney, Australia

Financial crises occur at regular and unpredictable moments in capitalist economies. However, an absence of shared theoretical approaches to and even definitions of the subject still plague the analysis of financial crises. This situation makes historical analysis even more important. This article compares two Swedish financial crises, one in the 1920s and the other in the 1930s. The comparison shows that despite their temporal and spatial proximity, the crises seemed to have had quite different underlying causes, links to international circumstances, severity, and government responses. The 1920s crisis in Sweden was for instance much deeper than the crisis in the 1930s, a marked contrast to the experience of most countries during these two periods. In focusing on the driving forces behind the crises, their development and governmental policies, the article also provides an opportunity to reflect on both financial crisis theories, on the current crisis and on recent historical research concerning crises.

In this paper I shall disregard them entirely, and deal merely with the question whether or not the capitalistic system is stable in itself – that is to say, whether or not it would, in the absence of such disturbances, show any tendency towards self-destruction from inherent economic causes, or towards out-growing its own frame. (Schumpeter, 1928, p. 361)

Introduction

The above passage reflects interwar anxieties about the economic and political state of the world. Schumpeter's 'them', however, is not referring to financial crises but rather wars and political unrest. In 1928, even before the Great Depression hit, the question whether capitalism was inherently unstable and, therefore, unsustainable, was more than just an idle question. It was a grave concern with important political consequences. Schumpeter's conclusions were pessimistic, not because of the benefits and costs of capitalism itself, but rather for its effects on the attitudes of economic and political actors, as well as on the general public. Schumpeter concluded the 1928 paper by writing that:

Capitalism, whilst economically stable, and even gaining in stability, creates, by rationalising the human mind, a mentality and a style of life incompatible with its own fundamental conditions, motives and social institutions, and will be changed, although not by economic necessity and probably even at some sacrifice of economic welfare, into an order of things which it will be merely matter of taste and terminology to call Socialism or not. (Schumpeter, 1928, pp. 385–386)

In many respects Schumpeter's views about the attitudinal issues created by economic crises paralleled the concerns of many of the most important figures of the time. But the emphasis on the emotive content of crises created a problem. If the main threat to capitalism involved such vague concepts as 'mentality', 'spirit', and 'expectations', empirical study of why crises occur, what effects they had, and how they could best be managed became more difficult.

For this task, historical study, comparing crises and their attending booms and busts, is a useful but complicated tool. Like all historical study, that dealing with business and finance is intrinsically important. But the history of financial crises has the added importance of addressing our immediate and pressing anxieties about our economic future. The alluring, but elusive, prospect here is that if we can better understand past financial crises, we may be better able to prevent them or at least minimise their impact in the future. Two recent contributions underpin both the intrinsic and contemporary importance of the historical research presented here.[1]

In a recent biography of Ivar Kreuger, buccaneering Swedish-based financier of the 1920s and former head of Swedish Match, Frank Partnoy argues that the neglect of the life and times of Kreuger has been unfortunate, because this was an extremely significant episode of its time. The size of the collapse, and the implications across many countries, was almost unprecedented (Partnoy, 2009). Compared to the much smaller and shorter-lived scheme of Ponzi, which has now become synonymous with speculative bubbles, the collapse of Kreuger's financial empire was truly breath-taking in scale and ramifications.

Beyond Swedish financial history, the publication of a recent and sweeping global empirical review of financial crises over several centuries provides an important counterpoint to this study. Reinhart and Rogoff (2009) assemble an impressively detailed empirical account of financial crises and remind us just how common they are. In doing so, they have produced not so much a general theory as a set of general attributes of crises and reopened the debate about the links between the extensive historical record of financial crises, and attempts to generalise their causes and attributes into theoretical models that are empirically testable or offer predictive propositions. Reinhart and Rogoff do not attempt to develop a new or modified general theory of financial crises, and instead opt for a more modest project of distilling a set of attributes that seem to be present or precede financial crises.

Both these historical accounts represent important accomplishments in themselves. The authors also use the results of their research to reflect on the current international financial crisis, and in so doing remind us that each new financial crisis generates renewed interest in the past, and thus invite historians and others to speculate on their common causes. Frank Partnoy makes a direct comparison between Kreuger's activities and those of Bernard Madoff, whose failed investment scheme has been emblematic of the current sub-prime financial crisis. Not only did Kreuger deploy many of the financial techniques and practices that are now commonplace, the collapse of the Kreuger group reveals many practices that were at the centre of the financial turmoil.[2] Sweden in the 1920s and 1930s, it seems, still has a lot to offer to the contemporary world of finance. It bears noting, despite Partnoy's excellent historical research, that there were important differences between Madoff and Kreuger, one being that the operations of the latter were connected more directly to actual industrial production.

In a similar vein, Reinhart and Rogoff make the case that based on their empirical research it was possible to see that a financial crisis of some form or another was looming. They suggest that many of the attributes that are associated with crises were present for several years, including the build-up of both leverage and hubris.[3] Despite their claim that the current financial crisis was foreseeable, their wider conclusion about the absence of general causal determination is a sobering one, both because of what their study included (financial factors), and did not (non-financial factors).

This paper extends work on the Swedish financial crises in two ways. It reviews the two crises in the light of recent historical scholarship, and in so doing compares their similarities and differences. This permits us to attempt to both develop an analysis of certain aspects of crises and to explain them as historical events. Before the two crises are addressed in turn, the next section seeks to situate them and the study of financial crises.

Background and conceptual approach

The study of financial crises has produced neither a single definition of crisis nor a widely held theoretical understanding of the phenomenon. Indeed, apart from the regular and costly experience of financial crises one reason for the ongoing interest by economists and economic historians has been the inability to produce a satisfactory understanding of the causes of crises.

In the absence of any strong consensus, two possible explanatory approaches can be discerned. One approach, which we have called the heterogeneity thesis, suggests a rather pessimistic view that whatever their common characteristics, each crisis is more or less unique. Bustelo (2000, p. 229) for instance, has observed that 'crises do not seem to present strong regularities over time'. An instrumentalist reading of the idiosyncratic nature of financial crises would be that the best that economists can do for policymakers or planners is to look for early warning indicators. A wider approach would involve treating crises and their causes as a normal part of the evolution of capitalism along with growth and stability. On the other hand, some economists continue to pursue the positivist promise that common predictable features of crises are discernable. This alternative approach, which we have called the *Holy Grailers*, is premised on the belief that a universal theory of crisis exists or is at least possible. While there are many suggested paths to the Holy Grail, they share a project of identifying or demonstrating general causal factors such as the presence of moral hazard, information asymmetry and other structural problems. Their disagreements often centre on the single most important or relatively most important of these elements (Allen & Gale, 2008; Kamin, 1999; Kindleberger, 1993; Kiyotaki & Moore, 1995).

The problem of developing a general theory of crisis has meant that the work of economic historians who document and analyse crises has been critical. With a number of competing theories of financial crises and several descriptive approaches, economic and business history is deployed in both developing and testing such approaches. In an earlier study of 150 years of financial crises in Sweden, a number of common attributes of crises were identified, as was the different influence of each in different periods of crisis. It was suggested that in the context of an absence of strong consensus there is considerable merit in an historical analysis of crises (Lönnborg, Rafferty, & Ögren, 2003).

But even conceding a lack of theoretical consensus only brings us to an even more alarming problem – what constitutes a financial crisis as an object of inquiry? We can see that the definition of crisis has been developed in a number of ways. Chan-Lau and Chen (2002, p. 53) define it simply as 'a large reduction in the amount of loans intermediated by the financial system (i.e. a large capital outflow or credit crunch)' while Eichengreen and Portes (1989, p. i) offer the more detailed description of 'a disturbance to financial markets, associated typically with falling asset prices and insolvency among debtors and intermediaries, which spreads through the financial system, disrupting the market's capacity to allocate capital'. Mishkin (1991, pp. 117–118) provides a more causal definition of crisis as a 'disruption to financial markets in which adverse selection and moral hazard problems become much worse, so that financial markets are unable to efficiently channel funds to those who have the most productive investment opportunities'.

What these definitions tell us is that financial crises can be understood partly in terms of the processes associated with them (reduced financial intermediation, declining liquidity, asset price reductions and banking fragility), as well as the factors that seem to have produced them (poorly structured incentives, over-expansion of credit, poor information and corporate governance). The definitional dilemma of studying financial crises parallels its theoretical understanding. Rather than despairing about the dilemma or attempting to force open a separation, this paper is based on the premise that the twin definitional nature of financial crisis (process and cause) can be utilised to develop an analysis of individual episodes.

Approaches to the driving forces of crises can also be seen to have been approached quite differently. The triggering factors behind crises have on several occasions been termed 'displacement' (Kindleberger, 1989). Displacement here is an outside event changing expectations, revealing previously hidden (profit or loss) opportunities and rapidly changing actors' behaviours. Such displacements are often connected to sudden and rapid political change such as wars, revolutions, restora-tions, changes of regimes or mutiny but can also consist of new innovations. Sjögren and Knutsen (2010) specifically focus on institutional changes as a reason for displacements.[4] To a certain extent all these events can be regarded as exogenous variables, so that displacement treats crises as caused by an outside event or development.

The other source of driving forces or triggers for crises is identified as an endogenous cause, something inside and often inherent to a system. As pointed out by Marx and Minsky and used by Kindleberger and others; the economic and finnancial system of capitalism is inherently unstable (Kindleberger, 1989). The potential for crises lies in its strength – the ability and necessity to expand credit after demand creates the potential for that expansion to create dis-proportionality – and crises are a way of revealing them and realigning processes.

Another important issue in this study concerns how crises have been dealt with and what measures and policies were introduced in order to deal with the repercussions of the crisis. We know for instance that a lender of last resort can be a double-edged sword as it may induce moral hazard, but we also know that it may end contagion through the spread of panics and thus can be seen as essential for mitigating crises.

The purpose of this brief review has been to motivate the study and outline its approach. The paper combines an empirical and theoretical framework to compare and contrast two different financial crises in one country. By focusing on a specific geographical area or nation state, we can limit the variables that affect the crises. However, the widespread diffusion of financial crises in different institutional settings and levels of economic development make comparative studies feasible in both time and space. Indeed, if economics is to provide useful advice that can be employed to help control any tendencies toward such crises, understanding the history of crises that have occurred is vital (Gavan & Hausmann, 1999).

This study thus focuses on three attributes of a financial crisis: (i) the causes, (ii) the developmental path identified and (iii) how the crisis was dealt with and the long-term consequences. With regard to causes the following sections compare variables related to both the institutional set-up (banking laws, regulations and their enforcement) as well as actual financial market performance (lending activities, market transparency and corporate governance). Regarding the handling of crises, a key focus is on the role of the state in resolving them, and the outcomes of such measures both for the banking structure and the regulatory system. The paper focuses on two crises from the 1920s and 1930s and analyses similarities and differences across the three attributes.

The industrial crisis of the 1920s

In the aftermath of World War I Sweden experienced perhaps its most severe crisis, which was industrial and structural in nature, caused by economic policies and accompanied by heavy deflation. An economic boom with increased credit advances in the banking system and accelerating inflation preceded the financial crisis, which involved deflation triggered by both international and domestic events. The driving forces behind the crisis were a combination of external displacement due to the war and more endogenous structural and institutional factors.

World War I led to an economic boom in Sweden that was mostly a result of increasing export surpluses. The trade balance became even more favourable through import restrictions and the result was high inflation. The ideal economic policy was to avoid shortages of goods and raw material and to promote self-sufficiency in production. This led to a) rationing of agricultural products and price controls and b) subsidies (through restrictions on imports) on domestic production which resulted in the establishment and growth of a large number of enterprises especially in manufacturing and industry.

The policies were not successful: the rationing led to extensive black markets and, probably, even higher inflation and the price controls were almost completely ineffective. Another factor contributing to inflation was that exporting enterprises treated the fall in the crown exchange rate as windfall profit. In this environment, stockpiling by firms and individuals grew as a way of avoiding shortages of raw materials and semi-manufactured products (Larsson, 1992).

With import controls in place, the war helped to stimulate the establishment and growth of a large number of new enterprises especially in manufacturing. These establishments were actively encouraged by the import substitution policy of the government to facilitate national self-sufficiency. At the end of the war, when international trade was re-established, a large number of these newly established firms in import-substituting industries (especially in iron and steel) went into bankruptcy.[5] But during the war shares in industrial companies became the main investment object as they skyrocketed in value.

After the war international political changes negatively affected the macro-economic environment for Swedish companies as important export markets disappeared. Sweden's biggest export market, Russia, vanished in the wake of the Bolshevik revolution in 1917 and several other important markets in Central and Eastern Europe could not purchase Swedish products due to their own postwar economic distress (Larsson & Olsson, 1992).

More important was the international economy. International production recovered quickly after the war, and as global supply of most commodities grew, increasing sales competition helped to push global prices downwards, leading to deflation. By mid-1920 the earlier inflationary pressures had disappeared and prices started to fall. In Sweden, the earlier stockpiling by enterprises to counteract goods shortage and higher prices ended abruptly and enterprises began running down stocks. This in turn lowered general demand for newly produced raw materials and semi-manufactured products. Enterprises also attempted to sell their products quickly to avoid further price cuts. This added further pressure to general deflationary trends. The international decrease in commodity prices and the domestic run-down of stock holdings was further strengthened by contractionary economic policy in Sweden.

Like many other European countries, Sweden had been attached to the gold standard before World War I (from 1873). Including the prior silver standard Sweden had kept a fixed exchange rate for 80 years (Ögren, 2003). Suspending convertibility during the war was seen as a temporary measure and one of the most important goals of the Swedish government after the war was to reconnect the currency to gold at the same value as in 1913. In order to achieve this, it was thought to be necessary to further feed deflation by cutting expenditures and restrictive monetary policy.

The general price level decreased by about 35% from 1921 to 1923, and wholesale prices fell even further. Swedish exporters were losing major international market shares due to the international recession and domestic deflation made Swedish products more expensive. Capital-intensive industries were especially hard hit as consumer industries could at least depend on domestic demand (Östlind, 1945, p. 602).

Table 1 shows the enormous increase in turnover at the Stockholm Stock Exchange with 1916 to 1918 as the peak years. Bank advances to the public lagged somewhat behind but accelerated, although at a more moderate speed, between 1916 and 1918. Also the money supply followed a similar development. Base money in terms of notes also started to increase in 1916 but was at its peak in 1918 to 1920 and the broad money supply, which includes inside money created by the banking system, rose steadily over the period.

An important aspect of the financing of industrial firms during the 1910s was that commercial banks had increased in importance as a source of finance. At the time, the government had been persuaded that existing bank legislation, which prevented banks from direct ownership of firms, was preventing banks from taking a more active part in the financing of new businesses. Accordingly, in 1911 the law was changed and banks were permitted to acquire shares on their own account. This meant that banks could now finance new business, take part in mergers and acquisitions and thereby take a more active part in financing industrialisation on a limited basis. The limitations on the extent of equity ownership were however easily circumvented. Banks established wholly owned holding (equity or issuing)

Table 1. Turnover on the Stockholm Stock Exchange (SSE), commercial banks' lending, credit losses, notes in circulation and M3, 1914–25.

Year	Turnover on SSE		Banks advances to non-bank public, annual change (%)	Loan losses/ advances (% total)	Notes in circulation 1914=100	M3
	Current prices	Fixed prices 1914=100				
1914	51.6	51.6	3.5	–	100.0	100.0
1915	50.9	44.3	6.3	–	96.6	110.4
1916	604.0	465.5	15.6	–	155.1	146.6
1917	1321.9	807.8	29.7	–	188.4	178.1
1918	1586.1	695.4	37.4	–	267.5	226.4
1919	526.2	199.6	10.8	0.2	245.9	251.6
1920	328.4	123.8	8.1	0.6	249.9	247.3
1921	161.8	71.2	–8.9	2.3	185.2	246.6
1922	195.0	105.8	–11.9	5.3	192.1	254.9
1923	161.1	94.2	–10.4	1.0	189.5	251.4
1924	169.6	99.2	–3.4	0.8	176.7	245.0
1925	232.6	133.4	–2.7	–	174.2	–

Note: M3 is a measure of the broad money supply that also includes bank money, i.e. notes and coins issued by the central bank (base money) plus the public's deposits in commercial and savings banks.
Sources: Statistics Sweden, on banks 1914–25.

companies, which meant they could now not only finance industrial firms through lending, but also become significant equity holders as well. This form of financing thus allowed banks to concentrate their lending and investment in a few interlocking firms. It was a practice that became widely exploited after the new Banking Act.

Since 1907 banks had been under supervision from a bank inspectorate, which was expected to monitor banks and counteract any excessive lending. However, the changing institutional environment made it very difficult for the inspectorate to monitor banks' positions in the evolving financial system. Consequently, banks were more or less given a free hand to expand their businesses. By 1918, there were 14 listed equity companies with close connections to one or more commercial bank (Larsson, 1989, pp. 7–12; Söderlund, 1978, pp. 1–28). This, combined with the expansion in relative importance of the banking sector in the economy, helped to increase financial fragility.

During the 1910s, a wave of new banks had established themselves in the Swedish banking market. There were also, as shown in Table 2, a substantial number of mergers as ownership concentration continued during the 1920s. The concentration was partly induced by the industrial sector's need for larger credit to support the rapid transformation of the economy, but partly due also to the changing regional nature of banking markets at that time. Mergers were used as ways to increase a bank's turnover but also as a strategy to spread their business to new geographic areas. In a fragmented banking market it was often easier and less costly to merge with a provincial bank than to establish new branch offices. In 1919, to counteract increasing bank concentration, the government changed the Banking Act to prevent banks from acquiring stocks in other banks.

One important factor behind the bank failures and higher concentration of the 1920s can be traced to the behaviour of several small regional banks. During the 1910s a large number of small provincial banks, which had received large deposits, started to expand outside their regional markets. The deregulation and increasing

Table 2. Number of banks and bank offices 1914–25.

Year	Number of banks	Liquidated banks	New banks	Number of bank offices
1914	67	8	0	659
1915	66	2	1	721
1916	60	7	0	805
1917	53	12	6	1050
1918	50	9	6	1319
1919	43	10	3	1408
1920	41	3	1	1210
1921	38	4	1	1398
1922	35	5	2	1356
1923	34	2	1	1307
1924	32	2	0	1253
1925	32	1	1	1091

Sources: Statistics Sweden, on commercial banks 1914–25.

competition stimulated banks that had earlier operated within definite client segments to expand to new business areas, chasing new business, particularly in Stockholm. In an environment where banks were competing for market share and spreading across market segments, the ability of banks to discriminate in lending decisions became compromised.

The bank crisis became visible in 1922 when prices of industrial shares on the stock market began to decline. This set off a process where the balance sheets of banks that had lent money against collateral on those shares with declining value began to be affected, at the same time that bank investment in those shares were declining in value. In the wake of the stock market collapse, banks were faced with a serious restructuring phase with very high credit losses and many non-performing loans.

Almost half of commercial bank credit had gone to the industrial sector and to protect their claims the banks often had to take over shares in these firms. Apart from the industrial sector, several equity companies and individuals were also affected by these credit losses (Larsson, 1992).

The equity companies had increased their ownership in the industrial sector significantly during the 1910s, with expansion financed largely by credit from the banks, and the share portfolios purchased by them used as collateral. With prices of those shares falling on the stock exchange, the assets of the equity companies became heavily discounted, and the banks were once again often forced to take over the shares to protect their claims. The system of financing and ownership that had developed with interlocking ownership, credit and boards of directors meant that banks were now extremely vulnerable to any price volatility on the stock exchange. In 1922, the government introduced new bank legislation to once again prohibit the banks from acquiring shares in equity, holding and investment companies. By the time the legislation was enacted in 1924, however, most of the equity companies were already bankrupt and speculation on the stock exchange had abated (Östlind, 1945, pp. 612–617).

One way commercial banks tried to overcome their financial distress was by removing non-performing loans and portfolios of worthless stocks to newly established firms with no direct connection to the bank. In this way it was possible to hide large amounts of bad loans, avoid extensive writing-off of loans and wait for better times to deal with these problem loans (Larsson, 1995).

In the early stages of the financial crisis, banks made a joint effort to stabilise the market through, for instance, Moneta (a consortium of banks) which acquired shares from the banks and attempted to prop up stock prices. These efforts could not however stabilise the fragile financial system, and the state was eventually forced to act as de facto lender of last resort.

The way the lender of last resort was organised followed in most important respects the way the role had been developed during the nineteenth-century crises. First the central bank would act to supply liquidity but as it was constrained by the fixed exchange rate the state had to include the taxpayers for the process of recapitalisation of the banks by the instigation of a specific fund called Kreditkassan (the Credit Institute) in 1922 after heavy pressure from the commercial banks. Originally Kreditkassan was a joint venture between the government, the central bank and larger commercial banks and at the outset the banks contributed one-sixth of the fund's capital but quite quickly the fund became completely funded and administered by the state.

The purpose of Kreditkassan was to support banks in crisis and to prevent *fire* sales of equity and other assets, which would have placed even greater downward pressure on the stock exchange. There was genuine fear that if the stock market fell much further the entire financial system would threaten the bank deposits of the public. Kreditkassan assisted the large banks by buying equity from them or lending to them at a normal rate, helping to stabilise their positions in the market (Ögren, 2007; Östlind, 1945). Later Kreditkassan was turned into the state-owned Credit Bank and later still became part of the state-owned bank Nordbanken (later renamed to Nordea).

In the face of the crisis, a large number of provincial banks also needed help to restructure their business. In the restructuring of these banks however a different pattern of assistance can be observed. During 1922 and 1923 the larger commercial banks, especially Stockholms Enkilda Bank (controlled by the Wallenberg family), and Skandinaviska Banken, acted as guarantor to several distressed provincial banks. This involvement showed the interdependence of the banks and recognition by the larger banks that they could be greatly affected by bankruptcy of even relatively minor banks (Östlind, 1945, pp. 612–515).[6]

Svenska Handelsbanken had especially great problems in avoiding bankruptcy and had to be saved by some creative accounting, sanctioned by the state, whereby debentures could be counted as share capital (Hildebrand, 1971).

One important effect of the deflationary crisis was a general suspicion of the stock market. In spite of the decreased importance of banks within the financial sector, the 1920s crisis actually served to consolidate the close connection between banks and industry, an ownership model which lasted for much of the rest of the twentieth century in Sweden.[7] The deflationary crisis also changed the institutional set-up of bank legislation and the limitation on banks acquiring shares changed the rules of the game on the Swedish capital market.

The earlier view that the bank inspectorate could monitor the bank market as well as business between industry and banks was proven to lack credibility. Instead, more rigid bank legislation was implemented as a way of preventing banks from becoming too heavily exposed to one or two firms. The view that emerged from the financial crisis was that commercial banks should only act as intermediators between savers and investors and not simultaneously act as investors. The idea of separating commercial banks and investment banks became even more prominent during the great depression, especially in the US.

The crisis also meant a restructuring of Swedish industry as several companies failed, which might to some extent explain the resilience of Sweden in the Great Depression in the 1930s despite being home to one of its main characters – Ivar Kreuger, the match king, whose story is taken up in the next section.

The Great Depression of 1930s and the collapse of the Kreuger empire

In the latter part of 1920s the international economy was booming, but in Sweden there was less of the asset price inflation seen in the 1910s. One factor that has been advanced to explain this phenomenon was that enterprises in Sweden were acting cautiously, following the previous crisis. For instance, finance was being sourced mainly from retained earnings and through the bond market, rather than the stock market. Capital flows from the US to Europe had been growing rapidly, but started to slow down toward the end of 1920s. In the wake of the Wall Street crash in October 1929 capital exports to Europe dried up almost completely (Cassis, 1992).

In the 1920s, economic pre-eminence had to a large extent shifted across the Atlantic from Europe to the US, but the US was not yet ready to act as the world's leading banker and carry an international responsibility for economic security. An important explanation was that unlike colonial rule by European powers, US capital exports were dominated by private enterprises, and directed to other metropolitan powers. Indeed, US policy was very domestically oriented. For instance, one consequence of US official trade policy that became evident in the late 1920s was that once US capital flows slowed, high US import barriers made it difficult to sell into the US and thus get hold of dollars to repay loans (Temin, 1989).

Debtor countries were then forced to raise short-term expensive finance in Europe to cover their fast-growing deficits. Central European countries for instance got extensive credits from the largest Austrian bank, Credit-Anstalt, and when several of these countries could not repay Credit-Anstalt was forced into bankruptcy in early 1931. As a consequence, the crisis spread through international credit markets. Banks from Berlin had supported the Austrian bank which in turn had funded their business in London. When Germany could no longer repay its foreign loans, the British finance market was pulled into the crisis. In turn, the effects of the European financial crisis were then exported to the US and added further fuel to the depression (Garside, 1993).

So how did these unfortunate international circumstances affect Sweden? An implicit assumption is that it should have had a major impact on the Swedish economy, not least as Swedish banks were closely tied to the expansion and breakdown of Ivar Kreuger's empire. In 1917, with financial support from Svenska Handelsbanken and an equity company, Kreuger had merged his company with the major match producer to form a single company, Swedish Match (STAB), which then began to acquire foreign competitors, especially in the Nordic countries (Hildebrand, 1985; Lindgren, 1979).

The ambitious global strategy for STAB was to create a monopoly position and thereby extract monopoly rents. The expansion of STAB, measured by increased market shares, was indeed impressive. By the beginning of the 1930s Swedish Match had control of 40% of the world market and, in addition, had agreements with collusive enterprises for another 22%. One major problem with the match industry was that the commodity was simple to produce so when prices increased, new entrants were attracted to the business, and thereby pushed prices down. The international cartel arrangements formed by STAB initially helped to prevent new entrants and thus to stabilise prices and profits.

In the 1920s Kreuger & Toll (an offspring of the original building company founded in 1908) was turned into a pure equity and holding company that acted as an internal bank to raise funds for the international expansion of the match industry. The industrial part of the company consisted of Swedish Match and the American subsidiary, International Match Corporation (IMCO), the latter established in 1923 as a coordinating unit for STAB's foreign branches.

For its time, the international acquisition of foreign match producers required immense capital mobilisation. During the early years this capital came mostly from the Swedish market, through the so-called Match Consortium, supported by Svenska Handelsbanken and Skandinaviska Banken. But even in 1922 the growing scale of this debt caused financial distress for the Kreuger companies, and it became clear that the Swedish credit market did not have the capacity to fund further expansion of the company. Therefore, STAB began issuing equity in London and one year later, in connection with the establishment of IMCO, a large bond issue was placed in New York (Hassbring, 1979).

In 1924 several countries, among them Sweden, reconnected to the gold standard, and this improved the international flow of capital, especially from the US to Europe. To a large extent, Ivar Kreuger exploited this financial opportunity, first to acquire funds for the international expansion of the match industry, but after 1925 he also redistributed loans to countries with capital scarcity. Kreuger was able to tie these loans to monopoly rights to produce and sell matches in these countries, thus forging a strong relationship between capital intermediation and the industrial sector in the Kreuger group (Wikander, 1979).

The Kreuger companies also started to acquire shares in other Swedish industrial firms. One important effect of the deflation crisis was the presence of cheap stocks, with majority holdings of international enterprises sometimes up for sale. In 1924 Kreuger was able to borrow capital on the American market to acquire more shares in the Swedish stock market. Another effect of the crisis in the 1920s discussed above was that banks, including the toxic asset funds from the crisis in the 1920s Kreditkassan and Moneta, had large holdings of shares in their portfolios, which made it possible for Kreuger to acquire several industrial firms and at the same time get bank loans using the shares as collateral. This meant that the banks still had the credit risk, as well as the business risk, even after the sale (Thunholm, 1991, pp. 212–213). The Stockholm Stock Exchange began to pick up again in the late 1920s, and to a large extent this can be explained by the injection of capital from the Kreuger empire to undertake large-scale mergers and acquisitions.

The business success of the Kreuger group was built on constant growth, which in turn demanded a constant in-flow of new capital. This depended on the continuing confidence of investors and creditors. Maintaining investor confidence required all the companies to show impressive profits and dividends. The ever-growing presence of Kreuger on the Swedish market led the conglomerate to generate these profits through an increasing number of internal transactions. In general, this often required assets in the different companies acquired to be re-valued several times. From this point of view, the Kreuger group ended up in a vicious circle. The higher the value of booked assets to show profits, the higher were the dividends required to attract new capital, which in turn was used to increase dividends in other companies. In the short term it was possible to survive through injections from the American capital market, but because of the close connection between different companies in the group, the whole group was vulnerable to any downturn.

Once the capital flow from the US to Europe slowed in the late 1920s and stopped after the Wall Street crash in October 1929, the financial platform of Kreuger's ambitious strategy began to break down. The value of Kreuger's most important equity in the US, the so-called 'participating debentures' (which had strong similarities with the so-called 'junk bonds' of the 1980s), dropped substantially (Galbraith, 1955). The falling prices on stocks and bonds made new issues of further equity virtually impossible. The international capital market entered a crisis when several countries stopped repaying loans, but in an effort to display confidence in his ability to weather it, Kreuger granted new international loans, and for instance the group advanced a loan to Germany in October 1929.

When foreign banks started to cancel loans in 1931, Kreuger faced severe liquidity problems. In order to cope with the situation, Kreuger secretly sold its majority stake in LM Ericsson to its American competitor, ITT. Kreuger also negotiated further loans from the Swedish central bank, guaranteed by Skandinaviska Banken, to amortise its loans to French banks. This loan, which was almost half of the Swedish currency reserves, put further pressure on the weak Swedish currency. The crisis became acute in February 1932, when ITT announced it was continuing action against Kreuger after it had become obvious that he had lied about the amount of available cash in LM Ericsson.

To solve these urgent financial problems, Kreuger once again turned to the Swedish credit market. On 23 February, with the group close to a total breakdown, and with several debts to be settled on that day, Kreuger approached the Swedish Prime Minister C.G. Ekman. After his direct intervention, the central bank and all the commercial banks, with the notable exception of Wallenberg's Stockholm Enskilda Bank, supplied capital to rescue the group. As a condition of the loan, the central bank demanded a total financial analysis of the Kreuger group. That report showed that Kreuger needed SEK 135 million to meet its financial obligations during 1932 (almost double the Swedish central bank's currency reserves). Kreuger was in New York but was instructed to return to Europe for a meeting with the head of Riksbank and Oscar Rydbeck, the CEO of Skandinaviska Banken. He returned to Europe, but on 12 March Ivar Kreuger was found dead in his apartment in Paris (Gäfvert, 1979, pp. 184–189; Glete, 1981; Lindgren, 1982).

The Kreuger group had received credit from the Swedish commercial banks which were almost two-thirds of the market's total lending. Skandinaviska Banken was the most important creditor and because of the close ties to Kreuger the bank had also guaranteed the central bank's loan. The losses for the bank were immense and it was subject to a bank run, leading the government to take measures to avoid a total collapse of the banking system by giving financial support through the central bank. But the central bank demanded that larger commercial banks also support the Scandinavian bank, that the bank not pay any dividends for 1931 and keep dividends low until all the loans were cleared. By 1936 the bank had repaid the loans both to the central bank and the commercial banks (Wigforss, 1932).

The crisis in Sweden in the 1930s, i.e. the Kreuger crash, had several effects on the Swedish financial market. The most immediate was to diminish the close connection between banks and industrial firms; bank legislation was changed back to the conditions before 1911, and the banks could no longer have any ownership ties with their customers.

The breakdown of the Kreuger group also changed the ownership structure in the Swedish industrial sector. The shares acquired by Kreuger returned to the bank's portfolios but with a new relation of power among the banks. Stockholms Enskilda Bank and Svenska Handelsbanken took over ownership as well as customers from Skandinaviska Banken, which had lost public confidence.

In terms of bank ownership, the new bank legislation made it impossible for banks to keep industrial shares in their portfolios. Instead commercial banks established holding companies, transferred the shares, and maintained control through a system where members of the board of directors were in charge of the shares in the holding companies. With the help of different classes of shares (A and B shares) the previous bank ownership was replaced by a banking group ownership, which remained in place until the 1970s, and to some extent still prevails today.

Another long-term effect of the crisis was to diminish interest among the public in investing on the Stockholm Stock Exchange (Table 3). Enterprises were thus also encouraged to look for alternative sources of finance, for instance through the bond market. The larger industrial enterprises to a great extent relied on self-financing through retained earnings, which meant that banks lost big business as clients. Instead they tended to focus on medium-sized companies as customers.

In spite of the Kreuger crash, the Swedish crisis in the 1930s was shorter and less severe than in other countries. Four explanations have been advanced to explain the limited effects of the international depression on Sweden. First, the devaluation of the Swedish currency (leaving the gold standard in 1931) improved the competitive position of industry and made it possible to continue exporting even into depressed markets. Second, rationalisation after the crisis in the 1920s had made Swedish firms more competitive internationally. Third, the domestic market expanded through consumption of products, i.e. automotive, textile, electricity and construction, and was not as dependent on international developments. The number of new entrepreneurs was also high in Sweden mainly because unemployment during the 1920s had seen many of them start up companies. Finally, the economic policy

Table 3. Turnover on the Stockholm Stock Exchange, commercial banks' lending, credit losses, notes in circulation and M3, 1926–35.

Year	Turnover on SSE		Banks advances to non-bank public, annual change (%)	Loan losses/ advances (% total)	Notes in circulation 1914=100	M3
	Current prices	Fixed prices 1926=100				
1926	285.1	285.1	0.8	–	100.0	100.0
1927	443.6	448.0	−4.6	0.6	100.2	110.5
1928	621.3	624.4	−0.5	0.5	92.6	111.7
1929	575.0	807.8	2.8	0.4	108.4	115.9
1930	638.2	667.8	6.5	0.8	113.1	119.7
1931	602.3	653.8	−1.8	0.8	111.0	116.8
1932	239.7	265.9	−8.4	4.6	113.9	120.7
1933	226.3	256.6	−9.8	0.9	123.3	132.2
1934	300.8	339.2	−3.0	1.2	134.8	136.1
1935	264.5	293.4	−2.8	0.4	149.7	139.7

Sources: Statistics Sweden, on commercial banks 1926–35.

introduced by the social democratic government was a Keynesian-type fiscal policy. For instance, the government introduced market-like wages to the unemployed, which along with other stabilisation-type policies increased purchasing power and facilitated a relatively rapid recovery phase (Lundberg, 1983).

Conclusion – eruptions, disruptions and financial crises

This paper has compared two financial crises in Sweden that occurred in the 1920s and 1930s which, while close together in time and place, were quite different in the forces driving them, how they were resolved and their effects on the wider economy and society. The final section attempts to draw some conclusions from our analysis of these financial crises. In an earlier study we had found five general attributes that have been identified as present in financial crises (Lönnborg et al., 2003).

The first common attribute with all the severe financial crises in Sweden is that they have coincided with an international downturn, and been closely associated with a flight of capital from Sweden. But in itself the coincidence of the international disruption to the financial system in Sweden was not enough to determine the magnitude of the crisis and the scale of the subsequent downturn. In the 1920s Sweden experienced a severe crisis during only a mild international downturn as opposed to only a mild downturn during the severe international crisis of 1930s. Perhaps crises should not be regarded as triggered by exogenous displacements, instead they are generally best understood as normal events within capitalism. Different outcomes, as in the case with the crises of the 1920s and 1930s in Sweden, demonstrate different institutional contexts, different vulnerabilities and different responses. This demonstrates that while crisis-like events are normal, they are not always the same, and analysing financial crises and their effects requires that the wider economic and institutional contexts of these events are brought into the framework.

A second attribute of financial crises in Sweden is that during the boom periods leading up to the crisis there had been a rapid growth in (typically international) credit and investment, and this flowed through to asset price inflation (especially in equity and real estate markets). But once again the magnitude of these expansions was very different. In the lead up to the crisis of the 1920s, expansion lasted several years, peaking with annual increases in lending to the non-bank public of 30% and more in 1917 and 1918. In the case of the 1930s crisis, the domestic expansion was shorter and much more moderate, with peak lending growth of 6.5% in 1930. The same difference was found for the expansion in the broad money supply in Sweden, including the non-bank publics' deposits in banks.

Third, changes in financial legislation and innovations in finance helped to increase the scope of activity of financial institutions within the economy (either through the possibility for circumventing existing regulation, or by changing the channels or institutional form through which credit growth occurred). This increased competition for activity and market share, which in turn increased risk-taking among financial institutions. Buoyant economic conditions, combined with credit growth and asset price inflation, encouraged financial institutions to take greater risks in concentrating credit expansion either to a few individuals or to particular sectors of industry or commerce, and these sectors were often quite new, or seemed so at the time. Recalling Reinhart and Rogoff's recent work (2009), buoyant conditions and ample liquidity often helped to produce the widespread belief that this situation was new and different. Borrowers were encouraged to increase leverage, which financial institutions facilitated in the expectation of continued growth.

Fourth, in each crisis state intervention was required to stabilise the financial system, however while responses were quite similar the results were quite different. In both cases studied here the initial response was to bail out the banks that were deemed as important for the financial system. But one striking difference concerns the monetary regime and the possibility to run flexible monetary policy; that is to provide discretionary liquidity. In the 1920s crisis the monetary objective above all was to readopt the gold standard which led to a monetary policy that worsened the deflationary spiral and rendered monetary authorities unable to counteract the effects of international business cycles on the domestic economy. In the 1930s, by contrast, the international crisis had already forced Sweden off the gold standard in 1931 so when the losses from the banks' involvement in the Kreuger Group became acute, the possibility to run more flexible monetary policy was not determined by an overriding need to be tied to a fixed anchor. This may have been of the utmost importance – especially as the losses in relation to the fall of the Kreuger Group were twice the total reserves of the central bank at the time.

Fifth, the outcome of each crisis, apart from state initiatives to absorb the losses and restart the financial and monetary system, was the instigation of governmental investigations to evaluate the role of banks in the Swedish economy and society. This resulted usually in new and stricter regulations for banking and a changing role for and reorganisation of bank supervision, which in many ways allowed the regulatory regime to catch up with the innovations that had been occurring.

The aftermath of financial crises have also been characterised by increased caution in the credit policy of banks, credit volumes have been reduced and the requirement to perform creditworthiness checks have increased. Rationalisation and inspection of cost development within banks have been recurrent issues in connection with financial crises.

In the wake of financial crises, the structure of the financial system has usually also undergone further change. The extent of concentration within the banking sector has often increased during the working out of financial crises, owing to the merger of distressed banks with larger banks. Financial institutions that have not been affected by the crisis on a large scale have thereby been able to increase their market share at the expense of those affected. And institutions that were not able to attract state support often failed, leaving commercial banks as the enduring financial institutions in the Swedish financial system.

Finally, five general consequences have usually occurred during crisis periods: i) financial institutions have themselves often acted cooperatively with affected banks receiving help from other financial organisations; ii) the government, though usually not the central bank, has acted as lender of last resort or established crisis management institutions; iii) banks have cut credit to the most severely affected sectors; iv) banks and other financial organisations have rationalised and emerged with increased efficiency, and often returning more to their core (pre-crisis) business; and v) through mergers and acquisitions financial institutions have been restructured and concentration on financial markets has increased.

There are obviously important questions that emerge from such a review. Given the regularity of financial disruptions, definitional issues about what constitutes a financial crisis are surely important but open. In particular, an issue for business and economic historians concerns the relationship between financial and wider economic and social crises. Much has been and is to be gained by focusing on financial crises, but much is surely also to be gained by looking at the changing relationship (and integration) between financial and economic processes. Eric Hobsbawm (2008) recently noted that capitalism seems to have an inherent crisis-prone tendency, yet thinking about instability and disruption in this historical context surely challenges us to ask what we mean when we think and talk about crises, financial and otherwise.

Notes

1. The two works are referred to here not as the only recent works on financial crisis, or even necessarily the most important. Rather, in their different ways they highlight some important points the authors seek to identify about the ways we historians and others have been approaching crises (others of note include Allen & Gale, 2009; Borio, 2010; Calomiris, 2007; Farlow, 2011; see also 'older' works such as Capie & Wood, 1986; Eichengreen, 2002; Hubbard, 1991).
2. Goetzmann and Newman (2010) also make a similar point aboüt securitisation of real estate mortgages.
3. Rheinhart and Rogoff (2009) make clear the role they see for hubris in financial crisis.
4. There are other studies about crises in the Scandinavian region (generally Drees & Pazarbasioglu, 1998; for Sweden Englund, 1999; Larsson & Sjogren, 1995; Lindgren, 1994; for Norway Knutsen, 1991, 2007; and for Denmark Hansen, 1996).
5. This postwar rationalisation of the Swedish industry has come to be known as the 'steel bath'.
6. Stockholms Enskilda Bank was controlled by the Wallenberg family and was considerably smaller than Skandinaviska Banken. However, these two banks merged in 1971 under the name of Skandinaviska Enskilda Banken (today SEB).
7. This is to be explained because the restructuring did not stop banks and industrial firms from having relationships, but rather changed the direction of ownership so that industrial groups (such as the Wallenbergs) came to exert control over banks.

References

Allen, F., & Gale, D. (Eds.). (2008). *Financial crises*. Cheltenham: Edward Elgar.
Bordo, M.D., & Munshid, A.P. (2000). *Are financial crises becoming increasingly contagious: What is the historical evidence on contagion?* (Working Paper Series 7900). Cambridge, MA: National Bureau of Economic Research (NBER).

Bordo, M.D., Taylor, A.M., & Williamson, J.G. (Eds.). (2003). *Globalization in historical perspective*. Chicago, IL: University of Chicago Press.

Borio, C.E.V. (2010). Ten propositions about liquidity crises. *CESifo Economic Studies*, *56*(1), 70–95.

Broadberry, S.N. (1984). The North European depression of the 1920s. *The Scandinavian Economic History Review*, *32*, 159–167.

Bustelo, P. (2000). Novelties of financial crises in the 1991s and the search for new indicators. *Emerging Markets Review*, *1*, 229–251.

Calomiris, C.W. (2007). *Banking failures in theory and history: The great depression and other 'contagious' events* (NBER Working Paper 13597). Cambridge, MA: National Bureau of Economic Research.

Capie, F., & Wood, G.E. (Eds.). (1986). *Financial crises and the world banking system*. New York: St. Martin's Press.

Cassis, Y. (Ed.). (1992). *Finance and financiers European history, 1880–1960*. Cambridge: Cambridge University Press.

Chan-Lau, J.A., & Chen, Z. (2002). A theoretical model of financial crisis. *Review of International Economics*, *10*(1), 53–63.

Drees, B., & Pazarbasioglu, C. (1998). *The Nordic banking crises: Pitfalls in financial liberalization* (Occasional paper (161)). Washington, DC: International Monetary Fund.

Eichengreen, B. (2002). *Financial crises and what do about them*. Oxford: Oxford University Press.

Eichengreen, B., & Bordo, M.D. (2002). *Crises now and then: What lessons from the last era of financial globalization?* (NBER Working Paper (8716)). Cambridge, MA: National Bureau of Economic Research.

Eichengreen, B., & Portes, R. (1989). *The anatomy of financial crises* (NBER Working Paper (2126)). Cambridge, MA: National Bureau of Economic Research.

Englund, P. (1999). The Swedish banking crises: Roots and consequences. *Oxford Review of Economic Policy*, *15*(3), 80–97.

Farlow, A. (2011). *Crash and beyond. Causes and consequences of the global financial crisis*. Oxford: Oxford University Press.

Gäfvert, B. (1979). *Kreuger, riksbanken och regeringen* [Kreuger, the Swedish central bank and the government]. Stockholm: Liber.

Galbraith, J.K. (1955). *The Great Crash 1929*. London: Hamish Hamilton.

Galbraith, J.K., & Lu, J. (1999). *Inequality and financial crises: Some early findings* (Inequality Project, Working Paper (9)). University of Texas.

Garside, W.R. (Ed.). (1993). *Capitalism in crisis. International responses to the great depression*. New York: St. Martin's Press.

Gavan, M., & Hausmann, R. (1999). *Preventing crisis and contagion: Fiscal and financial dimensions* (IADAB, Research Department Working Paper 401). New York: Inter-American Development Bank.

Glete, J. (1981). *Kreugerkoncernen och krisen på den svenska aktiemarknaden: Studier om svenskt och internationellt riskkapital under mellankrigstiden* [The Kreuger group and the crisis on the Swedish stock market: Studies about Swedish and international venture capital during the interwar period]. Stockholm: Almqvist & Wicksell International.

Goetzmann, W.N., & Newman, F. (2010). *Securitization in the 1920s* (NBER Working Paper no. 15650). Cambridge, MA: National Bureau of Economic Research.

Goodhart, C.A.E. (1999). Myths about the lender of last resort. *Journal of International Finance*, (2), 339–360.

Hansen, P.H. (1996). *På glidebanen til den bitre ende: Dansk bankvæsen i krise 1920–1933* [On the glide path until the bitter end: Danish banking during the crisis 1920–1933]. Odense: Odense Universitetsforlag.

Hassbring, L. (1979). *The international development of the Swedish Match Company 1917–1924*. Stockholm: Liber.

Herring, R.J., & Wachter, S. (1999). *Real estate booms and banking busts: An international perspective* (Financial Institutions Centre Working Paper 99–27). Wharton School, University of Pennsylvania.

Hildebrand, K.-G. (1971). *Banking in a growing economy: Svenska Handelsbanken since 1871*. Stockholm: Svenska Handelsbanken.

Hildebrand, K.-G. (1985). *Expansion, crisis and reconstruction 1917–1939: The Swedish Match Company*. Stockholm: Liber.

Hobsbawm, E. (2008). Eric Hobsbawm on the financial crisis. Interview with BBC, October 23. Retrieved May 13, 2009, from http://news.bbc.co.uk/today/hi/today/newsid_7677000/7677683.stm

Hubbard, G.R. (Ed.). (1991). *Financial markets and financial crises*. Chicago, IL: University of Chicago Press.

Kamin, S. (1999). *The current international financial crisis: How much is new?* (Board of Governors of the Federal Reserve System International Finance Working Paper no. 636). Washington, DC: US Board of Governors of the Federal Reserve.

Kindleberger, C.P. (1989). *Manias, panics, and crashes. A history of financial crises* (2nd ed.). Basingstoke: Macmillan.

Kindleberger, C.P. (1993). *A financial history of Western Europe* (2nd ed.). New York: Oxford University Press.

Kiyotaki, N., & Moore, J. (1995). Credit cycles. *Journal of Political Economy, 105*(2), 211–248.

Knutsen, S. (1991). From expansion to panic and crash. The Norwegian banking system and its customers 1913–1924. *Scandinavian Economic History Review, 39*(3), 41–71.

Knutsen, S. (2007). *Staten og kapitalen i det 20. Århundre – Regulering, kriser og endring i det norske finanssystemet 1900–2005* [The state and the capital in the nineteenth century. Regulation, crises and changes in the Norwegian financial system 1900–2005]. Oslo: Unipub.

Larsson, M. (1989). *Public control of commercial banks and their activities. The Swedish example* (Uppsala Papers in Economic History, no. 2). Uppsala: Department of Economic History.

Larsson, M. (1992). Government subsidy or internal restructuring? Swedish commercial banks during the crises years of the 1920s. In P.L. Cottrell, H. Lindgren, & A. Teichova (Eds.), *European industry and banking between the wars* (pp. 129–145). Leicester: Leicester University Press.

Larsson, M. (1995). Overcoming institutional barriers – financial networks in Sweden 1910–1990. In Y. Cassis, G.D. Feldman, & U. Olsson (Eds.), *The evolution of financial institutions and markets in twentieth-century Europe* (pp. 122–142). Aldershot: Scholar Press.

Larsson, M., & Olsson, U. (1992). Industrialiseringens sekel [The century of the industrialisation]. *In Sveriges Industri* [Swedish industry]. Stockholm: Industrilitteratur.

Larsson, M., & Sjögren, H. (1995). *Vägen till och från bankkrisen: Svenska banksystemets förändring 1969–94* [The road to and away from the bank crisis: The change of the Swedish banking system 1969–1994]. Stockholm: Carlsson.

Lindgren, H. (1979). *Corporate growth. The Swedish match industry in its global setting*. Stockholm: Liber.

Lindgren, H. (1982). The Kreuger crash of 1932. In memory of a financial genius, or was he a simple swindler? *Scandinavian Economic History Review, 3*, 189–206.

Lindgren, H. (1994). Att lära av historien: Några erfarenheter av finanskriser [To learn from history: Some experiences from financial crises]. In *Bankkriskommittén* (pp. 7–32). Stockholm: Fritze.

Lönnborg, M., Rafferty, M., & Ögren, A. (2003). One hundred and fifty years of financial crises in Sweden. In Y. Hasselberg & P. Hedberg (Eds.), *In it together* (pp. 113–144). Uppsala: Acta.

Lundberg, E. (1983). *Ekonomiska kriser förr och nu* [Economic crises in the past and now]. Stockholm: SNS.

Lybeck, J. (1992). *Finansiella kriser förr och nu* [Financial crises in the past and now]. Stockholm: SNS.

Mishkin, F.S. (1991). Anatomy of a financial crisis. *Journal of Evolutionary Economics, 2*(2), 115–130.

Ögren, A. (2003). *Empirical studies in money credit and banking. The Swedish credit market in transition under the silver and the gold standards, 1834–1913*. Stockholm: Stockholm School of Economics.

Ögren, A. (2007). Lender of last resort in a peripheral economy with a fixed exchange rate: Financial crises and monetary policy in Sweden under the silver and gold standards, 1834–1913. In P.L. Cottrell, E. Lange, & U. Olsson (Eds.), *Centres and peripheries in banking* (pp. 223–250). Farnham: Ashgate.

Östlind, A. (1945). *Svensk samhällsekonomi 1914–1922. Med särskild hänsyn till industri, banker och penningväsen* [Swedish economics 1914–1922. With particular regard to the industrial, banking and monetary system]. Stockholm: Swedish Bankers' Association.

Partnoy, F. (2009). *The match king: Ivar Kreuger and the financial scandal of the century.* London: Profile.

Petterson, K.-H. (1994). *Bankkrisen inifrån* [The bank crisis from the inside]. Stockholm: SNS.

Reinhart, C.M., & Rogoff, K. S. (2009). *This time is different – eight centuries of financial folly.* Princeton, NJ: Princeton University Press.

Schumpeter, J. (1928). The instability of capitalism. *The Economic Journal, 38*(151), 361–386.

Sjögren, H., & Knutsen, S. (2010). Why do banking crises occur? An evolutionary model of Swedish banking crises. In A. Ögren (Ed.), *The Swedish financial revolution* (pp. 193–203). Basingstoke: Palgrave Macmillan.

Söderlund, E. (1978). *Skandinaviska banken i det svenska bankväsendets historia 1914–1939* [The Scandinavian bank within the history of the Swedish bank market 1914–1939]. Uppsala: Norstedt.

Statistics Sweden. (1914–36). *Statistiska meddelanden: Uppgifter om bankerna* [Statistical messages: Information about the banks]. Stockholm: Statistics Sweden.

Statistics Sweden. (1980–95). *Statistiska meddelanden* [Statistical messages]. Serie K, Stockholm: Statistics Sweden.

Statistics Sweden. (1980–95). *Statistiska meddelanden* [Statistical messages]. Serie P, Stockholm: Statistics Sweden.

Stockholm Stock Exchange annual report. (1982–1995). Stockholm: Stockholm Stock Exchange.

Sveriges Riksbank. (1931). Statistical tables. In *Sveriges Riksbank 1668–1924–1931: Bankens tillkomst och verksamhet* [The Swedish central bank 1668–1924–1931: The emergency of the bank and the development] (Vol. V). Stockholm: Sveriges Riksbank.

Temin, P. (1989). *Lessons from the Great Depression.* Cambridge, MA: MIT Press.

Thunholm, L.-E. (1991). *Oscar Rydbeck och hans tid* [Oscar Rydbeck and his time]. Stockholm: Fisher.

Waara, L. (1980). *Den statliga företagssektorns expansion* [The expansion of the state enterprise sector]. Stockholm: Liber.

Wigforss, E. (1932). *Kreugerkris, banker och stat* [The Kreuger crisis, banks and the state]. Stockholm: Tiden.

Wikander, U. (1979). *Kreuger's match monopolies 1925–1930. Case studies in market control through public monopolies.* Stockholm: Liber.

Wood, G. (1999). Great crashes in history: Have they lessons for today? *Oxford Review of Economic Policy, 3*, 98–109.

Canada and the United States: Different roots, different routes to financial sector regulation

Donald J.S. Brean[a], Lawrence Kryzanowski[b] and Gordon S. Roberts[c]

[a]Rotman School of Management, University of Toronto, Toronto, Canada; [b]John Molson School of Business, Concordia University, Montreal, Canada; [c]Schulich School of Business, York University, Toronto, Canada

This paper explores the lessons to be learned from why the neighbouring banking systems of Canada and the United States, that share numerous commonalities, fared so differently during two major financial crises. The explanations are deeply rooted in different tolerances for industry concentration and state involvement, and the divergent routes of the development of their financial systems, founding institutions, on-going governance and regulation, and competitive structures. Canada's success during the more recent 2007–09 financial crisis is attributed to more effective regulation and conservative banking practices, including (self-) imposed stricter limits on bank leverage, much stricter limits on unconventional mortgages, and less reliance on the use of more 'creative' investment types (e.g. subprime lending) and structured products.

Introduction: the comeuppance of weak financial regulation

> Where a Lehman Brothers or Bear Stearns had neither parents with deep pockets nor prudential regulation to save it from disaster, our investment banks had both. (Coyne, 2009, p. 25)

The world economy was battered by the dramatic contraction of credit markets and the collapse of international trade during the 2007–09 economic and financial crisis. The turbulence began in the US, and spread to other countries, notably the United Kingdom. The crisis began in the nation known for the world's deepest, most liquid and seemingly most sophisticated financial institutions and markets. The depth, liquidity and faux sophistication of the US financial system were insufficient to ward off a systemic collapse that quickly engulfed the world.

As the US was engaged in an escalation of institutional failure, government intervention and nationalisation, the world came to realise that regardless of the proximate causes of the collapse – including global trade imbalances that attracted huge flows of foreign funds to the US, an unprecedented housing bubble and the explosion of securitisation and opaque financial engineering – regulation of the banking and financial sectors in the US (and many other countries) was deficient. Legislators, finance authorities and executives worldwide were soon embroiled in debates about the principles of financial regulation and the government's right and responsible role in overseeing the behaviour and operations of financial institutions, regulators and other market participants.

The passage of a major US banking bill in 2010 contained a range of interventionist steps including new limits on banks' involvement in 'proprietary trading' (the buying and selling of investments on financiers' own books unrelated to customers' needs), provisions to make it easier to liquidate large, financially interconnected financial institutions, and the creation of an independent Consumer Financial Protection Agency to guard against lending abuses. We will have to wait to find out if these initiatives adequately address the failed institutional heart of the collapse, specifically the fact that the systemic expansion of risk escaped the vigilance of regulation and regulators. A trio of financial techniques (securitisation, collateralised debt obligations and credit default swaps) were the means whereby financial institutions generated extraordinarily high leverage designed to be difficult for regulators to trace (Kane, 2010).

The real asset foundation of much of the financial expansion was the overheated housing market, especially the portion at the low end of creditworthiness or so-called 'subprime market' based on high debt-to-value ratios. The institutional interdependence of the creators, buyers and sellers of the derivative securities that levered this sector of housing finance tended to concentrate the risk to which US regulators seemed sanguine or unaware. Moreover, with so much finance pyramided on a narrow real asset base, the correlations among returns on the various financial products were much higher (consistent with higher systemic risk) than was reflected in their returns (Jarrow, 2009). When the housing bubble burst, driving financial institutions to failure, the once clever synthetic financial products became known as 'toxic assets'.

Meanwhile the US banking and financial system was left in disarray. The 2008 collapse of Bear Stearns, the Wall Street firm that pioneered securitisation and asset-backed securities markets, was both a significant casualty and contributor to the financial crisis. In 2006–07 Bear Stearns increased its exposure to the mortgage-backed assets that were central to the subprime mortgage crisis. Fear soon beset the markets as banks, and especially 'near' or 'shadow' banks (outside the regulatory perimeter), demanded unprecedented premia on short-term inter-institutional loans that led to a liquidity crisis among financial institutions.

As the financial crisis progressed, a huge amount of financial assets in the US had to be restructured due to 'failure' (e.g. Lehman Brothers, Merrill Lynch and Washington Mutual Bank) or taken over or guaranteed by the state (e.g. AIG) or brought under the too-big-to-fail safety net (e.g. Goldman Sachs and Morgan Stanley). Furthermore, Fannie Mae and Freddie Mac, two US government-sponsored enterprises, owned or guaranteed nearly $5 trillion in mortgage obligations at the time the US government placed them into conservatorship. With huge losses in 2008 and 2009, the cumulative loss for Fannie exceeded $72 billion since going public in 1970 (Bloomberg data).

Further north, Canada faced much the same external environments in the lead-up to the crisis as the US did. Indeed, the deep financial and economic integration of Canada and the US might suggest that Canada would inevitably be swept along by any shift in tides that emanate from or affect the United States. Nevertheless Canada did not experience a single bank failure, repeating its successful experience during the 1930s. When the US housing bubble burst, no similar spate of mortgage defaults occurred in Canada nor were there failures of or government equity injections into Canadian financial institutions. Short-term inter-bank loans flowed much as before. Ahead of banks in Singapore, Hong Kong and 92 other countries, Canadian banks were ranked first for 2008 and 2009 in Moody's annual ranking using standard debt rating criteria except for government support (Greenwood, 2009). The markedly superior financial performance in Canada was due in large part to fundamental differences in the structure and governance of the neighbouring financial systems.

Thus, the purpose of this paper is to consider two neighbouring countries which boast the world's longest common border, the world's largest flows of bilateral trade and cross-border investment, and many cultural similarities in language, law and new world heritage, to determine how and why these two countries fared so differently in the recent financial crisis, with a particular focus on the role of the financial sectors in the respective nations. The explanation for the dramatically different recent financial performance is deeply rooted in the divergent routes of the development of their financial systems, founding institutions, on-going governance and competitive structures. While the Canadian route to a system that successfully weathered the recent financial crisis is not unique (other countries such as Australia also emerged relatively unscathed), an understanding of the factors underlying Canada's success is likely to prove useful in informing future policy choices.

As discussed more fully below, the core of the Canadian financial system is a large, highly stable branch banking system. Banks dominate lending and credit creation nationally and account for over 60% of total financial assets in Canada. The six major banks represent about 85% of this total. These 'big 6' operate on a nationwide basis in commercial, retail and investment banking and also engage in wealth management and offer mutual funds. Combined with national branching, this wide range of activities allows them to benefit from both geographical diversification and economies of scale.

Since the 1920s, the highly concentrated Canadian financial system has enjoyed stability grounded on an implicit 100% guarantee of deposits at the large banks (Kryzanowski & Roberts, 1991). With continuity ensured, bankers in Canada have followed more conservative lending and funding practices. Further, universal banking came to Canada in the late 1980s and early 1990s providing investment banks with strong capital and unified regulation. While critics have argued that the Canadian financial system is too concentrated and protected from global competition, or that Canadian banks are too small and domestically focused relative to the big global players, such criticism does not stand up to empirical testing either in a historical context (Bordo, Rockoff, & Redish, 1994) or in the crucible of the financial crises of the Great Depression and 2007–09.

A brief history of the Canadian financial system[1]

As suggested above, the current Canadian financial system is widely acknowledged to be sound, secure and well-run. While this is in part due to good heritage, sound legislation and possibly good fortune, a number of important reforms came only as a reaction to bank failures. The heritage of English and Scottish financial legislation gave the various sectors a solid legislative framework even prior to confederation in

1867, while decennial revisions of the Bank Act ensured that amendments were timely. Several Royal Commissions examined threats, weaknesses and opportunities in banking and insurance and thus sped up the process.[2] The major types of financial institutions appeared early in Canada (e.g. fire and casualty insurers in 1809 and chartered banks in 1817), providing the system with a long evolution, at least by new world standards.

Neufeld (1997) suggests that a significant reason for the highly developed nature of the Canadian financial system was the absence of obstacles to the growth of national institutions. Whereas locally protective state legislation on banking and finance shaped (if not contorted) the US system, the Canadian system spread nationally as fast as banks could establish new branches (McDowall, 1993). Given Canada's far smaller population (one-tenth of the US today) and larger land area, it was important to ensure that economies of scale were never frustrated by legislative restrictions. In addition, the process enjoyed the flexibility of, for the most part, privately owned, publicly regulated institutions.

The rest of this selective history of Canadian financial development highlights the evolution of the structure of Canadian banking and finance with special regard for regulation and supervisory legislation as well as the institutions that oversee that function. We begin with the much better success of Canadian banks in weathering the Great Depression of the 1930s.

Survival of Canadian banks in the 1930s

Prior to 1929, the Canadian banking system enjoyed a number of features that served it well in the Great Depression. First, as discussed earlier, unrestricted national branching offered some diversification against regional shocks (e.g. rural versus urban). By promoting the growth of a small number of large banks, national branching reduced competition and facilitated government intervention. Second, although Canada did not have a central bank until 1934, an industry association, the Canadian Bankers Association (CBA), played a coordination role in times of panic, 'quickly arranging mergers between sound and failing banks, by encouraging cooperation between strong and weaker banks in times of stringency' (Bordo, 1986, p. 23, fn. 28). Third, forbearance (especially for the politically connected) and window dressing played an important role in preventing the failure of many Canadian financial institutions (primarily banks) during the 1920s (and subsequently in the 1930s). Furthermore, sophisticated and creative financial engineering was involved in the Quebec government financing to facilitate the merger between *La Banque Nationale* with *La Banque d'Hochelaga*, and various 'creative' (if not misleading or even fraudulent) reporting, accounting, repayment and taxation schemes were used to recapitalise the new *Banque Canadienne Nationale* resulting from the merger (Kryzanowski & Noiseux, 2004).

Fourth, and most importantly, after the failure of a major bank in 1923, successive governments backed forced mergers as an alternative to failure, setting in place an implicit guarantee of banks. This policy was articulated in records of the day. For example, speaking before the McKeown Commission investigating the failure of the Home Bank, a former finance minister stated:

> Under no circumstances would I have allowed a bank to fail during the period in question ... If it had appeared to me that the bank was not able to meet its public

obligations, I should have taken steps to have it taken over by some other bank or banks, or failing that, would have given it necessary assistance under the Finance Act, 1914. (McKeown, 1924, vol. 5, p. 324)

If I had believed that the Home Bank at that time was in danger of failing, closing its doors, was insolvent, I should have gone to the Bankers Association and told them to take over that bank. Either to one bank or more banks ... I would have made them do it. When I say that I had no legal power, but nevertheless I feel confident that I could have got them to do it. (McKeown, 1924, vol. 6, p. 359)

Additional archival evidence documenting the existence of the implicit guarantee is in Kryzanowski and Roberts (1993, 1998).

Beyond archival evidence, those researchers employ a market value model to restate the 1930s balance sheets of the ten large Canadian banks, all of which survived the Depression. Under a range of credible alternative assumptions on how credit and interest-rate risks affected bank balance sheets, their work demonstrates that nine of ten surviving banks were insolvent at market values between 1930 and 1935 (the lone solvent bank commenced operations in 1929). As an example, Canada's largest bank, the Bank of Montreal, had a model market value of -112% of book value in 1932 and the model estimated that 55% of current loans were bad. Given that no bank runs occurred and explicit deposit insurance began only in 1967, this result reinforces the archival evidence and strongly suggests that the banks enjoyed regulatory forbearance coupled with an implicit guarantee of all deposits.

Further evidence that an implicit guarantee of Canada's banks was in place from the mid-1920s is in Kane and Wilson (2002). Their work employs a statistical market value accounting model which recognises that observed share prices for banks include off-balance-sheet assets such as charter values and safety-net supports (SN). After extracting the net value to bank shareholders of safety nets as a percentage of market value (MV) for Canada's six largest banks and their predecessor companies, they conclude:

In Canada, blips in the value of SN/MV correspond broadly with crisis dates. SN emerges in 1896–1899, 1903–1905 (when three banks failed), in the mid-1920s (after the failure of the Home Bank) ... Our model indicates that large-bank stockholders benefited on occasion from implicit safety-net capital well before explicit deposit insurance was formally established. (Kane & Wilson, 2002, p. 668)

The implicit guarantee extended beyond banks to embrace Canada's largest life insurance company, Sun Life. During the 1920s boom, Sun Life invested heavily in equities, unlike its North American competitors who held negligible equity positions. After the 1929 crash, regulators mandated that Sun Life and its competitors employ backdated authorised values for securities in place of lower market values. This regulator-imposed accounting window dressing put a public face on capital forbearance and the implicit guarantee. After marking Sun Life's Depression-era balance sheets to market by replacing authorised values with actual market prices for common and preferred shares, Kryzanowski and Roberts (1998) report that Sun Life was insolvent with large negative surplus values in every year from 1930 to 1938. Due to a temporary stock price recovery (the apex in the upside-down V in a W stock market recovery), 1936 was an exception.

In contrast, Carr, Mathewson, and Quigley (1995) hold that prudent management and national branching promoted solvency and fully explain why there were no Canadian bank failures in the absence of explicit deposit insurance. They cite two pieces of allegedly conflicting evidence: positive stock prices for banks along with the results of a 1944 post-Depression historical audit of one major bank which affirmed solvency during the 1930s. Based on previous discussions, neither of these items is inconsistent with the presence of an implicit guarantee (Kryzanowski & Roberts, 1999). First, stock prices include off-balance-sheet assets such as charter values and safety-net benefits. It follows that positive stock prices are exactly what an economist would expect to observe when banks are insolvent at market values when an implicit guarantee is in place. Second, accounting window dressing typically accompanies an implicit guarantee so that an auditor's finding of solvency does not 'prove' that such a guarantee is absent or that the institution is solvent when marked-to-market.

Another lesson to be learned from examining archival evidence during this period is that the gap between the actual situations of financial institutions and public pronouncements by managements, elected officials and regulators tends to expand as the actual situations deteriorate. For example, while the Royal Bank 'technically tottered on the brink of insolvency throughout 1932–33', 'the bank persisted in viewing the hard times as an aberration, a moderate recession, as Holt told the shareholders, brought on by the speculative enthusiasm of the later 1920s' (McDowell, 1993, p. 252). This is an important caveat that should be kept in mind when reading contemporaneous assessments of financial crisis without the benefit of less restrictive access to archival evidence.

The Bank of Canada (BOC)

Until the BOC's establishment in 1934 due to political pressures,[3] large Canadian banks issued their own currencies. The federal finance department only issued small and very large denomination bank notes ($5 and under, and $500 and higher). The nation's largest bank, Bank of Montreal, acted as the government's banker. In the absence of a central bank, the system functioned well without a lender of last resort for three reasons. First, due to the stability discussed earlier, the banking system did not encounter the same liquidity problems as US banks. Second, the industry was self-regulated by the CBA in close concert with the government. Third, the gold standard or the prospect of returning to it served as a control over the money supply.

Canadian banks drew some criticism for aggravating the malaise during the Great Depression. The money supply was contracting and deflation was common, as the economy corrected from the high inflation in the 1920s. Farmers, manufacturing interests and other groups in favour of a depreciating currency all demanded a central bank. For example, the Royal Bank of Canada wanted the government's business diverted from the rival Bank of Montreal.

In 1933 Prime Minister R.B. Bennett called a Royal Commission on Banking and Currency on Canada with a mandate to study the functioning of the Finance Act and to make 'a careful consideration of the advisability of establishing in Canada a Central Banking Institution' (Macmillan, 1933, p. 5). Lord Macmillan, a prominent British jurist and known central bank supporter, was chosen as commission chair. Other members included British and Canadian bankers and John Brownlee, then Premier of Alberta, who petitioned in favour of a central bank because western farmers wanted cheap credit. The views of the commissioners reflected current-day sentiment supporting the creation of national institutions including the Canadian National Broadcasting Commission and Trans Canada Airlines (the predecessor to Air Canada).

Based on the positive recommendation in the Macmillian Report,[4] the BOC began operations on March 1935 after passage of the Bank of Canada Act. Initially the bank was founded as a privately owned corporation to insulate it from political influence. In 1938, under Prime Minister William Lyon Mackenzie King, the BOC became a special type of Crown Corporation with the governor appointed by Cabinet.

The BOC played an important role in financing Canada's World War II effort by printing money and buying government debt. The responsibility for creating small bills was transferred from the Department of Finance and the private banks were ordered to remove their currency from circulation. After the war, the bank's mandate was expanded to encourage economic growth in Canada. The subsidiary Industrial Development Bank (now called the Business Development Corporation) was formed to stimulate investment in Canadian businesses. The monetary policy of the BOC was geared towards increasing the money supply to lower interest rates and to achieve full employment with little concern about rising prices.

While it now had greater prospects for a more activist monetary policy, the BOC maintained the Bank Rate at the same 2.5% that it had inherited. It was not until February 1943, in the midst of the war, that the Bank Rate was cut.

The four pillars

Historically, the Canadian financial system was based on four principal groups: chartered banks, trust and loan companies, insurance companies and securities dealers. Each of these 'four pillars' was distinct in terms of market function, legislative control and ownership. Regulations enforced institutional separation of activities and prohibited cross-ownership. The rationale was that specialisation made all institutions less failure prone, and thereby the financial system more secure. The old-line financial institutions had clearly defined, non-overlapping but complementary functions.

Canada's *chartered banks*, incorporated and supervised under federal legislation, were and remain the dominant deposit-taking institutions with long involvement in commercial lending and significant sources of personal loans and residential mortgage credit since the mid-1950s. The nationwide branch-banking networks of the 'Big 6' banks are a defining characteristic of the Canadian financial system.

Trust and loan institutions tend to specialise in residential mortgages and term deposits. Unlike their provincially chartered counterparts, federally incorporated and supervised firms control the bulk of trusts' assets.

Canadian *life insurance companies* are under federal supervision. They invest the proceeds of life-insurance sales in portfolios of mortgages and financial assets such as bonds and equities.

Finally, Canadian *securities dealers* have traditionally operated under provincial legislation. The most influential provinces are Quebec for derivatives and Ontario for other traded assets, since they are homes to large concentrations of investment bankers, brokers, exchanges and associated financial industry personnel. Prior to June 1987, securities dealerships in general were owned by individuals actively engaged in the securities business. Today, following fundamental reform, as we shall discuss, each major chartered bank in Canada also owns an investment bank and is a sponsor to one or more families of mutual funds. At the time of writing in early 2011, the federal government is considering a shift to a national securities regulator, a move that faces opposition from a number of provinces.

Much of the history of the development of the Canadian financial system concerns how the functions of the financial pillars became less distinct. This, in turn, caused the tidy regulatory concept of pillar-distinction to become less defensible and less tenable as an underlying principle of regulation. By the 1950s, 'near banks' – credit unions, *caisses populaires*, trust companies and mortgage and loan institutions – emerged as significant national competitive forces. These upstarts moved imaginatively across the country, effectively capturing turf of the old-line chartered banks. Near banks offered a less stodgy system, more convenient locations and hours and generally a more customer-oriented approach to household and small business finance. Because they were not subject to the 6% cap on loan rates, the near banks undermined the chartered banks' comfortable intermediation margins by offering higher deposit rates and lower borrowing charges.

Due to increasing financial innovations by non-banks, the government launched a Royal Commission on Banking and Finance (1961), dubbed the 'Porter Commission' after its chairman. The time was right to explore whether the prevailing rationale of national financial policy may have been surpassed by events. This was the period when financial 'intermediation' had begun to be dispersed over a larger set of non-bank intermediaries, a harbinger of market-based finance with less reliance on banks with their predictable credit creation that the central bank had found relatively easy to influence.

For the stability of the Canadian chartered banking system in place at the time of the Porter Commission, the macro-financial environment comfortably accommo-dated the quasi-cartel that was in place. The statutory '6%' ceiling on bank lending rates along with other rigidly monitored features of conservative banking removed much of the incentive that Canadian banking might otherwise have had for financial product innovation. As with all cartels, an important common objective was stability.[5] The lasting Canadian banking innovations of the day tended to be in commercial (retail) banking processes, especially in the management and control of large branch banking networks. Without the incentive for aggressive financial innovation, especially in investment banking, the Canadian banking system had been sheltered from the sorts of competitive pressures that can systematically lead other banking systems to their peril.

The question was whether the move towards more competition in the Canadian banking and financial sector, along with a less rigid approach to the legislated structure, would compromise the longstanding stability of the system. The answer would depend on the nature and effectiveness of regulation.

The pillars crumble

Two Bank Act revisions are especially significant – the Act of 1967 that followed the Porter Commission, and the Act of 1980 which, among other things, introduced legislative flexibility by empowering the relevant Minister to amend 'regulations' from time to time involving issues such as the calculation of primary and secondary reserves and requirements for disclosure. The regulatory changes introduced by these two bank acts had a discernible theme. They allowed financial institutions in Canada to conduct their functions more efficiently, and to develop new products and services more effectively in an environment of competition and flexibility within the sector. While the Bank Act is restricted to federally chartered institutions, the drafters considered the impact of provincially chartered institutions and foreign players and, above all, the rapidly evolving market alternatives to intermediated finance.

To some extent the upstart near banks (primarily under provincial jurisdiction) enjoyed the shelter of constraints on chartered banks. This sub-sector of Canada's financial system grew rapidly, capturing an increasing portion of deposits and personal banking business from the chartered banks. This was a factor that posed a threat to the federal governance of major financial institutions. The chartered banks not only faced novel competition with respect to their deposit-taking function but they were also under mounting competitive pressure in their lending, especially to business. In the 1960s a growing share of short-term business finance was being done in the form of commercial paper and bankers' acceptances (marketable securities for which banks receive fees but not an intermediation margin). Indeed, the increasing use of securities by corporate borrowers is probably the single most important factor driving the eventual integration of Canadian banking and securities industries.

In view of the new realities in banking and finance, the Royal Commission on Banking and Finance reoriented Canadian banking policy, placing substantially increased emphasis on competition. This would foretell of the eventual dismantling of the independent pillars and move toward universal banking. En route, banks and the securities industry would emerge radically transformed in function, strategy, operations and ownership. Bank activities in restraint of competition were prohibited, deposit insurance was introduced and reserve requirements were reduced (eventually to zero), the scope of permitted business activities was expanded, restrictions on entry were eased, and foreign bank subsidiaries were permitted to operate in Canada.

The 1967 Bank Act and introduction of explicit deposit insurance

The 1967 Bank Act eliminated the 6% ceiling on the interest rate that banks charged on loans, signalling a shift away from a regulatory approach of rigid rules toward more market-determined results. Another significant development in regulatory policy introduced in 1967 involves substantially less onerous liquid reserve requirements that became similar to those of the near banks. For example, in place of an 8% cash reserve behind all Canadian dollar deposits, banks were required to hold 4% against Canadian dollar deposits 'payable after notice' and 12% on those that are 'payable on demand'. The assets permitted to satisfy the requirement (day-to-day loans and treasury bills as well as cash) included earning assets that banks would hold in any case.

This new flexibility in liquid reserve requirements, along with the removal of the interest rate ceiling and the broadening of lending authority, allowed banks to increase their average earnings on assets. This addressed the criticism that banks and their customers suffered a regulatory burden to the extent that banks could (or would) not pay competitive interest on savings deposits.

The new reserve requirement structure was particularly important for competition between banks and near banks. The required reserve ratio increased for demand deposits, but the near banks did not compete for this business. In contrast, lower reserve requirements for savings and term deposits made it profitable for the banks to compete vigorously in this market. As Canada and the world were about to enter a protracted era of high interest rates (and inflation) that would drive up the opportunity cost of non-interest-bearing deposits, the relative importance of demand deposits would decline sharply as people shifted their money into savings and term deposits. By 1980, the changed composition of deposits (with lower requirements on savings and term deposits) had the effect of lowering the average liquid reserve ratio from 8% to 5.3% of Canadian dollar deposits.

On the ownership front, the 1967 Bank Act introduced rules to maintain clear separation between banks and their customers. Banks were not to control important customers and vice versa. Chartered banks were prohibited from owning, directly or indirectly, more than 10% of the voting shares of any large Canadian company or more than 50% of a smaller corporation. An exception was stipulated for corporations that provide ancillary services directly to banks. One of many subsequent actions on ownership and control was introduced with concentrated bank ownership defined as no holdings greater than 10%. In response to two small trust company failures, explicit deposit insurance was introduced in 1967 with the founding of Canada Deposit Insurance Corporation (CDIC) covering deposits up to $60,000 (today $100,000).

1980 Bank Act

In addition to the negative effects of wealth destruction and redistribution, extraordinarily high inflation and the resulting financial uncertainty in the 1970s gave rise to unprecedented innovation and market-driven solutions to the financial problems of industry, households and institutions.

Inflation increases the opportunity cost of holding cash. Interest rate volatility creates risk that increases non-linearly with term, destroying the long-end of the financial market. In turn, industry faces great difficulty in financing investment of longer-lived capital projects while households find that cash flow requirements on mortgages are onerous. To address such problems, financial institutions and markets developed products tailored to the needs of savers and lenders, investors and borrowers. The new instruments, accounts and securities represented more creative and complex ways of assigning and distributing risk. For depositors, banks devised daily interest accounts to compete with the market alternative of money market funds. Banks and trusts offered variable rate mortgages. Derivative securities emerged as pure pricing of risk, allocated to those in the best position to bear it. Risk management was transformed into financial engineering. Although banks, trusts and insurance companies were innovative and adaptive, they were nevertheless constrained by out-dated regulation. The flexibility demanded of modern financial institutions called for lighter regulation.

The 1980 Bank Act allowed banks to 'factor' industrial receivables, a rudimentary form of securitisation, and to engage in capital asset leasing, a form of collateralised lending that in effect meant banks could 'sell' tax shields on depreciation. The Act extended the clearing system to any qualified financial institution – federal or provincial – that offered chequable deposits, thus removing a structural barrier to competition that only benefited the banks. Banks were permitted to establish 'captive mortgage companies'. By separating banks' mortgage accounts from the deposit-taking function and assigning no cash reserve requirement to mortgage business, this regulatory change substantially reduced the banks' overall cash reserve requirement. Given heightened competition, banks and near banks were now on the same reserve footing.

The 1980 Bank Act also introduced changes to regulations and requirements for entry into Canadian banking. First, the Act established a simpler method of incorporation for a new bank. This involved application to the Minister of Finance who had the authority to issue a charter ('letters patent') when s/he was satisfied that all the incorporation requirements were met. Previously, a new bank could only be established following a lengthy process that ultimately involved legislation.

More fundamentally, the Act relaxed the prohibition against the ownership of more than 10% of a bank's voting shares by a single 'interest'. While it continued to apply to ordinary chartered banks (now called Schedule I banks), it did not apply to Schedule II banks (foreign-owned deposit-taking subsidiaries). However, Schedule II banks were subject to higher minimum capital requirements, a limit on domestic assets of 20 times 'authorised capital' (an amount approved by the Minister of Finance), and a limit on the number of offices. Initially, a Schedule II bank could only have a head office and one other branch in Canada, with additional branches subject to ministerial approval. The 1980 Bank Act thus introduced fundamental change with respect to entry and ownership. While it did not elicit many new indigenous Canadian banks, it did provide a door for foreign bank entry. Today there are 44 Schedule II banks (41 foreign-owned).

In the 1980s, Canada introduced capital rules in harmony with the global move towards Basel I capital regulation. Insolvency regulation was tightened and the current centralised system of regulation of banks, insurance companies and pension funds under the Office of the Superintendent of Financial Institutions (OSFI) was established. OSFI replaced the previous system of inspection which failed to detect the weakness of two Western Canadian bank failures in 1985. In its early days in 1987, OSFI mandated that banks take provisions over three years to write down non-performing loans to Third World countries, principally Mexico, Brazil and Argentina (MBA countries). Because an immediate marking to market of these loans would most likely have impaired or wiped out bank capital, this act of regulatory forbearance was widely regarded as a modern manifestation of the implicit guarantee although it was never subjected to careful testing.

Move towards universal banking

As the pillars continued to crumble, banks were allowed to acquire businesses in competing areas. In the late 1980s, all the major banks entered the brokerage and investment banking businesses by acquiring existing brokerage firms or, in the case of Toronto-Dominion Bank, building its own (Kryzanowski & Ursel, 1993). In the 1980s, the growing role of pension funds and other institutional investors coupled with increasing market volatility magnified the risks faced by independent investment dealers. Under bank ownership, brokerage firms obtained access to capital and secure funding. One important result was the growth of the 'bought deal' in which underwriters purchase a stock issue and sell it to institutions within a day or two. A Canadian innovation also used in England, this form of underwriting addresses the need for issuers to place their securities quickly in volatile markets (DuVal, 1995–96).

In the real estate bust of the early 1990s, trust companies experienced difficulties and were bought by the major banks. The 1990s also saw banks expanding into mutual fund sales and wealth management. Two pairs of banks from the Big 6 were refused permission to merge on political grounds as this would have reduced the number of major banks to three. Faced with pressures for increased capital in the 1990s, insurance companies remained independent through ongoing prohibition against mergers with banks, and demutualisation that facilitated industry consolidation and new share issues. In 2008, Canada's largest life insurance company, Manulife, was discussed as a merger partner for a major bank. This move towards further merging of the pillars was never consummated, allegedly due to the relatively greater pressure exerted on elected officials by independent insurance agents. In 2009–10, federal finance minister Jim Flaherty was gearing for a showdown with the banks over their selling insurance on their websites, which went against the spirit of the law banning large banks from selling insurance products in their branches.

Significant and sustained differences between Canadian and American banking

This paper set out to identify significant and sustained differences between Canadian and American banking that explain the demonstrably greater stability of the Canadian system in the recent crisis.

The two most significant – and sustained – differences involve the institutional structure of financial systems in the neighbouring nations and the modes of financial sector regulation. A more subtle difference, although perhaps a driving force underlying the institutional and regulatory differences, is 'cultural' and historic as reflected in the founding principles of the two nations. This goes back to the US credo, 'Life, liberty and the pursuit of happiness' versus Canada's 'peace, order and good government'. Whereas the American Constitution and its subsequent interpretations were shaped by an inherent distrust of political influence on commerce and finance, Canadians have been generally more accepting of the state's role in overseeing, regulating and providing individual (e.g. health care) and corporate services. Examples of the latter include government-controlled entities such as the Canadian and Quebec Pension Funds; Central Mortgage and Housing Corporation (CMHC), which is Canada's premier provider of mortgage loan insurance, mortgage-backed securities, and housing policy and programmes; and Business Development Corporation (BDC), which helps create and develop Canadian businesses through financing, venture capital and consulting services, with a focus on small and medium-sized enterprises (SMEs). Canadians are also more accepting of greater concentration of corporate control and ownership as exemplified by greater family ownership of business and greater concentration in the financial sector.

System structure

The Canadian banking system, as outlined earlier, is dominated by six large banks each with an extensive national branch network. In contrast, between 1990 and 2009 the US banking system declined from over 12,000 to under 7000 commercial banks. A small percentage are large, and, until more recently, none had an extensive nationwide branch banking network. The atomistic institutional structure of the US banking system versus that in Canada underlies the weakness and vulnerability of the former.

Earlier we discussed the advantages of branch banking in Canada. Indeed, as American policy analysts explored the issue, they referred to the Canadian experience. According to Horwitz and Selgin (1987, unnumbered p. 6):

> Past experience in Canada demonstrates how branch banking can lead to a more efficient system for transferring funds between banks than that which has developed in the United States. Canadian banks were relatively free of government intervention until the middle of this century and were allowed to branch freely and circulate their own notes. Canada did not develop clearinghouses until much later than the United States, but not because its banking system was backward. Rather, with 13,000 banks in the United States and only 5 major banks in Canada, a far higher percentage of Canadian checks were cleared easily and quickly without multilateral clearings and transfers of reserves. The Canadian system was also very effective at moving funds between the vast farmland regions of the Canadian west and the urban areas of the east. Despite the overwhelming importance of agriculture in the Canadian economy, Canada never experienced the harvest season currency shortages and banking crises or the exposure to agricultural depressions that plagued (and to some extent continue to plague) the United States.

A dual banking system consisting of 'national' and state banks emerged in the United States during the Civil War. New national banking legislation was passed (1863, 1865) with the Comptroller of the Currency (1863) as the regulator. Federally chartered, national banks were 'national banks' in name only. As Sylla (2007, p. 136) points out:

> The early Comptrollers of the Currency also decided to interpret the National Banking Act in such a way that a federally chartered national bank could have only one office (unit banking) and was otherwise subject to the banking regulations of the state in which it was located. Hence a national bank could not open branches within a state or bank across state borders. Far from being national, as the Bank of the United States had been, the national banking system was in effect state banking with a federal charter and without a central bank.

In the United States, the Banking Act of 1933, based on the McFadden Act of 1927, and then the Bank Holding Company Act of 1956, continued to allow each state to establish its own policies concerning the scope for out-of-state banks to enter the state's market. Over time, some states (30 by 1990) and the District of Columbia reached reciprocal interstate banking agreements with states or other groups of states. Four other states permitted banks from any state to operate within their boundaries. Over 75% of these 34 states limited such interstate banking to purchases of in-state banks by out-of-state bank holding companies as opposed to allowing out-of-state banks to set up completely new branches. The other 25% permitted *de novo* branching. The remaining 16 states allowed no interstate banking at all.

The original law specified that the Federal Reserve Board of Governors (Fed) must approve the establishment of bank holding companies and prohibited bank holding companies headquartered in one state from acquiring a bank in another state. Over time, the strict prohibition was relaxed allowing bank holding companies to own banks across state lines and to benefit from diversification by pooling their capital at the holding company level (Baer & Mote, 1992). The interstate restrictions of the Bank Holding Company Act were formally repealed by the Riegle–Neal Interstate Banking and Branching Efficiency Act of 1994 (IBBEA). The IBBEA allowed interstate mergers between 'adequately capitalised and managed banks, subject to concentration limits, state laws and *Community Reinvestment Act* (CRA) evaluations'.[6]

The Gramm–Leach–Bliley Act, also known as the Financial Services Modernization Act of 1999, repealed part of the Glass–Steagall Act of 1933, opening up the market among banking companies, securities companies and insurance companies. The Glass–Steagall Act had restricted any one institution from acting as any combination of an investment bank, a commercial bank, and an insurance company. During the 1980s the Federal Reserve weakened Glass–Steagall restrictions by granting a wide range of investment banking powers to commercial banks. The 1999 Act allowed commercial banks, investment banks, securities firms, and insurance companies to consolidate formally. For example, Citicorp (a commercial bank holding company) merged with Travelers Group (an insurance company) in 1998 to form the conglomerate Citigroup. This corporation combined banking, securities and insurance services under a house of brands that included Citibank, Smith Barney, Primerica, and Travelers. This combination would have violated the Glass–Steagall Act and the Bank Holding Company Act of 1956 by combining securities, insurance, and banking, if not for a temporary waiver process. The Financial Services Modernization Act was passed to legalise such mergers on a permanent basis.

Developments other than market fragmentation and the movement to universal banking were the more direct causes of the recent instability of the US banking system. By December 2000, the US Republican Congress passed and President Clinton signed a bipartisan bill that freed banks to trade in derivative instruments outside the scrutiny of normal capital market regulators. The Commodity Futures Modernization Act of 2000 took a huge portion of derivative trading outside of the purview of the Commodities Futures Trading Commission (CFTC) and the Securities Exchange Commission (SEC). Passed after a decade-long debate about how to regulate derivatives and highly promoted by Treasury Secretary Robert Rubin, Alan Greenspan and other members of the 'Dream Economics Team', supporters of the bill based their view on several beliefs. First, the huge increase in OTC derivatives would continue. Second, its existence formed necessary linkages for users of derivatives, for whom standardised contracts were not sufficient. Third, OTC derivative trading gave US banks a huge competitive advantage. And, most importantly, self-regulation among banks provided adequate control and had blurred the distinction between organised and private markets (Kloner, 2001).[7] While many of the promoters came to regret their support and many to blame the Bush White House for reducing financial regulatory budgets, how the latest reforms will affect OTC trading is not yet clear.

Financial regulation

Under the influence of Hamilton, America had actually started out with a relatively centralised banking system, not unlike the Canadian one. The tension between the Hamiltonian and Jeffersonian visions of a financial system form one of the great leitmotivs of American history. The arguments continued for decades with both sides adapting as circumstances changed, clouding the battle lines. By the turn of the nineteenth century, Hamilton had lost much of his political clout. However, his Bank of the United States (the centrepiece of a centralised financial system that managed public debt, the dollar, banks, securities markets, corporations, and other enterprises, which was the envy of many European nations) lasted with a few years of financial turmoil some seven years after his death (its charter was 1791 to 1811). Against a good deal of Jeffersonian opposition, a second bank replaced it in 1816. The second bank also lasted only 20 years due to a renewal veto by President Andrew Jackson, heir to the Virginian's legacy (Sylla, 2007).

Based on subsequent events, the US paid a heavy price for the Jeffersonian aversion to large banks and a more concentrated banking system. While the Constitution gives the federal government control of the money supply, it is silent on the control of banks, which create money. This helped the Jeffersonians and their successors block the creation of a new central bank until 1912, when both bankers and Progressives agreed on its general necessity, if not its specific form. From the mid-1830s, through the first decade of the twentieth century, the American economy had been probably the most financially crisis-prone in the developed world (Fear & Kobrak, 2011). As already discussed, apart from the powers given to the Comptroller of the Currency (1863) and a few laws 'snuck' in by a Republican Congress during the Civil War setting up a 'national banking system', banks were still limited to doing one-state business, and basic banking regulation was left to the states in the US, unlike federal regulation in Canada. Some states provided firm regulation, others hardly any. Many states, influenced by Jeffersonian notions of the evils of powerful banks, made sure that their banks remained small by even forbidding inter-state branching. Much of the New Deal's financial legislation in the 1930s was designed to prevent 'fat cats' from wielding a great deal of financial power, while at the same time allowing the little guy new vehicles for small investment protected by diversification and transparency (Roe, 1994). During the 1980s and 1990s, regional and national banks emerged, a development that Richard Sylla (2007, p. 115) called 'reversing financial reverses'.

Beyond the advantage of federal regulation of a relatively small number of banks due to national branching, inter-pillar consolidation during the 1920s and intra-pillar consolidation more recently, the large Canadian banks benefited from stability with no bank failures between 1924 and 1985. Bordo et al. (1994) document higher rates of return on bank equity in Canada versus the US for the period 1920–80, attributed to a 'higher proportion of their portfolios devoted to lending' and greater leverage. Referring to the greater stability of the Canadian system they argue that:

> because the threat of failure was low, banks could reduce reserve ratios and increase leverage without alarming customers or provoking regulatory restrictions. The difference in net rates of return, in other words, might have been a return to an unmeasured component of the capital of Canadian banks – their reputation for soundness. (Bordo et al., 1994, p. 339).

Underlying the stability of Canadian banking is the implicit guarantee of large banks documented earlier. Coupled with higher rates of equity return discussed above, stability, along with a less competitive, integrated industry, led to conservative banking and regulatory cultures. An important aspect of Canadian bankers' conservatism is their tendency to fund assets with deposits as opposed to money market funding. Because deposits are far less subject to runs when banks experience difficulty, a high percentage of depository funding reinforced the stability of Canadian banks in the financial crisis of 2007–09 (Ratnovski & Huang, 2009).

Conservatism also extends to capital rules. The OSFI requires Canadian banks to hold higher levels of Tier 1 (equity) and total risk-weighted capital than mandated by the international Basel II capital rules. The banks, in turn, voluntarily choose to hold capital in excess of the required minimums. In addition to risk-adjusted capital, OSFI also sets a maximum level of leverage by limiting banks to a ratio of assets to capital not to exceed 20:1. Similarly to risk-adjusted capital, many Canadian banks choose leverage levels below the maximum of 20:1 (Saunders, Cornett, & McGraw, 2010). In contrast, many US and European banks had leverage levels of more than 25 and 30 to 1 during the recent economic crisis.

Bank regulation in the United States remains highly fragmented while most other G20 nations, including Canada, have only one bank regulator. Depending on its charter type and organisational structure, a US bank may be subject to numerous federal and state banking regulators. The US maintains separate banking, securities and insurance regulatory agencies at the federal and state levels in contrast to, say, Japan or the United Kingdom until more recently, where regulatory authority over the banking, securities and insurance industries is combined into one single financial service agency.[8] Even the US Federal Reserve System is fragmented as one of its five parts consists of 12 regional privately owned Federal Reserve Banks located in major cities throughout the nation based on a division of the US into 12 Federal Reserve districts. While all of these Federal Reserve Banks act as fiscal agents for the US Treasury, each has its own nine-member board of directors.

In contrast to detailed 'rules-based' or prescriptive regulation in the US, Canada adds a more discretionary 'principles-based' approach so that a financial institution must assure itself that it meets both the intent and what is explicitly prescribed in the legislation. For example, OSFI does not set out a fixed formula for what it considers adequate provision against loan losses, but it knows it when it sees it. OSFI has the power to step in to compel banks to make necessary adjustments. More generally, the mixed principles- and rules-based approach has the advantage of offering the regulator wider scope for action in the face of innovation designed to avoid regulation. This approach is also in place in Australia, which like Canada, did not experience any bank bailouts in 2007–09. Despite its merits, the principles-based approach by itself does not ensure successful regulation. Despite adherence to this regulatory style by its Financial Services Authority, the UK experienced major bank failures in the recent crisis.

In some important respects, Canadian banks benefit by being free from market distortions generated by political pressures facing their American counterparts. An important example of such distortions in the US is the home mortgage market where a number of institutional arrangements promoted overly rapid growth. Interest paid on home mortgages is tax deductible in the US but not in Canada. Mortgage insurance for home loans in excess of 80% of assessed value is required only on the excess amount rather than on the total loan value as in Canada. While US lenders extended 'Ninja loans' during the bubble period to borrowers with 'no income, job or assets' and 'liar loans' to borrowers who exaggerated their creditworthiness, Canadian lenders enforced lending guidelines and verified borrower credentials. Unlike in Canada, mortgages are non-recourse in some US states. Thus, the ratio of mortgages that had a high probability of being recovery deficient was much higher in the US than Canada. Finally, the US Community Reinvestment Act (CRA), mentioned above, requires federal financial supervisory agencies to encourage regulated financial institutions, including banks, to meet the credit needs of the local communities in which they are chartered. To enforce the statute, federal regulatory agencies examine banking institutions for CRA compliance and take this information into consideration when approving applications for new bank branches or for mergers or acquisitions. These requirements further encouraged banks to extend loans to unqualified home buyers, fuelling the US housing bubble.

History reveals that regulation significantly influences the path of financial sector development. The US and Canada demonstrate the point in a comparative sense. In 1967, Canada removed interest rate controls on deposits and loans whereas the comparable Regulation Q continued in effect in the US into the 1980s. When market interest rates exceed the controlled rate that banks can pay, the controls make intermediation uneconomic. In the 1970s when interest rates increased with inflation, there was no disintermediation in Canada. Canadian banks continued to have both a captive deposit base and secure loan portfolios as bank interest rates adjusted accordingly (Freedman, 1998). In contrast, the US banking system suffered serious disintermediation while a parallel banking system developed to channel savings through unregulated money market funds which then invested in bank securities or bank-sponsored products.

This explains in part the huge, largely unregulated 'shadow banking' securitisation market in the US conducted by stand-alone investment banks. Loans were repackaged to get them off the banks' balance sheets to avoid undiversified exposure. Similarly, the capital base weakness and the risk taken by depository banks such as Citigroup were opaque as US regulators and setters of accounting standards allowed them to move significant amounts of assets and liabilities off balance sheet into more legally and financially complex structured investment vehicles (SIVs). While the Toronto-Dominion (TD) bank exited its structured products business in 2005, no pre-crisis equivalent appears to have done the same in the US. After the financial deregulation of the 1990s described earlier, this process became accentuated as banks and investment banks worked with rating agencies to underwrite and sell asset-backed securities of dubious value.

Long before the 1999 US reforms that repealed the Glass–Steagall Act and its longstanding ban on American banks owning other types of financial institutions, Canadian banks were free to do the same. Following the 1987 deregulation, most of the country's large investment houses were bought by the Big 6 chartered banks (Kryzanowski & Ursel, 1993). While each subsidiary of an American banking conglomerate might be subject to a different regulatory authority, according to whether it was classed as an insurance company, investment bank or commercial bank, in Canada power was consolidated in OSFI to regulate the entity on both a stand-alone and consolidated basis. So, far from destabilising the banks, the brokers' absorption into the banks served to stabilise the brokers first in the late 1980s and later in the recent crisis. As our opening quote emphasises, by the time big American investment banks started to fail, neither financial muscle nor existing regulation was sufficient to ward off collapse. Such was not the case in Canada.

Conclusion

Canada's success in 2007–09 can be attributed to more effective regulation and conservative bank practices which includes imposed or self-imposed stricter limits on bank leverage as well as much stricter limits on unconventional mortgages and the use of SIVs. Subprime lending never gained an important market share in Canada. Canadian bank regulators moderate agency problems by placing well-defined limits on securitisation by requiring that lenders hold on to some of their loans. Further, although Canada experienced the seizure of its market for asset-backed commercial paper (ABCP), it did not develop a large shadow banking sector of independent investment banks and hedge funds taking on high levels of leverage. Further, Canadian banks had relatively lower exposures to various structured products such as collateralised mortgage obligations (CMOs), structured investment vehicles and credit default obligations (CDOs).

The historical foundations of the conservatism of Canadian banks are national branching which produced a small number of large banks given greater tolerance for concentration in Canada and the implicit guarantee of large banks in place since the 1920s. The result has been system stability which allowed banks to earn higher equity returns than their US counterparts while engaging in lower risk funding practices and holding greater capital. Going back to 1967, successive governments have implemented reforms eliminating interest-rate ceilings and encouraging a movement towards universal banking in a timely fashion. In addition to promoting stable growth, such legislative action largely prevented the development in Canada of US-style stand-alone independent financial institutions and securitisation markets with their attendant problems.

Some of the stability and high profits of Canadian banks are predicated on their being allowed to operate as cartels, which may reduce first-mover (and more risky) innovation and increase bank fees. Nevertheless, Canada provides a useful counterexample to some of America's excesses and may help us derive a more balanced approach than many countries have followed during the last few decades.

Acknowledgements
We thank Chris Kobrak, Joe Martin, Angela Redish and Mira Wilkins for helpful comments and suggestions. Financial support from the Social Sciences and Humanities Research Council of Canada is gratefully acknowledged.

Notes
1. This overview of the development of the Canadian financial system draws in substantial measure from Brean (2004) and Kryzanowski and Roberts (1991). It also owes a debt to Shearer, Chant, and Bond (1995), especially their Chapter 12, and to Freedman (1998).
2. A Royal Commission is a characteristically Canadian approach to addressing complex issues that may call for a shift in policy and law by the federal government.
3. The following discussion draws on Powell (2005), especially pages 44 to 51, 'The Depression Years and the Creation of the Bank of Canada (1930–39)', as well as on Bordo and Redish (1987).
4. The Canadian bankers on the committee opposed inter alia on the grounds that it was unwise to establish a central bank in the prevailing uncertain economic environment in which a newly established and untried central bank might hinder the government. Bankers favoured a return to the gold standard, contending that Canada's main problem was excessive debt. Other reasons for the negative raised by bankers included doubt about the availability of central banking expertise in Canada, the absence of a Canadian money market and the ineffectiveness of the Federal Reserve in countering the Depression in the United States.
5. At the height of the intense, risk-modifying 'cooperative' behaviour of Canadian banks during the 1950s and early 1960s, bank managers were provided with a for-your-eyes-only operational manual entitled 'Rates and Rules Generally Applied' that spelled out a common set of 'rates and rules' for bank loans. It even extended to other sorts of banking

commitments such as local advertising and promotion. The source of this information is a conversation with Robert Johnstone who was with the Research Department of the Bank of Canada and seconded to the Porter Commission.

6. The Community Reinvestment Act is a US federal law designed to encourage commercial banks and savings associations to meet the needs of borrowers in all segments of their communities, including low- and moderate-income neighbourhoods. Congress passed the Act in 1977 to reduce discriminatory credit practices against low-income neighbourhoods, a practice known as 'redlining'.

7. The name of the bill is somewhat of a misnomer since it actually deals with a wide range of derivative instruments, not just futures.

8. The UK government announced its intention to eliminate the Financial Services Authority (FSA) and give most of its power to a subsidiary of the Bank of England, the Prudential Regulatory Authority. It will also establish a Financial Policy Committee at the bank and establish a consumer protection and markets agency.

References

Baer, H.L., & Mote, L.R. (1991). The United States financial system. In G.G. Kaufman (Ed.), *Banking structures in major countries* (pp. 555–594). Boston, MA: Kluwer Academic Publishers.

Booth, L.D. (2009). The secret of Canadian banking: Common sense? *World Economics, 10,* 1–16.

Bordo, M.D. (1986). Financial crises, banking crises, stock market crashes and the money supply: Some international evidence, 1870–1933. In F. Capie & G.E. Wood (Eds.), *Financial crises and world banking system* (pp. 190–248). New York: St. Martin's Press.

Bordo, M.D. (2008). *An historical perspective on the crisis of 2007–2008* (Paper 14569). Cambridge, MA: National Bureau of Economic Research.

Bordo, M.D., & Redish, A. (1987). Why did the Bank of Canada emerge in 1935? *The Journal of Economic History, 47,* 405–417.

Bordo, M.D., Rockoff, H., & Redish, A. (1994). The U.S. banking system from a northern exposure: Stability versus efficiency. *Journal of Economic History, 54,* 325–340.

Brean, D.J.S. (1998). *Canadian extractive industries: Taxation, finance and foreign ownership.* Paper presented to the CIEPLAN Conference on Natural Resources and Development, Lima, Peru, September. Published (in Spanish) as 'Industrias Extractivas en Canada: Tributacion, Financiamiento y Propiedad Extranjera'. In D.J.S. Brean & M. Glave (Eds.), *Recursos naturales y desarrollo* (pp. 147–195). Santiago: CIEPLAN.

Brean, D.J.S. (2004). Financial liberalization: Historical perspectives, economic implications. In A. Berry (Ed.), *Critical issues in international financial reform* (pp. 125–151). New Brunswick, NJ: Transaction Publishers.

Carr, J., Mathewson, F., & Quigley, N. (1995). Stability in the absence of deposit insurance: The Canadian banking system, 1890–1966. *Journal of Money, Credit, and Banking, 27,* 1137–1158.

Coyne, A. (2009, April 13). Is Canada's banking system really so smart? *Maclean's*.

DuVal, G. (1995–96). The bought deal in Canada. *Canadian Business Law Journal*, *26*, 358–390.

Fear, J., & Kobrak, C. (2011). Banks on board: Banks in German and American corporate governance, 1870–1914. *Business History Review* [Special issue on Varieties of Capitalism], *84*(4), forthcoming.

Freedman, C. (1998). *The Canadian banking system* (Technical Paper no. 81). Ottawa, ON: Bank of Canada. Paper presented to the conference on Developments in the Financial System: National and International Perspectives, The Jerome Levy Economics Institute of Bard College, Annandale-on-Hudson, New York, April 1997.

Gordon, J.S. (2004). *An empire of wealth: The epic history of American economic power*. New York: HarperCollins.

Gordon, J.S. (2008, October 10). A short banking history of the United States: Why our system is prone to panics. *Wall Street Journal*.

Greenwood, J. (2009, October 8). Canadian banks top Moody's global ranking. *Financial Post*, Thursday.

Horwitz, S., & Selgin, G.A. (1987, December 15). *Interstate banking: The reform that won't go away* (Policy Analysis, no. 97). Washington, DC: The CATO Institute.

Jarrow, R.A. (2009). An expensive education: How last year's financial crisis taught us everything we needed to know about risk management. *Canadian Investment Review*, (Winter), 9–15.

Kane, E.J. (2010, January 22). *The importance of monitoring and mitigating the safety-net consequences of regulation-induced innovation* (Working Paper). Boston College.

Kane, E.J., & Wilson, B. (2002). Regression evidence of safety-net support in Canada and the U.S., 1893–1992. *Quarterly Review of Economics and Finance*, *42*, 649–671.

Kloner, D. (2001). The Commodity Futures Modernization Act of 2000. *Securities Regulation Law Journal*, *29*, 286–297.

Kryzanowski, L., & Noiseux, M.-H. (2004). *Too-connected-to-fail, window dressing, forbearance and the rescue of* La Banque Nationale *in 1924* (Working Paper). Concordia University.

Kryzanowski, L., & Roberts, G.S. (1991). Bank structure in Canada. In G.G. Kaufman (Ed.), *Banking structures in major countries* (pp. 1–58). Boston, MA: Kluwer Academic Publishers.

Kryzanowski, L., & Roberts, G.S. (1993). Canadian banking solvency, 1922–1940. *Journal of Money, Credit and Banking*, *25*, 361–376.

Kryzanowski, L., & Roberts, G.S. (1998). Capital forbearance: Depression-era experience of life insurance companies. *Canadian Journal of Administrative Sciences*, *15*, 1–14.

Kryzanowski, L., & Roberts, G.S. (1999). Perspectives on Canadian bank insolvency during the 1930s. *Journal of Money, Credit and Banking*, *31*, 130–136.

Kryzanowski, L., & Ursel, N. (1993). Market reaction to announcements of legislative changes and Canadian bank takeovers of Canadian investment dealers. *Journal of Financial Services Research*, *7*, 171–185.

Macmillan, Lord. (1933). *Report of the Royal Commission on Banking and Currency in Canada*. Ottawa, ON: Government of Canada.

McDowall, D. (1993). *Quick to the frontier: Canada's Royal Bank*. Toronto: McClelland and Stewart.

McKeown, H.A. (1924). *Report of the Royal Commission to enquire into and report upon the affairs of the Home Bank of Canada* (18 vols). Ottawa, ON: F.A. Acland.

McQueen, D. (1997). Economic research at the Bank of Canada, 1935–65. *Canadian Business Economics*, *5*, 89–95.

Neufeld, E.P. (1997). Reshaping Canada's financial system: Who wins, who loses? In P.J.N. Halpern (Ed.), *Financing growth in Canada* (pp. 419–429). Calgary, AB: University of Calgary Press for Industry Canada Research Series.

Organisation for Economic Cooperation and Development. (2000). *Economic survey: United States*. Paris: OECD.

Powell, J. (2005). *A history of the Canadian dollar*. Ottawa, ON: Bank of Canada. Retrieved February 14, 2011, from http://www.bankofcanada.ca/en/dollar_book/

Ratnovski, L., & Huang, R. (2009). *Why are Canadian banks more resilient?* (Working Paper WP/09/152). Washington, DC: International Monetary Fund.

Roe, M. (1994). *Strong managers, weak shareholders.* Princeton, NJ: Princeton University Press.

Safarian, A.E. (1959). *The Canadian economy in the Great Depression.* Toronto: University of Toronto Press. Reprinted by McGill-Queen's University Press in 2009.

Saunders, A., Cornett, M.M., & McGraw, P.A. (2010). *Financial institutions management: A risk management approach* (4th Canadian ed.). Whitby, ON: McGraw-Hill Ryerson.

Shearer, R.A., Chant, J.F., & Bond, D.E. (1995). *The economics of the Canadian financial system: Theory, policy and institutions* (3rd ed.). Toronto: Prentice-Hall Canada.

Sylla, R. (2007). Reversing financial reversals: Government and the financial system since 1789. In P. Fishback et al. & D.C. North (Preface), *Government and the American economy: A new history* (pp. 115–147). Chicago, IL: University of Chicago Press.

The effect of banking crises on deposit growth: State-level evidence from 1900 to 1930

Carlos D. Ramirez

Department of Economics, George Mason University, Fairfax, VA, USA; Center for Financial Research, Federal Deposit Insurance Corporation, Washington, DC, USA

Using a newly constructed database of bank failures for the period 1900 to 1930, this paper estimates a dynamic regression model to examine the extent to which banking instability at the state level affects the proportion of state deposits relative to national deposits. The main results indicate that banking failures reduce the proportion of state deposits by approximately 0.04% in the short run and by nearly 1% in the long run. In the eight states that adopted deposit insurance systems during the 1910s, however, there is little evidence that banking crises affected deposit growth. In addition, there is no evidence that the banking crisis of the 1980s and 1990s had any significant effect on state deposit growth. These results suggest that deposit insurance may have lessened the effects of banking instability on deposit growth.

Mr. Bissel, a farmer, having no faith in banks, kept his money hidden about his farm ... The other day he hid it up in flue. The next day his wife put up a stove and started a fire and burned up $3,000 in bank notes. (*New York Times*, 18 May 1897, p. 1)[1]

The bank commissioner of Kansas is quoted as saying that while there is no way of getting accurate figures, he has reason to believe that there is as much money hidden in socks and under carpets or buried or carried as is on deposits, and Commissioner Royce, of Nebraska, agrees with his opinion. (*Washington Post*, 25 June 1905, p. 9)

Introduction

One of the most serious and devastating consequences of banking crises is the loss of deposits from the banking system. In the absence of deposit insurance or any other (privately or publicly implemented) programme aimed at restoring confidence in a nation's banking system, bank failures lead to a systemic decline in deposits, not just because the deposits of failed institutions are lost (temporarily or permanently) but also because people may lose confidence in the banking system altogether – they simply stop trusting banks. As a result, they end up adjusting their portfolios of liquid assets away from the banking sector and into more rudimentary forms of savings, such as keeping their money under the mattress, literally or figuratively. That is, they simply take their money out of the banking system. If this happens – if the loss of confidence becomes institutionalised (as it has in many developing countries in recent years) – the systemic loss in deposits leads to long-lasting financial disintermediation and a permanent destruction of bank lending capacity, thereby affecting economic growth.

To empirically examine whether banking crises lead to long-lasting decline in deposits, one must find instances of sudden financial disintermediation that were not accompanied by broad and direct government intervention aimed at restoring confidence in the banking system. Only in the absence of such government intervention can the direct link between banking crises and long-term deposit growth be discerned. The experience of the United States between 1900 and 1930 – in other words, before the Depression – offers a valuable opportunity for examining the issue. This was a period when the United States endured not only several major banking crises (the Panic of 1907, the agricultural crisis of the early 1920s, and others) but also some relatively minor ones (Wicker, 1996, 2000). Such periods of banking crises were common in US history before the 1930s, but three aspects of the period 1900 to 1930 make it particularly useful for our purposes.

First, an important feature of these (pre-Depression era) crises is that for the most part they were regional in nature. Even the more serious Panic of 1907 was concentrated in New York, with limited fallout elsewhere (Moen & Tallman, 1992; Wicker, 2000). The regional nature of these crises allows us to identify on a regional basis the effect of banking crises on subsequent deposit growth.

Second, before 1930 the financial system was not subject to an orchestrated effort by the federal government to engage in counter-cyclical fiscal and monetary policy, and therefore the relationship between banking crises and deposit growth was uncontaminated by such intervention. Although the Federal Reserve had been created in 1913, its initial objective was to smooth out the regional credit cycles that were associated with agricultural borrowing demands (Kupiec & Ramirez, 2009; Miron, 1986). Notwithstanding the agency's impact on the seasonal agricultural cycle, early Federal Reserve policies did not seek an explicit counter-cyclical role for monetary policy. That is, monetary policy was not aimed at smoothing out business cycles (White, 1983). In the 1930s, however, this view of monetary policy would change, and the banking crises of the Depression era would be immediately followed by orchestrated efforts from the federal government that, as noted above, were aimed at restoring the public's confidence in the financial system.

Third, during the sample period eight states made an effort to stop (or at least slow down) the incidence of banking crises by adopting some form of deposit insurance, and the existence of these deposit schemes should help us identify the effect of banking crises on deposit growth.[2] As discussed in more detail below, none of these deposit insurance schemes effectively reduced the incidence of banking failures. However, even if they failed in stopping or slowing down banking crises, they could still have been effective in slowing down the contraction in deposits stemming from the crises. If deposit insurance served to reassure depositors that their funds would not be permanently lost, one would expect the relationship between banking failures and deposit contraction in these eight states to be weaker than the relationship in states without deposit insurance.

This combination – the regional nature of the crises, the absence of federal intervention, and the presence of some state deposit insurance schemes – allows for a relatively clean investigation of the hypothesis that sudden episodes of financial disintermediation (financial panics) affected long-term deposit growth. To this end, I make use of a newly constructed database that identifies the incidence of banking crises in every state in the nation between 1900 and 1930 and for all banks, not just national banks. I then fit an Arellano-Bond dynamic panel model to analyse the extent to which bank deposits at the state level were affected by the severity of state banking crises. The evidence suggests that a state that endured a banking crisis also experienced a statistically significant reduction in its share of aggregate deposits – a reduction of about 0.02% to 0.04% after one year, with a long-term decline at between 0.4% and 0.8%. At first, this effect is seemingly small – less than 1% in the long run. However, we must bear in mind that this estimated effect represents the cost in terms of the loss of deposit growth *per crisis*. Hence, in the absence of intervention, the accumulated effects of having repeated crises can be quite significant.

I find further confirmation of this hypothesis by comparing the results for states that had adopted deposit insurance with the results for states that had not. For states with deposit insurance I find that banking crises did not affect state deposits in any systematic manner. For states without deposit insurance, however, the effect of banking crises on deposits is both statistically and economically significant. States that endured banking crises and did not have deposit insurance see a long-term decline in their deposits (relative to deposits nationwide) of almost 1%.

As a final confirmation of the hypothesis, I re-estimate the same dynamic regressions for the 1975–2008 period. During the entire period, nationwide deposit insurance was in force; but in the 1980s and early 1990s, the US banking system suffered various crises. Just as I found for the eight states with deposit insurance in the earlier period, for the later period I find no evidence that under deposit insurance, banking crises had any systematic effect on state deposits.

Taken together, the results suggest that the costs of financial crises are not negligible and are likely to affect long-term economic growth through a reduction in deposits. The results further suggest that the establishment of institutions aimed at restoring confidence in the banking system, institutions such as deposit insurance, may help to forestall the effect of banking crises on deposit growth. In addition, they suggest that national deposit insurance may be helpful for promoting banking and financial market stability.

Of course, this conclusion does not necessarily imply that deposit insurance is, on the whole, socially desirable. Before drawing the inference that it is, one has to net out the costs of deposit insurance – for it is already well known that deposit insurance is not costless. A significant strand of the banking and finance literature has documented the fact that when deposit insurance is mispriced, it distorts bank behaviour by introducing a moral hazard problem.[3]

The rest of this paper is organised as follows: the next section discusses the underlying data and presents summary statistics. The third section presents the empirical methodology and discusses in more detail the equation to be estimated. Section four discusses the results. Section five offers concluding remarks.

Data and summary statistics

The data underlying this paper come from several sources. For the 1900–30 period, state-level deposits for all banks as well as data (interest expenses, etc.) for national banks are from Flood (1998), and liabilities of failed banks by state are from Kupiec and Ramirez (2009). For the 1975–2008 period, state-level deposits for all banks, interest expense on deposit accounts, and liabilities of failed banks by state are from the *Historical Statistics on Banking*, published online by the FDIC.[4]

Table 1 presents basic summary statistics. 'State deposits' is defined as deposits for all banks in state i at time t, divided by total (national) deposits, also at time t, all multiplied by 100. This variable measures the state's deposits as a percentage of national deposits. Naturally, it will vary by the size of the state, with larger proportions in the larger states. This observation can be confirmed by comparing the mean and the median statistics. Over the entire 1900–30 period, the average comes to a little over 2%, while the median is 0.74%. A similar pattern can be observed for the 1975–2008 period. Of course, this state-to-state variation will have to be controlled for in the regressions. A more detailed discussion of this issue is provided below, in the section on the empirical methodology.

'Crisis' is a constructed indicator variable that measures the incidence of banking crises. Constructing it is tantamount to defining it. Unfortunately, there is no precise definition in the literature of what constitutes a 'banking crisis' (Caprio & Klingebiel, 1997). Different researchers resort to somewhat different definitions, depending on data availability as well as other issues. For example, Demirguc-Kunt, Detragiache, and Gupta (2000) use a variety of indicators, any one of which could be used to justify the determination that a banking system was in crisis. These indicators include, among others, periods when non-performing loans are at least 10% of total assets, when the cost of rescue operations is at least 2% of GDP, when banking troubles result in the nationalisation of banks, or when governments implement emergency measures such as bank holidays, and deposit guarantees. Unfortunately, none of these measures can be determined during the sample period covered in this paper. Thus, I must rely on other measures.

Undoubtedly, an excellent candidate for identifying episodes of banking crisis would be the price of bank stocks relative to other stocks in the market. Because stock prices are forward-looking measures, it should be possible to identify the likelihood of a banking crisis from the behaviour of bank stock prices. However, bank stock prices are generally not available because most banks during the period

Table 1. Summary statistics.

Statistic	Period	Median	Mean	Standard dev.
State deposits	1900–1930	0.74	2.08	4.51
	1975–2008	0.94	1.96	3.31
Crisis	1900–1930	0	0.133	0.340
	1975–2008	0	0.134	0.341
Spread	1900–1930	0.001	–0.0001	0.019
	1975–2008	–0.024	–0.026	0.020

Notes: This table presents basic summary statistics for the variables included in the regressions. See text in the Data section for specific definitions as well as sources.

1900 to 1930 were not publicly traded companies. Reinhart and Rogoff (2008) suggest that, in the absence of stock price data for banks, a viable alternative is to use bankruptcies and bank closures. This is the measure used in this paper.

To that end, I construct an indicator variable entitled 'crisis', which equals 1 if, in a particular year, the liabilities of failed banks in the state are above 1% of the state's deposits. The choice of 1% as the threshold is justified on empirical grounds. The total cost of the S&L crisis during the 1980s and early 1990s, arguably one of the most serious crises in recent history, was approximately $160 billion, or about 0.6% of bank deposits.[5] Thus, the 1% threshold is a reasonably conservative level. In fact, it delivers nearly identical frequencies across the two different time periods: 0.130 for 1900 to 1930 versus 0.134 for 1975 to 2008.[6]

The last variable in the summary statistics is 'spread'. This variable is meant to capture the behaviour of the interest on deposits in each state, relative to the 'general', nationwide level of interest rates. It is possible that, during periods of local (state-level) banking turmoil, the interest rate on deposits may change. This change in deposit rates may, in turn, influence depositor behaviour. For this reason, a measure of the spread is included in the empirical analysis.[7]

Because actual deposit rate figures for each state are not available, I construct a proxy for this spread. Specifically, for the 1900–30 period, the spread is defined as the ratio of total expenses to total deposits for national banks, minus the end-of-year 90-day time money rate in New York City.[8] For the 1975–2008 period, this spread is defined as total interest on deposits divided by total deposits, minus the six-month time money rate, available from the Federal Reserve.

As one would expect, the mean and median spreads are statistically zero.[9] This follows from the fact that the average rate over all states should be reasonably close to the nationwide interest rate.

Empirical methodology

To investigate the long-term effects of banking crises, I estimate a dynamic transfer model where the dependent variable is bank deposits at the state level relative to nationwide deposits (that is, the ratio of state deposits to total national deposits) and the independent variables include factors known to influence the demand for bank deposits, as well as a measure of banking crises. Specifically, the regression model is

$$D_{i,t} = \alpha_0 + \sum_{k=1}^{n_D} \alpha_k D_{i,t-k} + \sum_{k=1}^{n_r} \gamma_k \left(r_{i,t-k} - r_{US,t-k} \right) + \sum_{k=1}^{n_C} \beta_k C_{i,t-k} + \phi_1^T SFE + \phi_2^T YE + \varepsilon_{i,t}$$

$$(1)$$

where $D_{i,t}$ is the share of state i's deposits in national deposits at time t and, $r_{i,t-k}$ is the ratio of total expenses (primarily interest expenses) to total deposits for national banks. As pointed out above, this variable is a proxy for the interest rates on deposits in state i at time t. $r_{i,t-k} - r_{US,t-k}$ is the spread of the interest rate in state i's deposits relative to the nationwide interest rate at time t. $C_{i,t}$ is an indicator variable equal to 1 if, at time t, the share of state i's failed-bank liabilities in state i's deposits is above 1%. This variable picks up whether there is a banking crisis in state i at time t. SFE stands for state fixed effects. YE stands for year effects. The residual term, $\varepsilon_{i,t}$, picks up any remaining unexplained variation of the model.

The intuition for selecting $D_{i,t}$ as the dependent variable is straightforward. With the possible exception of the panics of the 1930s, banking panics in the United States have been essentially regional in nature. For example, as indicated in the introduction, even the more serious Panic of 1907 was concentrated in New York, with limited fallout elsewhere (Moen & Tallman, 1992; Wicker, 2000). Similarly, the banking problems of the early 1920s originated in the Midwest, and although failures spread throughout most agricultural states, it did not affect all states equally (Calomiris, 2000; Wicker, 2000). We can exploit this feature of the data to investigate the extent to which deposits in a given state were influenced by banking problems in that state *relative* to nationwide deposits. It is natural to hypothesise that banking problems in state i should affect deposits in state i more strongly than they affect deposits in other states.

It is worth adding that the ratio of state deposits to total deposits also serves to ensure that desirable properties of the dependent variable are maintained when the regression is estimated. For example, any cyclical or seasonal pattern that affects the demand for deposits in levels is unlikely to drive the ratio as long as the pattern applies to all deposits. Similarly, any macroeconomic factor that may influence deposits in levels will not necessarily bias the ratio as long as the shock is truly macroeconomic in nature. That is, as long as the shock affects all states more or less equally. Nonetheless, it is possible that some macro shocks affect deposits in different states differently. It is precisely for such reasons that the regression includes year effects.

There is also justification for the inclusion of state fixed effects when one estimates Equation (1). As pointed out in the data section above, the 'state deposit' variable varies by state, with the larger states having the largest proportion of national deposits. The state fixed effects control for this source of variation in the regressions.

In order for the model to account for dynamic effects, Equation (1) includes a lagged dependent variable. Because past events may have a long-lasting effect on the relative demand for deposits, it is important to consider various lag lengths. To be as comprehensive as possible, I allow the lag length to vary from 1 to 5. The α_k's are the coefficients of the lagged dependent variable. I use these coefficients to compute the long-run effect of crises on deposits.

The standard portfolio choice model motivates the inclusion of $r_{i,t-k} - r_{US,t-k}$ in Equation (1). This model assumes that the fraction of wealth invested in a particular asset is a function of all asset returns in the portfolio. Under gross substitutability, the fraction of wealth invested in a particular asset is increasing in that asset's returns, and decreasing in other assets' returns. Hence, the effect of $r_{i,t-k} - r_{US,t-k}$ on relative deposits is expected to be positive. As this spread increases, the demand for deposits in state i should also increase, all else held constant. Thus, I expect the γ_k's to be positive. Just as indicated above for the lagged dependent variable, I consider different lag structures to allow for a robust estimate of this effect.

The inclusion of $C_{i,t}$ in Equation (1) serves to test the hypothesis of this paper, which is that periods of banking instability should be associated with a long-lasting reduction of deposits in that state. The logic behind this hypothesis relies on an intuitive modification of the standard portfolio choice model. An increase in banking instability can lead to a behavioural change among depositors if they lose trust in the banking system and there is no credible mechanism for restoring public confidence in it. In a sense, people simply stop trusting banks. Such a loss of confidence would almost certainly lead to a decline in relative deposits that is unlikely to disappear in the short term.

It is important to highlight the long-lasting nature of such a decline. Why? Because such protracted declines cannot be attributable only to the bank closures or suspensions that inevitably take place during crises. A reduction in bank deposits stemming *only* from the suspension of banks should be temporary in nature. The intuition behind this argument is straightforward. Pre-Depression banking panics per se tended to be very short-lived events. The majority of banks that suspended operations during pre-Depression panics reopened a few weeks after panics subsided (Calomiris, 2000; Wicker, 2000). Hence, if public confidence in the banking system were not at stake, once the panic subsided deposits would return to pre-panic levels as suspended banks reopened and *de novo* institutions arose to pick up the business left behind by the institutions that closed during the crisis.

This argument implies that banking crises that were accompanied by general loss of confidence in the system should result in a long-lasting impact on the ratio of state deposits to national deposits. By contrast, episodes of banking crises that were not accompanied by loss of confidence in the banking system should have, at most, a temporary effect on the decline of state deposits relative to national deposits.

To test this hypothesis, I estimate Equation (1) for different regimes: one characterised by the existence of institutions aimed at instilling confidence in the banking system, and one characterised by the lack of such institutions. Comparing these results will allow us to make appropriate inferences regarding the long-lasting nature of the effect of banking crises on deposits.

The most obvious candidate for an institution designed to instil confidence in the banking system is deposit insurance. By design, deposit insurance is supposed to reassure depositors that their funds will not disappear from the banking system in the event of a bank failure. To the extent that such an institution is credible, it should dampen the effect of banking crises on deposits. This is not to say that deposit insurance is free of negative aspects. Recent research has demonstrated that deposit insurance has had quite a number of drawbacks. In particular, it introduced the well-known and documented issue of moral hazard into the system because it removed depositor discipline from banks, thereby encouraging banks to take on more risk. Nonetheless, depositors' knowledge that their deposits are insured should have alleviated the reservations they had about the viability of the banking system. Thus, it is possible that deposit insurance, although aggravating risky behaviour from the banker's perspective, also lessened the depositor's concerns about the viability of the banking system during periods of distress. In fact, there is some empirical support for this claim. Chung and Richardson (2007) provide evidence suggesting that these deposit insurance schemes reduced bank suspensions due to runs, but ended up increasing suspensions due to mismanagement.

As noted above, between 1900 and 1930, deposit insurance existed at the state level for eight states. Oklahoma was first when it introduced its deposit insurance scheme in 1908, and Washington State was last when it introduced it in 1917. These state deposit insurance schemes differed somewhat in their implementation and logistics (insurance coverage, bank participation eligibility, premium assessment costs, etc.).[10] However, they all shared enough features to justify looking at them as a group. Most importantly and as previously discussed, they all intended to instil depositor confidence in the banking system. But besides having this common objective, they shared other features as well: they all had an insurance fund that was created by assessing premiums on participating institutions (normally state banks). These premiums were not risk-based. When the state deposit insurance fund was

Table 2. GMM regression results, 1900–30, for all states.

	Reg. 1	Reg. 2	Reg. 3	Reg. 4	Reg. 5
$D_{k,t-1}$	0.797***	0.725***	0.732***	0.776***	0.796***
	(0.014)	(0.027)	(0.028)	(0.029)	(0.031)
$D_{k,t-2}$		0.019	−0.243***	−0.227***	−0.276***
		(0.025)	(0.032)	(0.035)	(0.038)
$D_{k,t-3}$			0.286***	0.415***	0.394***
			(0.024)	(0.033)	(0.036)
$D_{k,t-4}$				−0.164***	−0.242***
				(0.026)	(0.036)
$D_{k,t-5}$					0.100***
					(0.027)
$Spread_{k,t-1}$	0.037***	0.031**	0.027***	0.025*	0.023*
	(0.013)	(0.013)	(0.013)	(0.013)	(0.014)
$Spread_{k,t-2}$		0.017	−0.011	−0.010	−0.014
		(0.014)	(0.013)	(0.013)	(0.014)
$Spread_{k,t-3}$			0.012	0.026**	0.023*
			(0.013)	(0.013)	(0.014)
$Spread_{k,t-4}$				0.006	−0.007
				(0.013)	(0.014)
$Spread_{k,t-5}$					0.024*
					(0.014)
$Crisis_{k,t-1}$	−0.041*	−0.041**	−0.053***	−0.051**	−0.041**
	(0.022)	(0.020)	(0.019)	(0.020)	(0.021)
$Crisis_{k,t-2}$		−0.025	−0.029	−0.021	−0.026
		(0.021)	(0.019)	(0.019)	(0.021)
$Crisis_{k,t-3}$			−0.048**	−0.036*	−0.041**
			(0.020)	(0.019)	(0.020)
$Crisis_{k,t-4}$				−0.011	−0.009
				(0.021)	(0.021)
$Crisis_{k,t-5}$					−0.069***
					(0.023)
Implied LT effects	−0.203*	−0.260**	−0.581***	−0.591***	−0.820***
	(0.109)	(0.110)	(0.147)	(0.194)	(0.202)
Year effects?	Yes	Yes	Yes	Yes	Yes
Fixed effects?	Yes	Yes	Yes	Yes	Yes
No. Obs.	1392	1344	1296	1248	1200
Wald Chi-sq	3059.34	2702.67	2653.72	2454.37	2022.01
Prob > Chi-sq	0.000	0.000	0.000	0.000	0.000

Notes: Dependent variable: $D_{k,t}$, which is defined as deposits in state k at time t, divided by nationwide deposits at time t, all multiplied by 100. '$Spread_{k,t}$' is the interest rate spread. '$Crisis_{k,t}$' is the banking crisis indicator variable. 'Implied LT effects' is the implied long-term effect of '$Crisis_{k,t}$' on $D_{k,t}$. Standard errors are provided in parentheses. ***Significant at the 1% level or better. **Significant at the 5% level. *Significant at the 10% level.

below a threshold, banks could be assessed additional premiums until the fund was deemed to be adequate. In addition, most of these deposit insurance schemes handled depositor payoffs in a similar manner. In the event of a failure, depositors were to be paid in cash. If the fund was insufficient, depositors would be given either interest bearing certificates, certificates of indebtedness, or warrants. In fact, it is precisely these common (and arguably ill-conceived) features that researchers highlight as key for understanding their demise.[11]

For the purposes of this empirical exercise, we can use the fact that eight states experimented with deposit insurance between 1908 and 1930, along with the fact that national deposit insurance has been in effect in the United States since 1934. It is this variation in deposit insurance across states and over time that the paper exploits to evaluate the hypothesis that banking crises had a long-term effect on deposits. To that end, I estimate Equation (1) for the following four distinct regimes.

(a) 1900 to 1930: No national deposit insurance. Regressions are estimated for all states, including those with deposit insurance.
(b) 1900 to 1930: Regressions are estimated only for states that had deposit insurance during the time it was in effect.
(c) 1900 to 1930: Regressions are estimated only for states that did not have deposit insurance.
(d) 1975 to 2008: National deposit insurance in effect. This period saw one of the nation's most severe episodes of bank failure (during the late 1980s and early 1990s). Hence, the period can usefully be compared with the 1900–30 period. Regressions are estimated for all states.

If the hypothesis set out in the introduction is valid, we should observe banking crises having long-term effects on deposits only under (a) and (c), when deposit insurance was not present. For (b) and (d), the effect of banking crises on deposits should be either nonexistent or temporary at best.

Equation (1) is estimated with panel data, and it contains a lagged dependent variable. It is well known that, under such conditions, OLS estimates are biased,

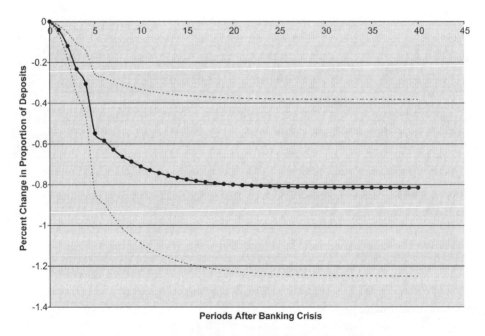

Figure 1. Effect of banking crisis on the proportion of state deposits over time, 1900–30. Notes: This figure plots the dynamic effects of a banking crisis on state deposits as implied by the regression model. The bands represent 95% confidence intervals.

Table 3. GMM regression results, 1900–30, for deposit insurance states.

	Reg. 1	Reg. 2	Reg. 3	Reg. 4	Reg. 5
$D_{k,t-1}$	0.820***	0.688***	0.688***	0.690***	0.667***
	(0.064)	(0.111)	(0.114)	(0.029)	(0.119)
$D_{k,t-2}$		0.154	0.193	0.169	0.180
		(0.108)	(0.139)	(0.141)	(0.144)
$D_{k,t-3}$			−0.061	−0.245*	−0.253*
			(0.114)	(0.142)	(0.145)
$D_{k,t-4}$				0.249**	0.171
				(0.115)	(0.143)
$D_{k,t-5}$					0.107
					(0.119)
$Spread_{k,t-1}$	0.016	0.008	0.005	0.006	0.006
	(0.015)	(0.018)	(0.018)	(0.018)	(0.018)
$Spread_{k,t-2}$		0.000	0.006	0.011	0.012
		(0.017)	(0.021)	(0.021)	(0.021)
$Spread_{k,t-3}$			−0.004	−0.024	0.023
			(0.016)	(0.020)	(0.020)
$Spread_{k,t-4}$				0.020	0.011
				(0.017)	(0.020)
$Spread_{k,t-5}$					0.014
					(0.017)
$Crisis_{k,t-1}$	−0.027	−0.032	−0.037*	−0.040*	−0.044*
	(0.020)	(0.021)	(0.022)	(0.022)	(0.023)
$Crisis_{k,t-2}$		0.000	0.010	0.017	0.015
		(0.021)	(0.024)	(0.025)	(0.026)
$Crisis_{k,t-3}$			−0.020	−0.027	−0.029
			(0.024)	(0.026)	(0.027)
$Crisis_{k,t-4}$				−0.014	−0.015
				(0.024)	(0.025)
$Crisis_{k,t-5}$					−0.014
					(0.025)
Implied LT effects	−0.152	−0.197	−0.262	−0.477	−0.677
	(0.120)	(0.171)	(0.196)	(0.350)	(0.494)
Year effects?	Yes	Yes	Yes	Yes	Yes
Fixed effects?	Yes	Yes	Yes	Yes	Yes
No. Obs.	122	122	122	122	122
Wald Chi-sq	517.77	571.67	553.97	553.71	545.81
Prob > Chi-sq	0.000	0.000	0.000	0.000	0.000

Notes: Dependent variable: $D_{k,t}$, which is defined as deposits in state k at time t, divided by nationwide deposits at time t, all multiplied by 100. '$Spread_{k,t}$' is the interest rate spread. '$Crisis_{k,t}$' is the banking crisis indicator variable. 'Implied LT effects' is the implied long-term effect of '$Crisis_{k,t}$' on $D_{k,t}$. Standard errors are provided in parentheses. ***Significant at the 1% level or better. **Significant at the 5% level. *Significant at the 10% level.

even with the inclusion of fixed and year effects (Arellano & Bond, 1991; Holtz-Eakin, Newey, & Rosen, 1986). For this reason, in estimating Equation (1), I make use of Arellano and Bond's (1991) GMM difference estimator.

Empirical results

Table 2 presents the regression results of Equation (1) for all states during the 1900–30 period. The table presents five different regressions, corresponding to different lag

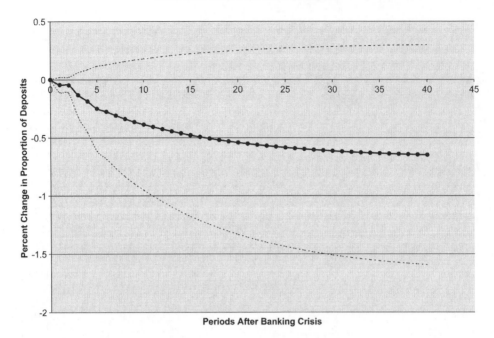

Figure 2.   Effect of banking crisis on the proportion of state deposits over time, 1900–30, for deposit insurance states.
Notes: This figure plots the dynamic effects of a banking crisis on state deposits as implied by the regression model. The bands represent 95% confidence intervals.

lengths.[12] The purpose of including five lags in Equation (1) is to obtain a robust result of the short- or long-term effect of banking crises on deposits. Virtually all five regressions demonstrate that banking crises indeed had a long-lasting effect on deposits. The coefficient for the first lag of the banking crisis variable is negative and statistically significant at standard levels, indicating that a year after a crisis began, deposits in that state had declined relative to nationwide deposits.

To evaluate the hypothesis that banking crises had a long-lasting effect on deposits, I use both the coefficients of the banking crisis variable and the autoregressive coefficients of the dependent variable. The long-term effect of the crisis on relative deposits measures the dynamic impact of the crisis shock on relative deposits in the long run, all else held constant. It is calculated at the steady-state in order to identify the implied equilibrium effect. More precisely, if $A(L)D_{i,t} = B(L)C_{i,t} + \varepsilon_{i,t}$, where $A(L)$ and $B(L)$ are polynomials in the lag operator, the long-term effect is given by the rational polynomial $B(L)/A(L)$.[13] Table 2 shows that the estimated long-term effects are all negative and statistically significant at standard levels. This result implies that a banking crisis in a particular state is associated with a long-term decline in that state's deposits relative to national deposits.

Because the banking crisis variable is an indicator variable, its coefficient can be interpreted as the magnitude by which the proportion of deposits in the state relative to total US deposits is affected. Using the coefficient estimates from regression 5 as an example, we observe that, one year after a banking crisis hits, the typical state

Table 4. GMM regression results, 1900–30, for states without deposit insurance.

	Reg. 1	Reg. 2	Reg. 3	Reg. 4	Reg. 5
$D_{k,t-1}$	0.790***	0.720***	0.729***	0.777***	0.798***
	(0.015)	(0.029)	(0.028)	(0.031)	(0.033)
$D_{k,t-2}$		0.015	−0.249***	−0.237***	−0.287***
		(0.026)	(0.034)	(0.037)	(0.039)
$D_{k,t-3}$			0.291***	0.425***	0.405***
			(0.025)	(0.034)	(0.038)
$D_{k,t-4}$				−0.170***	−0.251***
				(0.027)	(0.037)
$D_{k,t-5}$					0.102***
					(0.029)
$Spread_{k,t-1}$	0.035**	0.031**	0.026*	0.023	0.019
	(0.015)	(0.013)	(0.015)	(0.015)	(0.016)
$Spread_{k,t-2}$		0.019	−0.008	−0.005	−0.009
		(0.015)	(0.015)	(0.015)	(0.016)
$Spread_{k,t-3}$			0.008	0.024	0.020
			(0.015)	(0.015)	(0.016)
$Spread_{k,t-4}$				0.006	−0.005
				(0.015)	(0.015)
$Spread_{k,t-5}$					0.018
					(0.016)
$Crisis_{k,t-1}$	−0.041*	−0.043*	−0.055**	−0.051**	−0.044*
	(0.022)	(0.023)	(0.022)	(0.023)	(0.024)
$Crisis_{k,t-2}$		−0.025	−0.032	−0.024	−0.031
		(0.024)	(0.022)	(0.022)	(0.023)
$Crisis_{k,t-3}$			−0.045*	−0.036	−0.043*
			(0.023)	(0.022)	(0.023)
$Crisis_{k,t-4}$				−0.015	−0.016
				(0.025)	(0.024)
$Crisis_{k,t-5}$					−0.078***
					(0.026)
Implied LT effects	−0.196*	−0.256**	−0.575***	−0.619***	−0.915***
	(0.119)	(0.125)	(0.171)	(0.229)	(0.243)
Year effects?	Yes	Yes	Yes	Yes	Yes
Fixed effects?	Yes	Yes	Yes	Yes	Yes
No. Obs.	1270	1222	1174	1126	1078
Wald Chi-sq	2655.15	2338.46	2315.42	2148.55	1764.39
Prob > Chi-sq	0.000	0.000	0.000	0.000	0.000

Notes: Dependent variable: $D_{k,t}$, which is defined as deposits in state k at time t, divided by nationwide deposits at time t, all multiplied by 100. '$Spread_{k,t}$' is the interest rate spread. '$Crisis_{k,t}$' is the banking crisis indicator variable. 'Implied LT effects' is the implied long-term effect of '$Crisis_{k,t}$' on $D_{k,t}$. Standard errors are provided in parentheses. ***Significant at the 1% level or better. **Significant at the 5% level. *Significant at the 10% level.

initially experiences a decline of 0.041% in its proportion of deposits. The autoregressive coefficients as well as the remaining lagged crisis variables indicate that this effect is persistent. Three years after the banking crisis, the decline is approximately 0.24%. After five years, it is 0.55%. In the long run, it reaches 0.82%. Figure 1 displays graphically the dynamic pattern of this effect, along with 95% confidence intervals. It is evident that the effect of banking crises on the proportion of state deposits is persistent.

Table 3 presents the regression results for the eight states that had deposit insurance during the 1900–30 period. In order to ensure that the regression results are measuring the effect of deposit insurance, I included in this subsample only the years during which the insurance was in effect. Because not all eight states implemented deposit insurance at the same time, and they ended it in different years, this subsample is necessarily unbalanced. Nevertheless, one may still evaluate the extent to which banking crises affected deposits. Table 3 supports the hypothesis that deposit insurance appears to have lessened the effect of banking crises on deposits. In virtually all regressions, the crisis indicator variable is small and statistically insignificant. Indeed, the implied long-run elasticities, while negative, are not as large as those estimated for the states without deposit insurance. In addition, they are not significant in a statistical sense at standard levels.

This result can be graphically confirmed by a plot of the dynamic effects. Figure 2 shows that the effect is negative. However, the 95% confidence interval bands include the horizontal axis. Hence, it is not possible to reject the hypothesis that there is no effect.[14]

Table 4 completes the analysis of the 1900–30 period. It presents the regression results for the states that did not have deposit insurance. As expected, the results mimic those of Table 2: banking crises do lead to long-lasting declines in relative deposits. Indeed, the coefficients presented in Table 4 are nearly identical to those obtained in Table 2. In particular, the implied long-term effects are statistically significant at a standard level in virtually all the regressions. And just as Figure 1

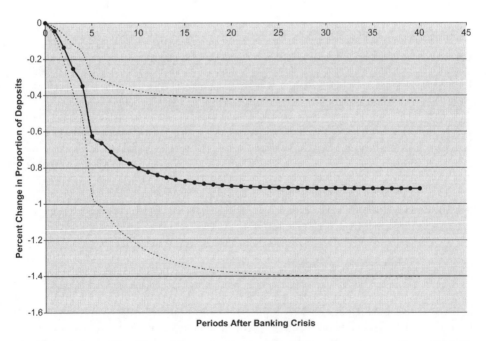

Figure 3.   Effect of banking crisis on the proportion of state deposits over time, 1900–30, states without deposit insurance.
Notes: This figure plots the dynamic effects of a banking crisis on state deposits as implied by the regression model. The bands represent 95% confidence intervals.

Table 5. GMM regression results, 1975–2008.

	Reg. 1	Reg. 2	Reg. 3	Reg. 4	Reg. 5
$D_{k,t-1}$	0.011	0.010	0.016	−0.005	−0.011
	(0.027)	(0.027)	(0.026)	(0.029)	(0.030)
$D_{k,t-2}$		0.052**	0.058**	0.059	0.050
		(0.026)	(0.026)	(0.027)	(0.030)
$D_{k,t-3}$			−0.087***	−0.088***	−0.088***
			(0.030)	(0.031)	(0.031)
$D_{k,t-4}$				−0.059*	−0.066**
				(0.031)	(0.032)
$D_{k,t-5}$					−0.008
					(0.043)
$Spread_{k,t-1}$	0.153***	0.085	0.017	0.037	0.050
	(0.043)	(0.059)	(0.058)	(0.059)	(0.061)
$Spread_{k,t-2}$		0.087	−0.049	−0.050	−0.047
		(0.058)	(0.066)	(0.068)	(0.071)
$Spread_{k,t-3}$			0.132**	0.100	0.108
			(0.058)	(0.068)	(0.071)
$Spread_{k,t-4}$				0.027	−0.047
				(0.060)	(0.072)
$Spread_{k,t-5}$					0.074
					(0.061)
$Crisis_{k,t-1}$	−0.033	−0.037	−0.031	−0.026	−0.022
	(0.061)	(0.059)	(0.058)	(0.059)	(0.060)
$Crisis_{k,t-2}$		−0.011	−0.018	−0.017	−0.010
		(0.058)	(0.055)	(0.056)	(0.057)
$Crisis_{k,t-3}$			−0.001	−0.003	0.010
			(0.006)	(0.056)	(0.056)
$Crisis_{k,t-4}$				0.053	0.059
				(0.058)	(0.057)
$Crisis_{k,t-5}$					0.081
					(0.059)
Implied LT effects	−0.033	−0.052	−0.048	0.012	0.106
	(0.061)	(0.088)	(0.097)	(0.108)	(0.124)
Year effects?	Yes	Yes	Yes	Yes	Yes
Fixed effects?	Yes	Yes	Yes	Yes	Yes
No. Obs.	1581	1530	1479	1428	1377
Wald Chi-sq	12.75	18.86	23.44	26.41	26.30
Prob > Chi-sq	0.000	0.000	0.000	0.000	0.000

Notes: Dependent variable: $\Delta D_{k,t}$, which is defined as the change in deposits in state k at time t, divided by nationwide deposits at time t, all multiplied by 100. '$Spread_{k,t}$' is the interest rate spread. '$Crisis_{k,t}$' is the banking crisis indicator variable. 'Implied LT effects' is the implied long-term effect of '$Crisis_{k,t}$' on $D_{k,t}$. Standard errors are provided in parentheses. ***Significant at the 1% level or better. **Significant at the 5% level. *Significant at the 10% level.

does, Figure 3 confirms graphically that the effect of banking crises on state deposits is indeed persistent.

As a robustness check, I also investigate the effect of banking crises on state deposits for the 1975–2008 period.[15] Because deposit insurance at the national level was already implemented during this period, the expectation is that the crises the banking system in the US endured during the 1980s and early 1990s would not have affected state deposits. Table 5 presents these results. They unambiguously indicate that these banking crises did not affect state deposits in any systematic manner. None of the banking crises coefficients is statistically different from zero. Furthermore, none of the estimated long-term effects is statistically significant. This result is consistent with the hypothesis that the existence of credible institutions can lessen or even eliminate the long-term effects of banking crises on deposits.

Concluding remarks

This paper investigates the dynamic effects of banking crises on state deposits. In particular, using data from 1900 to 1930, I estimate a dynamic regression model to examine the extent to which banking instability at the state level affects the proportion of state deposits relative to national deposits. The main results indicate that banking failures reduce the proportion of state deposits in national deposits by approximately 0.04% in the short run, and by nearly 1% in the long run.

To evaluate the hypothesis that this long-lasting loss in deposits following a banking crisis is attributable to a loss of confidence in the banking system, I re-estimate the dynamic regression model for the eight states that adopted deposit insurance between 1908 and 1929, and compare these results with those obtained for the subsample that did not have deposit insurance. If deposit insurance increased depositor confidence in the banking system, we should observe that the effect of banking troubles on deposits should be smaller or even nonexistent in deposit insurance states.

The results are consistent with this hypothesis: the evidence shows that the adverse effect of banking instability on deposits occurs only for the subsample of states that did not have deposit insurance. By contrast, banking troubles do not appear to have any significant effects on deposits in states that did adopt deposit insurance.

I obtain further confirmation of these findings by comparing the results obtained for the 1900–30 period with those obtained for the 1975–2008 period. This comparison is illuminating because both periods experience similar frequencies in the incidence of banking troubles, but during the first one, institutions aimed at restoring confidence in the banking system were lacking, whereas during the second one, banking benefited from the existence of nationwide deposit insurance.

Taken together, these results imply that without confidence-building institutions (deposit insurance), banking crises can have long-lasting adverse effects on deposit growth. Straightforward intuition can explain these results. Depositors who lose access to their money, even temporarily, tend to become more apprehensive about keeping their money in the banking system. To the extent that they adjust their liquid portfolios away from banks and into more rudimentary forms of savings, such as hiding the money under the mattress literally or metaphorically, bank deposits and therefore financial intermediation are compromised in the long run. The long-lasting nature of such shocks is particularly damaging because, by destroying bank capacity, these shocks end up affecting economic growth.[16]

One important policymaking implication of this research is the desirability of implementing policies that prevent the economy from getting bogged down in an inefficient equilibrium, with depositors keeping some or all of their wealth away from the banking system. But identifying and implementing the correct policies is not that simple. Between 1908 and 1930, eight states adopted deposit insurance. Although the results here support the contention that those schemes may have alleviated the effect of banking instability on deposit growth, a large literature has documented that those schemes magnified the incidence of banking crises by introducing the well-known moral hazard problem in banking. Mispriced deposit insurance encourages banks to take on more risk (Chan, Greenbaum, & Thakor, 1992; Kane, 1989; Merton, 1977; and others).[17] Not surprisingly, by 1930 all eight deposit insurance schemes had failed.

In modern times, during periods of serious financial market turmoil, governments face political and social pressure to implement policies whose purpose is to ameliorate the adverse consequences of the crisis as well as try to prevent future crises. In fact, this is an issue of current prominence, given the 2007–09 meltdown of the US (not to mention globally) financial system. But recent history tells us that many of such policies may not have completely restored confidence in the banking system. In both Russia and Argentina, for example, a sizeable proportion of the population has indicated in recent surveys that it does not trust banks or does not even have a bank account.[18] Evidently the policies adopted by the Russian and Argentine governments in the aftermath of the two countries' crises have not gained complete credibility. Investigating such issues is certainly worthy of further research.

Acknowledgements

I would like to thank, without implicating, Christopher Kobrak, Mira Wilkins, Lee Davison as well as two anonymous referees for very helpful comments and suggestions on an earlier draft. Ashley Carreon provided very valuable research assistance. Financial and logistical support from the FDIC's Center for Financial Research is gratefully acknowledged. The paper's findings and conclusions do not necessarily represent those of the Federal Deposit Insurance Corporation.

Notes

1. According to http://www.measuringworth.com, $3000 in 1897 is equivalent to $80,100 in 2009, using the Consumer Price Index.
2. The eight states were: Oklahoma (1908–23); Kansas (1909–29); Nebraska (1909–30); Texas (1909–25); Mississippi (1914–30); South Dakota (1909–30); North Dakota (1917–29); and Washington (1917–29) (Sources: Calomiris, 1989; White, 1997).
3. This literature is too large to be listed in a footnote. For a recent paper, see Demirgüç-Kunt and Detragiache (2002) and the references cited therein. For historical evidence, see Calomiris (1990, 2000).
4. For more details, see http://www2.fdic.gov/hsob/
5. Ergungor and Thomson (2005), and author's calculations.
6. As a robustness check, I redefined the indicator variable 'crisis' to equal 1 whenever the proportion of failed banks was above 1% of the total number of banks (as opposed to the liabilities of failed institutions relative to total deposits). The empirical results were very similar in terms of magnitude and statistical significance.
7. A more detailed discussion of the importance of this variable in the regression specification is provided in the empirical methodology section below.
8. The 90-day time money rate in New York City is available from the NBER macrohistory database: http://www.nber.org/databases/macrohistory/contents/chapter13.html
9. By a one-sample t-test I fail to reject the null hypothesis that the mean spread is zero for both periods.
10. For a more in-depth analysis of these deposit insurance schemes see Federal Deposit Insurance Corporation (1956).
11. See Vaughan and Wheelock (2002) for an analysis of the deficiencies of these insurance schemes.
12. Tests of autocorrelation show no significant evidence of autocorrelation with 1 or more lags.
13. For more details, see Enders (2004, chap. 1).
14. Undoubtedly, the number of observations used to estimate the regressions in Table 3 is substantially smaller than that used to estimate the regressions in Table 2 (or, for that matter, Table 4). This is due to the nature of the data – only eight states adopted deposit insurance, and the period during which deposit insurance was in effect ranged from 4 to

20 years. Hence, altogether I only have 122 state-year observations on which to perform the test. Although the number of observations is limited, it is still large enough to reliably estimate the regression coefficients. Even the dynamic GMM specification with the longest lag consumes about 33 observations from the sample to compute the lag coefficients, and for estimating state and year effects. This implies that the regressions in Table 3 still have nearly 90 degrees of freedom, which is adequate for making statistically reliable inferences.

15. The regressions for the period 1975 through 2008 are estimated in changes for the dependent variable, since the Im, Pesaran, and Shin (2003) panel unit root tests show that this variable has a unit root in levels, but it is stationary in differences. It is worth pointing out, however, that regardless of whether the regression is estimated in changes or in levels, the effect of banking instability on deposits is nearly identical.

16. For evidence that financial disintermediation can have a long-lasting effect on economic growth, see Ramirez (2009).

17. For evidence on how the deposit insurance schemes of the 1920s distorted bank incentives and encouraged risk taking, see, for example, Alston, Grove, and Wheelock (1994), Calomiris (1990, 2000), Wheelock and Kumbhakar (1994), White (1983, 1997).

18. For example, a survey done in Argentina in 2004 revealed that 86% of the population does not trust banks (*Russian Business Monitor*, 2 June 2004). On 28 July 2004, *The Moscow Times* reported that according to polling done by the All Russian Public Opinion Survey, approximately two-thirds of the people in Russia do not have bank accounts.

References

Alston, L.J., Grove, W.A., & Wheelock, D.C. (1994). Why do banks fail? Evidence from the 1920s. *Explorations in Economic History, 31*, 409–431.

Arellano, M., & Bond, S. (1991). Some tests of specification for panel data: Monte Carlo evidence and an application to employment equations. *Review of Economic Studies, 58*, 277–297.

Calomiris, C.W. (1989). Deposit insurance: Lesson from the record. *Economic Perspectives, Federal Reserve Bank of Chicago*, (May), 10–30.

Calomiris, C.W. (1990). Is deposit insurance necessary? A historical perspective. *Journal of Economic History, 50*, 283–295.

Calomiris, C.W. (2000). *U.S. bank deregulation in historical perspective*. Cambridge: Cambridge University Press.

Caprio, G., & Klingebiel, D. (1997). Bank insolvency: Bad luck, bad policy, or bad banking? In M. Bruno & B. Pleskovic (Eds.), *Annual World Bank conference on development economics 1996* (pp. 29–62). Washington, DC: World Bank.

Chan, Y.S., Greenbaum, S., & Thakor, A. (1992). Is fairly priced deposit insurance possible? *Journal of Finance, 47*, 227–245.

Chung, C.Y., & Richardson, G. (2007). Deposit insurance altered the composition of bank suspensions during the 1920s: Evidence from the archives of the Board of Governors. *The B.E. Journal of Economic Analysis & Policy, 5*(1). Retrieved April 12, 2009, from http://works.bepress.com/gary_richardson/1

Demirgüç-Kunt, A., & Detragiache, E. (2002). Does deposit insurance increase banking system stability? An empirical investigation. *Journal of Monetary Economics, 49*, 1373–1406.

Demirgüç-Kunt, A., Detragiache, E., & Gupta, P. (2000). *Inside the crisis: An empirical analysis of banking systems in distress* (Research Working Paper no. 2431). Washington, DC: World Bank.

Enders, W. (2004). *Applied econometric time series*. Hoboken, NJ: John Wiley and Sons, Inc.

Ergungor, O.E., & Thomson, J.B. (2005). *Systemic banking crises* (Discussion Paper no. 9). Cleveland, OH: Federal Reserve Bank of Cleveland.

Federal Deposit Insurance Corporation. (1956). State deposit insurance systems. In *FDIC Annual Report 1956* (pp. 47–73). Washington, DC: Federal Deposit Insurance Corporation.

Flood, M.D. (1998). U.S. historical data on bank market structure, 1896–1955 [Computer file]. Ann Arbor, MI: Inter-university Consortium for Political and Social Research (distributor). Retrieved February 1, 2002, from http://www.icpsr.umich.edu/icpsrweb/ICPSR/

Holtz-Eakin, D., Newey, W., & Rosen, S. (1986). Estimating vector autoregressions with panel data. *Econometrica, 56*, 1371–95.

Im, K.S., Pesaran, M.H., & Shin, Y.C. (2003). Testing for unit roots in heterogeneous panels. *Journal of Econometrics, 115*, 53–74.

Kane, E.J. (1989). *The S&L insurance mess: How did it happen?* Washington, DC: Urban Institute Press.

Kupiec, P.H., & Ramirez, C.D. (2009). *Bank failures and the cost of systemic risk: Evidence from 1900–1930* (Report no. 2009–06). Washington, DC: Federal Deposit Insurance Corporation. Retrieved December 1, 2009, from http://ssrn.com/abstract=1421885

Merton, R.C. (1977). An analytic derivation of the cost of deposit insurance and loan guarantees: An application of modern option pricing theory. *Journal of Banking and Finance, 1*, 3–11.

Miron, J.A. (1986). Financial panics, the seasonality of the nominal interest rate, and the founding of the Fed. *American Economic Review, 76*, 125–140.

Moen, J., & Tallman, E. (1992). The bank panic of 1907: The role of trust companies. *Journal of Economic History, 52*, 611–630.

Ramirez, C.D. (2009). Bank fragility, 'money under the mattress,' and long-run growth: U.S. evidence from the 'perfect' panic of 1893. *Journal of Banking and Finance, 33*, 2185–2198.

Reinhart, C.M., & Rogoff, K.S. (2008). *Banking crises: An equal opportunity menace* (NBER Working Paper no. 14587). Cambridge, MA: National Bureau of Economic Research.

Vaughan, M.D., & Wheelock, D.C. (2002). Deposit insurance reform: Is it déjà vu all over again? *The Regional Economist, Federal Reserve Bank of St. Louis*, (October), 5–9.

Wheelock, D.C., & Kumbhakar, S.C. (1994). The slack banker dances: Deposit insurance and risk-taking in the banking collapse of the 1920s. *Explorations in Economic History, 31*, 357–375.

White, E.N. (1983). *Regulation and reform of the American banking system, 1900–1929*. Princeton, NJ: Princeton University Press.

White, E.N. (1997). Deposit insurance. In G. Caprio & D. Vittas (Eds.), *Reforming financial systems: Historical implications for policy* (pp. 85–100). Cambridge: Cambridge University Press.

Wicker, E. (1996). *The banking panics of the Great Depression*. Cambridge: Cambridge University Press.

Wicker, E. (2000). *Banking panics of the Gilded Age*. Cambridge: Cambridge University Press.

Concluding thoughts on the use and abuse of financial history: Panics and public policy

Christopher Kobrak

ESCP Europe, Paris and Rotman School of Management, University of Toronto

> In my opinion it is a grand book. We all have the greatest reason to be grateful to you for saying so well what needs to be said. You will not expect me to accept quite all the economic dicta in it. But morally and philosophically I find myself in agreement with the whole of it; and not only in agreement with it, but in a deeply moved agreement.
>
> Keynes to Hayek, June 28, 1944, on the publication of the latter's *Road to Serfdom*

Introduction

Much has changed since the publication of our Special Issue on history and financial crises in April 2011, and much has remained the same. The Eurozone witnessed another crisis in confidence, nail-biting negotiations to restructure current debt, to put limits on future sovereign debt, and to create a financial safety net to ward off future threats to the single currency zone. Europe fell back into recession and both Chinese and American economic growth weakened. Confidence in America's ability to deal with federal and state indebtedness eroded. Rating agencies, perhaps traumatized by their errors in 2008, downgraded the borrowings of several sovereign countries, including those of the United States. The financial fragility of American states became more evident. The trading activities of JPMorgan Chase, an organization that had been considered exemplary during the crisis, called into question whether banks and regulators have developed adequate models and procedures to assess and control risk (*Financial Times*, May 14, 2012). With the Libor scandal, faith in market signals and the integrity of bankers as well as their regulators has weakened still further (Several articles in The *Financial Times*, July 2012). But perhaps of greatest concern is a marked decrease in many countries' public confidence in mainstream politicians' ability to reduce the impact of the current crisis and to avoid future ones. The likelihood that by the time this chapter appears events will make some points made here obsolete or worse still, dead wrong, is high and sobering. Nevertheless, as of this writing, July

2012, stock markets and foreign exchange rates have stabilized somewhat since the tumultuous summer of 2011, and in Europe and the United States some measures have been agreed to evaluate and bolster banks.

A great many new publications dealing with the recent crisis have come out, many with an historical outlook. Some that we had not seen before the publication of the Special Issue have used recent history to put flesh and blood on major actors (Lewis, 2010; Johnson and Kwak, 2010); others have placed blame on the welfare state and speculated on the doom of Western Civilization (Moyo, 2011). Some have highlighted the role of fraud and pure greed in financial crises, a subject that regrettably played little role in our Special Issue (Morgenson and Rosner, 2011). Defining terms is still a major problem, as Mira Wilkins and I noted in our introduction to the Special Issue. Some recent texts include periods of high interest rate and foreign exchange rate volatility as a "financial crisis," even when that volatility is connected with high growth and for the most part vibrant capital markets (Kindleberger and Aliber, 2011, p. 310, U.S. 1982-87). Much has been written about how faith in market mechanisms and in their resulting prices brought us to the precipice. But surprisingly, despite the severity, length, forewarnings and broad geographic reach of the crisis, little has been written since fall 2011 about the ill-preparedness of American and European regulators once the problems became evident in 2007 and early 2008 (Engelen et al, 2011). Very few participants and regulators took seriously dangers inherent in the organizational and institutional transformation that made the explosion in over-the-counter derivatives trading possible, what one of the best books on the crisis calls somewhat dismissively the "plumbing" of the financial system (Reinhart and Rogoff, 2009, p. 221). While new financial instruments play a great role in many accounts, the mutation of financial trading from largely public markets to private ones, one of the defining transformations of our time, has received considerably less attention (Haldane and Alessandri, 2009; James and Kobrak, 2010). Public discussion of bank practices have focused on calls for reinstating Glass Steagall and implementing the Volcker Rule, which rather miss, among other things, the magnitude and complexity of changes to the relationship between public markets and banks since the beginning of the 20th century. Anyone who has owned a house knows that "plumbing," not just macroeconomic statistics, affects the value of their investment.

In short, nothing has changed, though, to shake our basic conviction that examining history is a useful starting point for coming to grips with our current malaise, but that too little and too much historical analysis both entail dangers. More precisely put, ignoring both historical precedents and believing that history just repeats itself, as Nietzsche famously warned, knowing too little or too much about the past, may have been equally important catalysts to the recent financial crisis and blockages in finding political and economically viable policies for it and future crises. Even those who were making policy and steeped in historical study evidenced many blind spots about aspects of history useful during and even after the crisis broke. Ironically, both getting into and out of the crisis may have and will follow a rockier road due to potholes dug from mistaken historical analogies (Vinokurova, 2012). Perhaps A.J.P. Taylor was right that the best we can learn from history is to make new, rather than old, mistakes. Sadly, whether we have learned from history or not in shaping financial policy remains as much an open question today as it was when our Special Issue appeared.

The body of this chapter – added as the Special Issue is transformed into a book – is divided into four parts. In all four parts, I will discuss some literature published since the Special Issue or work published earlier that has received a lot of attention over the past 18 months. I have tried to group my comments into themes that capture some of the ongoing issues in the use of history to shape policy. The purpose of these concluding thoughts is to relate that literature to the themes of the Special Issue and to highlight some financial crises and aspects of crises we and others have neglected. I will use but try not to duplicate some of the extensive literature reviews that have come out recently (Neal, 2011). The first section deals with the tendency of many scholars to focus on one crisis in the past, for purposes of historical comparisons. The second explores the topic of seeking one or a set of causes for financial crises, which will allow us to predict them. The third section looks *at* the problem of financial innovation and government's role in creating crises. The last discusses those financial crises that fell off of our radar because regulators and financial practitioners avoided catastrophe (and thus few perceived them to be "crises"). Although I will draw on the texts of the articles in the Special Issue, which were international in scope, regrettably we did not include many regions, for example, South America, Asia, and Africa. My comments here will do little to rectify this omission. I will draw principally on lessons from American crises and policy. This chapter is not intended to provide new empirical data, but rather to make some arguments – beyond what was in our introduction – about how history has and has not been used to understand the current crisis. The chapter is by nature polemical, for which I hope the reader will excuse me. The opinions expressed here, intelligent or not, are my own and do not reflect those of my co-authors in this text.

One Crisis Fits All

Panics elicit simplistic explanations of many sorts. One, I will call the mono-analogy; a second the mono-set-causal approach, a subject that I will discuss in the next section. From the very beginning of the recent crisis, the lessons of the 1930s dominated historical analogies with the present. Avoiding the mistakes of the Depression seems uppermost in policy makers' minds. They measure success based on the extent to which we dodged a second Depression (*The Economist*, 2011). Some books that purport to analyze the recent financial crisis using history do not even bother to look at any other historical crisis, never questioning whether other crises might provide better explanations or guideposts for recovery (Desai, 2011).

The Great Depression analogy has rekindled interest in the master economist John Maynard Keynes and Keynesian solutions to the present problems, some with little regard for contextual differences between the two periods, and perhaps even some of Keynes's subtle points about how financial markets function. These differences include, but are not limited to, the far greater share of national product government expenditures play today compared with then and the overhang of the effects of World War I during the interwar period; for example, overcapacity in many areas created by national policies designed to foster independent strength in key sectors. All of these factors may have made Keynesian remedies more adapted to the specific maladies of that time. For at least 60 years, many governments – for economic, humanitarian, and perhaps for self-serving reasons – have been employing fiscal stimulus, even at times when the master himself might have cautioned them about the political and economic dangers.

Understandably, politicians and the people they represent have in many countries tried to address low overall demand, high debt, and infrastructure issues with extreme measures. But government actions (or inaction) may have already distorted market responses. Although government borrowing and poor oversight may not have driven up interest rates in some countries, governments' inability to address sufficiently investor uncertainty may have "crowded out private investment" by creating a veritable bubble in some alternative government assets (Zappia, 2012). Some governments are profiting from historically low interest rates, amassing levels of indebtedness hardly known in peacetime, as of this writing, precisely because anxieties abide about the appropriateness and reliability of financial regulation and market organizational devices, like Libor. Fear seems to have drained both western companies and individuals of much of the "animal spirits" necessary for vibrant economies. Neither stimulus nor savings that are not very specifically tailored to our times have been able to restore reputation and faith in economic discourse, which are so important to reviving the economy (Flandreau, 2012, for the importance of reputation and economic discourse).

Yet economists and policy makers today still seem wedded to fiscal, monetary, or austerity measures, alone and sometimes in combination, which may not be well adapted to our precise problems, relying on past theories and policies derived from very different times and revealing a lack of creative dynamism, or as Keynes himself quipped, perhaps even a slavish devotion "to some defunct economist." While some economists recognize that the reliability of highly mathematical modeling used to test theory and derive policy may be vitiated by political actions, for example, faith in the continuity of historical relationships – the basis of the models – seems more the rule than the exception (Sims, 2012). But our failure to address many of the causes of the current crisis is by no means unique. As Youssef Cassis's recent account of the mixed record of financial architecture reforms following many financial crises of the past 100 years argues, historical precedent offers only small hope that this "time will be better" (Cassis, 2012). There would be a certain irony if reinvigorated Keynesians stood out among those deficient in understanding what was happening when Keynes wrote (as compared to our crisis), and what has happened since the 1930s (King et al, 2012; Skidelsky, 2009). They are, to be sure, not alone.

Paul Krugman goes a step further. In papers calling for a huge increase in public spending, he refers to our present period as a depression and blithely reminds readers of how we got out of the last depression, namely with war spending and World War II, conveniently forgetting the social costs of both, and for some countries the overall levels of government and spending indebtedness in the 1930s compared to now (Krugman, May 2012). Leaving aside, the mixed evidence about government stimulus pulling countries out of the depression, given the quotation at the start of this chapter, one should wonder at least how Keynes, let alone Hayek, might react to further deficit spending.

There is still some confusion about what part of the interwar crisis is comparable with our own. As Harold James and others have pointed out, many commentators still focus on the spectacle of the 1929 stock market crash in the United States, rather than the more important worldwide banking crisis of 1931, which ignited most of the worst aspects of the Depression hit (James, 2009). Some analyses of the effects of the recent crisis still measure it against the 1929 downturn, rather than the much more severe and significant 1931 crisis, while recognizing that the recovery in trade, equities, and other key indicators were recovering quickly by the end of 2009 (Almunia, et al, 2010). Along these lines, scholars differ in dating the beginning and end of the Great Depression. Some papers combine the mono-analogy with the mono-causal approaches (Reinhart, 2012).

Nevertheless, no discussion of history and financial crisis should or can avoid the Great Depression, but here and in the Special Issue, we took a broader view. We tried to integrate other crises into our introduction and articles and to emphasize that the 1931 banking crisis differed from country to country. Including the American experiences before 1929 and those of Canada and Sweden, as we did, provided a useful reminder of what was commonplace and unique in the causes and effects of our recent difficulties. By the Great Depression's nadir in the early 30s, unemployment in Germany and the United States had risen to approximately a quarter of each country's workforce. For the rest of the decade, U.S. unemployment remained above 14%, while Germany, as Krugman reminds readers, enjoyed labor shortages by 1939, thanks to its "deficit spending".

Not only have most countries been so far spared most of these horrifying economic effects, a fact for which some central bank intervention is rightly praised, many of the preconditions of the 1931 banking crisis were absent in 2008. Fixed exchange rates among major currencies, falling commodities prices prior to the crash in 1929, an equity crash before the 1931 banking crisis, high tariffs and other obstacles to trade in the 1930s, the absence of many near-automatic economic stabilizers and deposit insurance in key countries alongside very fresh psychological and economic war wounds were just a few significant contexts for policy makers in the early 1930s, and not in 2008. All this calls into question whether policy-makers should be congratulating themselves on avoiding the 33% decline in GDP witnessed in the United States during the Great Depression. When the banking crisis began in 1931, many western economies were already in a severe downturn. By the end of 1930, Germany's economy had shrunk by 13% and America's by 12% from their respective peaks in 1929. At the end of 2007, five years ago, world economic growth was slowing but still running at nearly 5%, in the developed (G7) world it stood above 2%, whereas emerging markets were churning out nearly 8% increases over 2006.[1] Unemployment in Germany and the United States in 1930, for example, was already approximately 14 and 9% respectively, nearly one-third higher than their spring 2008 levels in both countries, with far less social protection and automatic economic stabilizers, especially in the United States.[2] Although several countries today are suffering from similar levels of unemployment and drops in GDP, those nations, individually or even collectively, represent nowhere near America's and Germany's combined economic weight in 1931.

That said, the financial crisis that hit the world in summer 1931 still contains many lessons for our own time, many of which central bankers have heeded, perhaps over-zealously to be absolutely sure not to make the same mistakes. Indeed, like our own crisis, that in the early 1930s involved a seizing up of the banking system, a massive explosion of counterparty risk, interruptions in normal trade, and then a huge number of bank failures, which contributed to a tremendous increase in government intervention in the banking system in nearly every developed country. Although the 1931 Crisis, like our own, may actually have had American origins, both quickly exposed the "fault lines" in world finance, requiring coordinated central bank efforts to keep liquidity and confidence in the system. Indeed, several countries, including the United States, suffered a more severe banking crisis in their own systems a few years later. Like our own period, too, many banks and their customers had made speculative or just foolish purchases funded by debt, worse still by debt then and now in currencies other than that of their own country.

But here, as in many aspects of the crisis, reasoning from history entails many difficulties. Actual borrowing in many countries by some measure was not particularly high in 1931. Then, like now, our methods of calculating indebtedness, for example, fell short of providing an adequate picture. Statistics often fail to capture the combined financial stress of the amount and type of financial instruments, and "off-balance sheet" government commitments. Should the present value of reparations payments have been included with German government debt in 1931, and U.S. and European promises for future pension and healthcare today? Do these "off-balance sheet debts" present special, perhaps greater risks, because of the political frictions they represent? One might argue with good reason that the issues raised by fixed-exchange rates during the 1930s might provide some insights for European bankers struggling with the fates of Greece, Portugal, Ireland, Italy and Spain now. But are the experiences of Britain in 1931 or the United States in 1934 devaluing and leaving the Gold Standard, for example, useful for countries that have completely given up their own currencies in circulation, and whose fiscal, employment and banking systems contain weaknesses requiring major, long-term repair. Moreover, given the very specific conditions of the European Union and the Eurozone, and our overall financial architecture, which includes hot-money and trillions of dollars of derivatives, can any historical precedent tell us whether it would be a good idea for Greece to give up the Euro or not?

Perhaps the most important lessons of the 1930s are not economic but rather political. In desperation, the populations and governments of many countries turned to various forms of autarky and authoritarianism, a fate that we have so far avoided. The lesson of the 1930s should be to avoid allowing our success to date to make us complacent or deterministic. Many well informed commentators during the interwar period, with good reason, feared or predicted the end of capitalism and democracy (Overy, 2009). At the very least, the calamities of the first half of the 20th century contributed to a consensus among leading economists and politicians about not only avoiding earlier mistakes but what those mistakes were and how to avoid them in the future. Although postwar investment aid packages helped, the transformation did not rely solely on "stimulus packages" before or after the conflagration, but rather new confidence and wisdom forged by a successful war effort against Fascist regimes and concerns about new rivals.

The Bretton Woods system, first developed at the close of World War II, was intended to restore much of the pre-World War I macro-economic stability. Unlike those efforts in the 1920s, it included a realistic assessment of each country's ability to contribute – with a U.S. pledge to replace Britain as banker of last resort – foresaw a gradual return to free trade and fixed exchange rates and created institutions to aid the process. For approximately 25 years, Western Europe, North America and Japan enjoyed high economic growth, increased trade and relative interest rate, inflation and foreign exchange stability. Success relied on governments accepting certain constraints, namely the trilemma: they could not simultaneously permit free capital movements, maintain fixed exchange rates and pursue an independent monetary policy oriented towards their own domestic needs (Ferguson, 2008). Only two of the three were sustainable at any one time. Eventually the system broke down due to governments (and their constituencies) losing that discipline. In this, they were aided by new financial institutions that served their short-term interests, but which ultimately added system risk and reduced public control (See section 3).

"This Time is Different"

As Mira Wilkins and I noted in our introduction, finding explanations and predictive mechanisms for all financial crises has been the Holy Grail for many economic historians. We understand and sympathize with the undertaking, but the ambition itself may lead to overgeneralization, to ignoring useful counter-examples and much of the specificity of each crisis necessary to formulate reasonable approaches to its cure.

Along these lines, I particularly regretted not including more about the 1907 Bankers' Panic, which in many ways resembled our recent crisis. Although it too had worldwide implications, following on the heels of a speculative bubble and a natural disaster (San Francisco Earthquake as opposed to Hurricane Katrina), and being precipitated by organizational innovations – the formation of trusts to handle business forbidden to more regulated banks – its causes and cure have received relatively little ink. The Panic was severe and left a long-term impact on finance, but the recovery was faster and stronger than what we have experienced so far and was accompanied by large scale private recognition of wrongdoing and self-imposed corrective action.

For many reasons and according to many observers, the American system had been broken for a long time. American finance lacked many stables of our current financial architecture, a FED and an SEC to name just two, and was more crisis prone than the financial systems of other industrial countries. During several dramatic months in fall 1907 what appeared like an endless series of financial institutions' failures and potential failures eroded confidence in the entire system that only a heavy dose of leadership and courage could restore. Oddly, this crisis gets little press in financial histories.[3] The actual panic, which lasted only a few months, may have been the first financial crisis in the United States that was fueled and then calmed by media frenzy.[4] As the crisis unfolded, more and more fraudulent or merely flamboyant investing was revealed. When credit from New York banks dried up, there were numerous runs on banks and trust companies all over the country. Runs on three trust companies spooked other financial institutions to hoard cash, boosting lending costs (or cutting lending off altogether) to equity markets and corporations. Like today, even public institutions had difficulty borrowing. Major manufacturing companies reported steep declines in demand. The crisis quickly spread to Europe and interest rates in London and Paris tightened. The volume of bills traded in London dropped 90%. International customers of U.K. banks, especially those in Spain, Italy and the United States, three economies highly dependent on foreign funds and with weak banking systems, found themselves deprived of credit.

Obviously, the crisis affected equity markets and the so-called real economy in the United States and other countries. Mercifully, the downturn was shorter and less severe than might have been expected or in comparison to the Great Depressions of the late 19th and early 20th centuries. Commodity prices fell by 21% and industrial production fell more than during any other previous U.S. crisis. Bankruptcies grew in November by 47% over the same month a year earlier, making it the second worst month in U.S. history up to that point. Wholesale prices fell by 5%. While dipping as much as 50% during the year, from year-end 1906 to 1907, the U.S. stock market fell 33%. By 1908, unemployment nearly tripled from its 2.5% 1906 level. According to some estimates, by the end of 1908, GNP had fallen 15% in real-terms from year-end 1906. Foreign money left in droves, threatening the finances of New York City's and other local administrations.

Although some very recent research suggest that the return of foreign funds (namely French gold) played a much greater role in stemming the panic than had been previously recognized (Rose, 2012), private bankers, led by J.P. Morgan, came to the rescue, albeit in part to save institutions he and his friends had a large hand in creating, notably the trusts. Without public pressure on him personally, and to a large degree without government intervention, J.P. and his friends saved the country from a far worse meltdown and helped engineer a financial recovery. They stood behind key banks and shored up the country's financial reserves. He examined the records of many trusts and devised financial plans for saving the weaker ones. Early in the crisis (the end of October), within hours of hearing about the collapse of stock prices, Morgan lined up nearly $25 million from New York bankers to ensure sufficient liquidity for brokers, who paid very high rates but were able to keep their doors open. Acting independently of federal and state authorities, Morgan called together the leading financiers of his day and forced the consolidation or closure of other financial institutions. His actions and words were designed to calm markets and investors, not excite them. The first private bailout was followed by many others. Many public statements followed expressing the willingness of financiers to do whatever was needed to solve the crisis. He even urged religious leaders to preach calm. By the end, the Morgan group had intervened in saving many banks, brokers, the stock exchange and even the finances of the city of New York.

The degree to which Morgan engineered the bailout – and thereby made a lot of money for himself and his friends – infuriated many contemporary observers, ushering in greater public rather than private management of the economy. Some even accused him of precipitating the crisis for his own pecuniary ends.[5] In contrast to today when the public and politicians rant and rave about public funds being used to bailout greedy bankers, then the bailout contributed to the sentiment that this sort of market intervention – if it is going to be done at all – should be done with public control. Both Morgan's power to influence American finance and distrust for his seemingly tyrannical disdain for the interests of the common man reached their peaks after the crisis. Many companies disappeared by merger, bankruptcy or both and the economy took nearly two years to recover - a time during which many adjustments were made but one that would appear politically intolerable today. By the end of 1909, however, in real terms, with little inflation, U.S. GDP had surpassed its 1906 level by 11%, unemployment was down to 5.7%, and the stock market surpassed all previous highs. Some patient investors made excellent returns by buying in the face of panic. The U.S. and other economies were once again on a relatively fast track after a relatively short but painful and scary interlude.

Nevertheless, the crisis unleashed regulatory soul searching. Like today, the idea that the banking system, financial innovators working on the fringe of regulation, could cause widespread and substantial economic hardship, indeed threaten the whole world's stability, understandably terrified not only the man and woman on the street but also experienced regulators and investors. In 1908, the U.S. Congress established a commission to study the banking system. Its efforts finally led to the establishment of the Federal Reserve as well as other changes in banking regulation. Unlike most other developed countries with a strong public-private partnership for control of the economy, thenceforth in the United States the handling of crises would be much more of a public function rather than one of private financial actors cleaning up the messes they themselves had created. Regulatory changes were not confined to the United States. Even countries with much more solid banking systems initiated reforms. But particularly in the United States – and later in other countries influenced by its economic and political power – the uproar and reforms coincided with or helped cause a shift in attitudes about responsibility for maintaining the public good. Once a joint undertaking of powerful private figures and government officials, each ostensibly was to have very separate agendas, at times pursued in balanced harmony, at times in open conflict, and at times in cozy corruption. By the time the 2008 crisis hit, bankers seemed to have a very diminished sense of their public responsibility. The Bankers' Panic of 1907 suggests that individuals and institutions help shape the contours of crises and their remedies, and that reform of both will almost always entail unintended consequences (North, 1990).

Perhaps one reason for the neglect of the Bankers' Panic is that it does not fit readily into a mono-causal explanation of financial crises. It was not proceeded by an excessive debt build up and even though it involved a freezing up of the banking system, it was of short duration. Since the Special Issue appeared, Reinhart and Rogoff's study of eight centuries of financial folly, which came out in 2009, has become even more influential. Their thorough analysis has crept into many accounts and reinforced the positions of those searching for patterns of financial crises, even those who do not quote them (Kindleberger and Aliber, 2011).

Reinhart and Rogoff's detailed economic analysis of leverage and financial crises helps us go beyond simple narrative about panics and certainly serves as a useful antidote to those in the ten years running up to the recent crisis who seemed drunk on "new paradigm Cool Aid." Reinhart and Rogoff's view that excessive levels of debt, whatever the form, adds system risk to society has much to recommend it and serves a useful caution. Increased debt-loads, in many forms, certainly preceded many financial crises and complicated policy-making once bubbles burst. But that debt adds to risk is a truth easily found in finance textbooks. Although Reinhart and Rogoff acknowledge that different forms of debt pose different levels of risk, admittedly and intentionally, there is little in their work about the context of a period that helps explain why and when debt burdens become unmanageable, because "no time is different." In more recent articles, they have tried individually and jointly to use some of their original insights to produce a predictive model. Oddly, by some of Reinhart and Rogoff's own data the 1932 debt levels of the United States and Germany – the two of the countries hardest hit by the Depression – were very high as measured by GDP and compared with other countries that suffered financial distress (Reinhart and Rogoff, 2009, p. 120). In short, determining what excessive debt is requires understanding how funds are being used and more about the institutional and organizational contexts within which it is raised. The more Reinhart and Rogoff seek to generalize, the more they rely on averages that can mask important differences.

Some critics have taken them to task for exactly this point. Christina Romer, for example, notes that Reinhart and Rogoff's use of averages of 9.3% declines in real per gross domestic product and 4.4 years of duration for the 14 major crises since 1929 ignores huge variations among countries and periods. Norway and Argentina had very different reactions to their crises in 1987 and 2001 respectively (1 and 20% declines), and even during the 1930s the United States witnessed very different output reactions to its many banking panics. Likewise, Sweden and Japan had very different trajectories after their respective banking crises in the 1990s (Romer, December 17, 2011). Some have pointed out that even the pre-crisis debt levels differ greatly and that the notion of public debt does not encompass all state obligations, like those for healthcare, which Reinhart and Romer in part acknowledge. While economic historians tend to agree that economic downturns associated with financial crises tend to be long and severe, others have called into question Reinhart and Rogoff's view that growth, once it comes, is modest. Understanding why recoveries differ and judging policy remedies, then, requires a better understanding of the specific historical causes of any crisis, and particularly the transmission mechanisms of our own (Bordo and Haubrich, 2012).

Even Reinhart and Rogoff's defenders have produced somewhat strange results. One study claiming to find evidence for their predictive FEM model (housing prices, equity prices, current account balances as percent of GDP and real GDP growth per capita and public debt) turn up evidence themselves from the 1907 crisis that runs contrary to what the model would predict (Horan and Ononiwu, 2010). Although they agree that some common factors triggered financial crises in prior periods and other countries, Saktinil Roy and David M. Kemme found that not all the common factors – asset price growth, government debt, and cross-border capital flows – are always significant predicators of banking crises. Moreover, for policy-makers and investors none of this literature, even work by Shiller and Roubini, can answer the all-important question of when the bubble will burst and how deep or long the crash will be (Roubini, 2006 and Shiller, 2008). Averages are important, but as Reinhart readily admits in their average (hers and Rogoff's) is a range from 2 to 22% drop in employment and one to twelve years of duration (Reinhart, 2012).

The articles in the Special Issue individually and collectively embody the view that each event, our recent crisis included, contains aspects that are commonplace and unique. To be sure, we are not alone in holding this view. Several studies have taken an eclectic approach to using history to better understand our current predicament (Claenssens, et al, 2010; Atack and Neal, 2009). Brean et al, and Billings and Capie in the Special Issue, for example, presented evidence that a tradition of prudent banking can have a great deal of influence over how a country can avoid or reduce the impact of global bank panics. Unfortunately, "This Time is Different and the Same" makes a far less catchy title and perhaps a more complicated book. Avoiding tautology by describing just how complex and multifaceted private and public contexts interact with underlying and more general economic phenomena is never easy.

Innovation and Regulatory Contexts: The Public and Private Sectors as Midwives to Crisis

Most of the blame for the recent panic has understandably fallen on the private sector. In the run up to 2008, banks and capital markets were reinventing themselves at a dizzying pace. Like capitalism itself, or as Marx and Engels wrote of the bourgeoisie in *The Communist Manifesto*, finance is restless and always innovating, but the record of the past 30 years is impressive by the standards of any age. It witnessed the death of virtually all the Glass Steagall restrictions on domestic and foreign banking in the

United States, the creation of many huge multinational banks, banking's internalization of many capital market transactions, an explosion of new financial derivatives (including securitization of debt) and their trading, a huge increase in the amount and speed of financial trading, the spread of financial activity to many countries once on the periphery of capitalism and the disintermediation of many once bread-and-butter services of financial enterprises to name just a few. Some distinguished regulators have questioned whether these innovations have brought any value, a view that for obvious reasons has been heard more often since than before the crisis. But taking financial innovation to task is a little too easy today, requiring a selective amnesia about how much we owe our economic development in the past and even desired aspects of our current living circumstances to financial innovation (Ferguson, 2008; Rajan, 2010). Since the crisis, many narratives about the run-up to the crisis have detailed how reckless innovation brought on the crisis (Shiller, 2008; Roubini and Mihm, 2010; Tett, 2009, and McClean and Nocera, 2010). Few of these, however, have addressed the topics of innovation and regulation historically to glean out some insight as how we can better govern "animal spirits" for public good.

Regulators have always had real difficulty keeping up with innovation and crises (Kindleberger and Aliber, 2011). They seem behind the curve of financial innovation and this gets us into trouble. Christopher Kopper argued here very convincingly that even the vaunted Reichsbank was ill-prepared for its post-World War I banking oversight duties. From the narrow focus of the U.S. Fed on inflation and employment to European blindness about the dangers of its own real estate boom and highly indebted nations, public officials did not distinguish themselves in their concern about and preparations for a crisis. Almost all of the articles in our Special Issue addressed this issue. Carlos Ramirez, for example, pointed out that U.S. officials had examples of good American banking measures among the states, just because of that country's fragmented banking regulation. Innovation of any kind entails costs and poses risks, a long-standing dilemma for society's ability to adapt to new circumstances and improve productivity and an ongoing challenge to assess costs and benefits of control versus freedom. But history in general, and our Special Issue in particular, may not be able to address some aspects of our current regulatory framework, which seems overwhelmed by the relentless innovation and distorted incentives of our "new financial order." (Shiller, 2003) The relative size, resources, complexity and degree of international internalization and ability to play regulatory arbitrage seem individually or in combination in our period to have added a layer of difficulty to governance of the banking system that may truly be unprecedented.

Most of the efforts to draw lessons from the past about this financial crisis recognize that government action or inaction is an important precursor to bubbles and panics. It is hard to find a financial crisis whose origin cannot be traced to some positive action by governments or at the very least to some grievous flaw in regulatory control. From John Law to the recent U.S. housing bubble, most financial meltdowns were precipitated by government's attempts to solve some political or social problem with economic policies, whose consequences, positive and negative, are often unforeseen or unforeseeable.

But this is where the agreement ends. On the one hand, several economists argue from the experience of the Great Depression that we need more economic stimulus, others that stimulus is ineffective or that, in the required amounts, has dire consequences, like autarky and even war. Everyone admits that American financial regulation before 2008 was wanting, but Democrats lay the blame primarily on Republican measures, Republicans on Democratic (FCIC and two dissenting reports). Both seem to forget that one of the most serious errors, The Commodities Futures Modernization Act of 2000, which allowed banks to trade derivatives internally and led to the explosion in exotic, illiquid derivatives trading, was the product of by-partisan agreement supported by many of the leading lights in economics from both parties including Larry Summers, Alan Greenspan and Robert Rubin, and signed into law by a Democratic president. Some commentators recognize that the abuses in the housing market, particularly the weaknesses in Fannie Mae and Freddie Mac procedures, were the product of decades of government intervention in the housing market designed to stimulate demand and quell protest against the losses in purchasing power, and that international regulations helped foster reckless risk taking in the United States and Europe (Friedman, 2006 and 2011). Some analyses of the recent financial crisis recognize that government efforts to spend their way out of the breakdown of Bretton Woods was the first of a long line of Keynesian measures, whose efforts have required a lot of off-balance-sheet public financing and created precarious opportunities for the private sector (Rajan, 2010).

We hope that the collection sheds some light on the age-old issue of when and how governments should intervene in markets, an answer that may change in different economic environments. Several of the chapters – Canadian and U.K. banking and state deposit insurance stories – highlight regulators' capacity to perform better. But unfortunately, the issue contained little about the unforeseen consequences of government intervention. For this a discussion of the 1970s and governments' efforts to shelter their constituencies might be helpful.

The breakdown of the Bretton Woods Agreement did not occur overnight or even over a period of months as most of the crises discussed here. Even though I use the year in which Nixon pulled the United States off the gold standard, it was a process that built up over many years and continued with incremental changes to the world financial system. The reasons for its demise, in reality, were much more complex than many commentators admit now or contemporaries admitted at the time (Eichengreen, 2007). Fixing a precise date or even a month is difficult. Clearly, though, in 1965 the Free World's financial architecture was the Bretton Woods Agreement. By 1975, it was not. For twenty-five years, governments succeeded in convincing most businesses and individuals that they could count on relatively stable exchange and interest rates, increasing freedom of movement of goods and capital, and a high degree of intra-government and financial coordination of remedies to crises, a series of macro-political conditions that encouraged trade and business in general to a remarkable degree. The often-heard explanation that the United States' loss of fiscal and political discipline created an overabundance of dollars on world markets, thereby threatening the U.S.'s ability to hold the gold-dollar standard, is only part of the story. In reality, a combination of conflicting national priorities – American as well as other nations' short-sightedness – and capital markets becoming more international in scope shattered much of a system based on governments' ability, alone or in tandem, to control financial actors and markets.

Very much like today, one might argue about Bretton Woods that economic circumstances – such as the increase in foreign direct investment and the creation of off-shore banking – simply made the existing financial architecture obsolete. Unlike the first two crises, this was not a banking crisis to begin with, although the breakdown of

Bretton Woods contributed to one or several later. It was a crisis of macroeconomic regulation that provided the necessary backdrop for a revolution in financial markets and institutions, as well as how governments perceived the social contract. Although some areas and periods enjoyed wonderful growth and stability, in comparison to the 20 years preceding it, the first decade of the post-Bretton Woods period ushered in stagnation and turbulence. In the longer run, it was characterized by a huge increase in the geographic breadth of globalization, massive foreign investment, highly volatile interest, inflation and foreign exchange rates, as well as periods of high growth and stable markets, the restructuring of many high value-added sectors, new business practices and technologies and low real income growth in the developed world. But in 1971, these outcomes were unknown. For investors, then like now, a new era of unwelcome uncertainty seemed at hand, a fact that can be seen in stock market valuations. While economies were still growing, investors were spooked. From 1971 to 1984, the Dow Index hardly budged. During the decade that began in 1971, U.S. stock prices gained only 20%, less than 2% per year not including dividends. With high inflation, however, the returns were in real terms negative.[6]

What only became clearer during the 1970s was that the demise of Bretton Woods led to two separate extreme antidotes: a greater willingness to give into whatever the market dictated and to use economic intervention to spare individuals the pain of economic distress, or in some cases just diminished ability to keep up with high expectations. Although under the circumstances of the external and internal economic shocks of the 1970s, imagining politically and economically sustainable alternatives to the new policy orientations is difficult, the combination of the two set in motion the configuration of many of our current problems and had unintended negative consequences. The first orientation entailed an abdication of government responsibility for macroeconomic stability and less control of economic variables; the second, its opposite, a huge increase in government responsibility for human welfare in most of the world, an orientation that had its roots in the interwar period but was bolstered in Japan, Western Europe and the United States during the 1970s with one of the greatest increases in government spending during peace time. It was a widespread phenomenon. In Britain welfare expenditures went from 10% of GDP in 1960 to 17% in 1980. In America, during roughly the same period, expenditures for health, Medicare, income security and social security doubled as a percentage of GDP, outstripping defense for the first time. Japan witnessed similar increases, but its vibrant economy and great increases in productivity made them more tolerable.[7] For much of the developed world it makes up a huge proportion of domestic product (if you include private expenditures for health care), one that with an aging population is destined to continue to climb rapidly.

Ironically, ultimately both entailed what seemed like a privatization of economic risk. As governments realized that their expenditures were unsustainable, the private sector was encouraged to fund them. With no effective way of managing economic variables, new market devices (such as financial derivatives, the cause of many of our current woes) were developed to manage risk. With government expenditures unsustainable, social expenditures were privatized too. Private pension, house ownership and health care schemes, funded privately, either individual or corporate debt, tried to fill gaps between the promised safety net (and expected consumption) and reality in many developed and emerging markets. Hard as it may be to imagine now, in some sense, markets came to the rescue. Governments, companies and individuals could not increase taxes, pass on costs or keep up with their expectations through earnings, so they borrowed, requiring ever increasing international financial flows to fund the debt from the cash rich to the cash poor. As many of us have conveniently forgotten, just over 20 years ago the debts of many developing countries, similarly burdened with expenditures for public services, almost brought the whole financial system to its knees, adding to the effects of inflation, stagnant growth in productivity in much of the world, and, of course, uncertainty. Even the rising star of most of the post-Bretton Woods period, Japan, seemed to be finally falling. As much of the world relished the fall of communism, its vaunted economy faltered under the weight of over-investment, wasteful public works and huge social outlays, one of the most rapid and nightmarish transformations from economic powerhouse to sick man that the world has ever known.

Like those applied by Japan in the 1990s, all the stimulative efforts brought little growth. The period after the fall of Bretton Woods will probably always be remembered for high inflation and the perception of stagnant growth. By 1980, the Misery Index (unemployment plus inflation), popularized by President Carter, was well over 20%. Efforts to tackle inflation until the 1980s were fruitless. When the FED used interest rates to squeeze out inflation, unemployment climbed to over 10%. The sharp downturn was followed, however, by a steep pick-up in growth. Unlike some countries, though, in the 1980s, the United States witnessed three major economic changes. It ran large government deficits, created in large part by reduced taxes and increased military expenditures rather than new social welfare programs; it deregulated many sectors and allowed, indeed encouraged, the restructuring of commercial enterprises. Perhaps most importantly, both public and private debt surged as a percentage of GDP and began a long period of pulling in funds from the rest of the world using an ever-increasing web of intricate financial instruments. By the new century, though, despite the housing bubble, the only things Americans were spending significantly more on than 30 years before were health care and education (James, 2009).

"Good Financial Crises"

As a distinguished business historian has pointed out, business history suffers from a selection bias. Following a biological model, we treat failed cases as trivial and focus on successful companies (Fridenson, 2004). Financial history inclines toward the opposite. System threats that run amok get the lion's share of attention. We tend to pass over the ones that seem to have been easily survived, forgetting perhaps that we have dodged a bullet and that the gun holds several rounds. In the Special Issue, Mira Wilkins and I used the Long-term Capital Management collapse as an example of just such a "crisis," the successful handling of which encouraged complacency among bankers and their regulators at the end of the last century. Little in the way of stricter regulation of hedge funds or derivative instruments followed. Indeed, in less than a decade derivatives trading had increased tenfold, with private (over-the-counter) transactions accounting for nearly 90% of the total $500 trillion (ten times world output).[8] New instruments were developed, outside of markets, allowing many to become so incomprehensibly complicated that even the banks which wrote them often did not know all of their financial consequences. Some successes, however, should be used more often to illustrate that treating a financial problem often has far less cost than letting it fester.

During the 1980s, much of the world questioned whether the sovereign and bank debt that had been used to bolster consumption would bring down the world's financial system. America was not the only country that used debt to finance consumption. Indeed, the phenomenon seemed in the 1980s to be most dangerous in the developing world. But just as the third-world debt crisis seemed to abate, and America's chief economic and political rivals, Marxist countries, ran amok, the United States once again became the focal point of financial fears. The Savings and Loan (S&L) Crisis, which came to a head in the late 1980s but had been developing for at least a decade, was a product of long- and short-term American regulatory decisions. As the crisis unfolded, many politicians, journalists, and the public at large were convinced that the Savings and Loan crisis was further evidence of the end of America's century. The American thrift institutions, many of which were in dire straits due to changing economic circumstances, poor regulation, and some unsavory business practices accounted for nearly $2 trillion in financial assets. At the creation of the Resolution Trust Corporation (RTC), empowered to deal with the crisis, the amounts at risk to the U.S. taxpayer were in excess of $230 billion, a far greater percentage of GDP and the federal government's budget than the $700 billion committed to the Troubled Asset Relief Program (TARP). After several years of taking over and liquidating over 700 financial institutions, working through the sale of assets, the final cost to the U.S. government was less than $100 billion (Kohn, 1994; Greenspan, 2007 for the RTC details).

The Savings and Loan crisis in the United States serves as testimony that few, if any, financial crises have single causes and that even severe banking system breakdowns need not have catastrophic long-term negative consequences. It also illustrates the dangers of cozy relationships between regulators and the regulated as well as politicians postponing uncomfortable choices. Contrary to the perceptions of some analysts, the staid world of Savings and Loan banks was often beset by crises. Although required to file financial statements to state and federal regulators and confined mostly to taking deposits and making real estate loans, in 1907 and in 1931, S&Ls were heavily hit by falls in credit from money center banks, bank runs and falls in housing prices. With the inflation of the 1970s they lost depositors to larger banks and money market funds, who had fewer restrictions on rates and offerings. Allowed finally to offer higher rates to depositors, guaranteed up to $100,000 in 1978, a tenfold increase, they were still stuck with mortgage assets paying 4-6%. By 1980, it was clear to some that they needed a bailout (perhaps as little as $15 billion), but neither the President nor Congress acted. They did, however, loosen the restrictions on S&L's investments, which created an ideal scenario for unscrupulous business people, a mismatch between riskless sources of cash (deposits guaranteed by the government) and risky investments in supporting the debt and equity of leveraged buyouts, for example (Krugman, 1997).

Although the government investment of between $50-100 billion led to a useful restructuring of the sector with less cost to the government than previously thought, the crisis pointed to several weaknesses in the financial system. The first was poor supervision of financial institutions matching of assets with liabilities. The second is a whole slew of hidden potential government liabilities from private pension funds to mortgage-backed securities. In order to get financial institutions to lend more and provide other services, several quasi-governmental agencies gave tacit guarantees to many facilities, some of which are only now clear. The crisis in 1989 in part led to an economic downturn. Despite much hand wringing and foreboding prophesies it was a weak and short-lived recession, leading many to believe that the U.S. government and the Federal Reserve were well positioned to handle future bank failures, a comforting but perhaps erroneous misconception. Unfortunately, its successful conclusion contributed to the widespread conviction that financial crises, the business cycle in general, were vanquished parts of our historical legacy, appropriately relegated to a place in the "dustbin." A more modest conclusion drawn from the past – namely that committing large sums of money for the orderly reorganization of banking activities in a crisis *may* end up costing much less than the original commitment and *may* represent a much cheaper alternative than doing nothing – was too rarely evoked in the heat of public debates. As Billings and Capie argued here, at the very least, highly capitalized and liquid banks have more time to work out problems than highly leveraged ones.

Conclusion

Making public policy based on historical analogy is a seductive practice, fraught with pitfalls, a fact which, as with other forms of addictive behavior, may only add to its allure. If history teaches us anything it is that events, like people, are defined by both their similarities and uniqueness. But under pressure or in distress we seem to be more prone to grope for some simple way of ordering human behavior, guiding future actions and predicting outcomes. As with people and families, just when we need to concentrate our attention and intervene, historical events splinter into a huge array of complex patterns and causal factors defying precise and reliable prediction. This in no way implies that economic historians are unable to highlight interesting patterns associated with financial crises, such as the added risk arising out of large increases in debt financing. Rather it merely suggests that economic historians should recognize the contributive perspectives of both their parent disciplines – economics and history – namely, that there is both repetition and uniqueness in events. We may learn through history how to treat financial diseases with economic policies, but the precise dosing and timing of medicines need to differ with each occurrence.

One of the essential lessons of history is that crises come and go. This lesson may seem painfully obvious, but those who have studied manias and panics should be struck with how investors and regulators forget that bubbles burst when their animal juices are flowing in a mania, and that they end when they despair during the panic. Some recent books use the current crisis as evidence of the end of Western Civilization (Moyo, 2011). Oddly, the same author writes incorrectly that "The past fifty years have been the longest period in the history of man without a major world conflict destroying plant, property, and people," forgetting simultaneously the long 19th century (1815-1914) and the recovery of the West after the Great Depression and World War II, the "long fifty-year revival," that count as evidence against her own thesis about the end of the West (Moyo, 2011, p.192). Both the factual mistake and prediction based on extrapolation from the recent past evidence lack a balanced historical perspective.

Avoiding extrapolation is precisely what I hope to have achieved here by discussing several financial crises of the last century. My choice, though international in scope, is skewed toward the United States for several reasons. The first is that for much of the past 100 years most financial crises, like this one, seem to have been bred in the United States. America for all its economic strengths has a rather checkered, to be generous, history of regulating financial markets and a low capacity for controlling populist sentiment, two causally connected features of the American landscape. Second, for most of the past 100 years the vast size of the American economy in general and its financial markets in particular have ensured that most of U.S. strengths and weaknesses have had a global reach.

These short histories of financial crises are not intended to be comprehensive. Although financial crises do share some common patterns, I hope to show that they have many contours, that is, causes, duration, depths and cures, which have to be carefully considered before we make policy. To be sure, the facts are selected to illustrate those points. Some were precipitated by external shocks that had nothing to do with finance; others had their origin in the financial system. In fact, it helps illustrate how little we really know going into a crisis and about their short- and long-term consequences; in short, the dangers of rushing to judgment.

Knowing what is happening and what is important as it is happening is almost impossible. Actions almost always have unintended consequences. Crises can turn out worse or better than they appear at first blush, as evidenced by the S&L and LTCM experiences, which did not bring down our financial system as some feared. But what we perceive is happening at any time can have as much influence on events as actual conditions, perhaps more (Soros, 2008). The future is difficult to predict, in part, because our perceptions of what is going on, which is both a reflection of reality and something based on our own interests and predilections, affect the underlying economic reality as much or more than the reality itself, a long-known truth that George Soros, an enormously successful hedge fund manager, calls "reflexivity" (Soros, 2008). Over-as well as under-reaction to events can make a crisis more severe. While sober analysis and knowledge of history are no panacea, their absence – especially in the context of unabashedly seeking political advantage, a desire to sell media time or space, or worse still a propensity to manipulate markets for greater profit – is particularly harmful because it undermines the whole system. So too, is uncritical faith in markets, governments, or financial and economic theory and models, perhaps all symptoms of decline in belief and the need to re-establish social meaning and purpose. But whatever our sentiments become, they are part of the economic reality. A measured response and public assurance coupled with behind the scenes actions, moreover, helps subdue fears that themselves ignite panic; a fact which J.P. Morgan appreciated better in 1907 – or whose interest lay in appreciating it – than many politicians, business leaders and other pundits do today. Given the current sense of trauma and what some forecasts indicate is yet to come, further postponement of a financial day of reckoning seems to pose unimaginable risk. As with so many things, readjustment is painful and generally becomes more difficult the longer that it is postponed.

Even though we had several advantages going into this crisis, which government and business leaders did not have in 1931, we have at least two issues which make dealing with the crisis very hard. The first is the huge power and lack of effective transparency of financial institutions, despite hundreds of pages of accounting documents, the readers of which – and I daresay even writers – do not fully understand. One of the core elements of this crisis is the degree to which banks and other financial markets have created internal, cross-border financial markets, circumventing market pricing and clearing mechanisms, thereby creating a morass of instruments whose specificity defy valuation and control. Not only does finance absorb a much larger portion of world product than it did say in 1907, it does so behind the corporate veil and beyond the effective reach of domestic regulations.

This regulatory blind spot combined with an ever-growing lack of responsibility on the part of not only financial leaders, but also their regulators, politicians and the man on the street creates an environment in which irresponsibility is rewarded. While journalists, politicians and their constituents rail, with a great deal of justification, about the culture of greed, few recognize how the unchecked expectations of the masses and capitalists together reinforce one another to create a political culture designed to avoid pain and to postpone confrontation with unwelcome truths.

Perhaps understandably after nearly twenty years of growth, in part furthered by financial innovation and freedom, we forget that innovation and freedom have their price. This is not to say that we cannot do better, but at the very least we must begin with a better understanding of the strengths and weakness of the system that has brought the world unparalleled prosperity. Both the bankers and borrowers deluded themselves that anything was possible, including blatantly unsustainable financial instruments and asset price growth. Each in his own way wants freedom without the responsibility of keeping himself in check. Compare the bankers' lack of social responsibility in 2008 with those bankers of 1907, who stepped in to save a system from problems they themselves had created. Moreover, with banks using the crisis to restore old businesses and profitability with high interest rates, perversely they and their regulators may have the same effect as central banks did in 1930s, namely choking off credit precisely when it should be made easier to acquire. The bankers feel, with some justification, that they can use their huge economic weight to force a government bailout, the same way the masses of people use their political weight to do the same. As government intervention becomes the norm, few seem worried about the safety of the entire system, the huge economic, political and social effects of failing to address each segment's own shortcomings. While we ostensibly work towards unwinding the debt which helped get us into this precarious position, we replace the private forms with public, as if that changes the level of debt. Instead of saving and investing in goods and activities that will really create the productivity gains necessary for sustainable growth of our living standards, increased consumption is offered as a political bribe and social palliative. Not surprisingly many of those who unquestioningly enjoyed the fruits of excessive borrowing made possible by an overly complex and under regulated financial architecture are now equally impatient with its defects. Continuing to socialize risk and privatize gain across broad social strata is moral hazardousness as well as intellectual laziness applied on a system-wide scale.

Notes

1 *The Economist*, November 8, 2008, p. 84. Gross National Product numbers are notoriously subject to a great deal of interpretation, and definitions of terms like recession and depression hard to pin down. Nevertheless, the banking crisis hit at a time when the world economy, despite high commodity prices, was relatively robust. This does not imply that forecasts of doom and gloom for 2009 are wrong, but it is useful to remember the track record of economic forecasters for this crisis as well as myriad other up- and downturns in economic growth.

2 (Berghahn, 1989, p. 284) and (Morrison, 1965, pp. 942-943) for the statistics.

3 (Kindleberger, 1993) has only a few pages on the crisis and those devoted mostly to Italy and Spain. The same is true of his *Manias, Panics, and Crashes: A History of Financial Crisis.* Walton and Rockoff in their *History of the American Economy* (1998) devote a few sentences

to the 1907 Panic. A very recent study (Bruner and Carr, 2007) has done a lot to correct this lacuna in the literature.

4 (Kobrak, 2008, pp. 152-156) The crisis spread like wildfire, in part because of new media giants' ability to publish all over the nation.

5 (Carosso, 1987, pp. 547-549) Carosso cites evidence that Morgan even lost money because of the crisis, but even many of his banking brethren had already begun to fear his extraordinary power.

6 Even the U.S. economy grew on a per capita basis at approximately the same rate from 1971 to 1984 that it had from 1945 to 1971. Cambridge, Historical Statistics, CJ.

7 (Ferguson, 2008 pp. 199-211).

8 (Erturk 2008, p. 8).

References

Almunia, et al. (2010). From the Great Depression to Great Credit Crisis: Similarities, Differences, and Lessons, *Economic Policy, 25*(62), 219-265.

Atack, Jeremy, and Neal, Larry, eds. (2009). *The Origins and Development of Financial Markets and Institutions from the Seventeenth Century to the Present.* Cambridge: Cambridge University Press.

Berghahn, V.R. (1989). *Modern Germany: Society, Economy and Politics in the Twentieth Century.* Cambridge: Cambridge University Press.

Bordo, Michael D. and Haubrich, Joseph G. (2012). Deep Recessions, Fast Recoveries, and Financial Crises: Evidence from the American Record, Federal Reserve Bank of Cleveland, Working Paper, www.clevelandfed.org/research.

Bruner, Robert F. and Carr, Sean D. (2007). *The Panic of 1907: Lessons Learned from the Market's Perfect Storm.* Hoboken: John Wiley & Sons.

Carosso, Vincent P. (1987). *The Morgans: Private International Bankers, 1854-1913.* Cambridge, MA: Harvard University Press.

Cassis, Youssef. (2012). *Crisis and Opportunities: The Shaping of Modern Finance.* Oxford: Oxford University Press.

Claenssens, Stijn, et al. (2010). The Global Financial Crisis: How Similar? How Different? How Costly? *Journal of Asian Economics, 21*, 247-264.

Desai, Padma. (2011). *From Financial Crisis to Global Recovery.* New York: Columbia University Press.

Eichengreen, Barry. (2007). *The European Economy Since 1945: Coordinated Capitalism and Beyond.* Princeton: Princeton University Press.

Engelen, Ewald, et al. (2011). *After the Great Complacence: Financial Crisis and the Politics of Reform.* Oxford: Oxford University Press.

Erturk, Ismail. (2008). *Financialization at Work: Key Texts and Commentary.* London: Routledge.

Ferguson, Niall. (2008). *The Ascent of Money: A Financial History of the World.* New York: Penguin Books.

Financial Crisis Inquiry Commission. (2011). *The Financial Crisis Inquiry Report.* Washington, D.C., GPO.

Flandreau, Marc. (2012). The vanishing banker. *Financial History Review, 19*(1), 1-19.

Fridenson, Patrick. (2004). Business Failure and the Agenda of Business History, *Enterprise & Society, 5* 562-582.

Friedman, Jeffry, ed. (2011). *What Caused the Financial Crisis.* Philadelphia: University of Pennsylvania.

Friedman, Jeffry. (2006). *Global Capitalism: Its Fall and Rise in the Twentieth* Century. New York: Norton and Company.

Greenspan, Alan. (2007). *The Age of Turbulence: Adventures in a New World*. New York: Penguin.

Haldane, Andrew G. and Alessandri, Piergiorgio. (2009). Banking on the State, Twelve Annual International Banking Conference, Chicago, September 25.

Horan, Peg, and Ononiwu, Ifeanyi Timothy. (2010). Centennial Repeat of History: Testing the Veracity of Reinhart and Rogoff Model. *Review of Business*, *31*(1), 98-110.

James, Harold. (2009). *The Creation and Destruction of Value: The Globalization Cycle*. Cambridge, MA.: Harvard University Press.

James, Harold and Kobrak, Christopher. (2010). From International to Transnational Finance: The New Face of Global Capital Markets. Working Paper, Infiniti Conference 2011.

Johnson, Simon, and Kwak, James. (2010). *13 Bankers: The Wall Street Takeover and the Next Financial Meltdown*. New York: Vintage Books.

Kindleberger, Charles P. and Aliber, Robert Z. (2011). *Manias, Panics and Crashes: A History of Financial Crises*, sixth edition. New York: Palgrave Macmillan.

Kindleberger, Charles P. (1993). *A History of Western Europe*. Oxford: Oxford University Press.

King, Lawrence, et al. (2012). Making the same mistake again – or is *this time* different? *Cambridge Journal of Economics*, *36*(1) 1-15.

Kobrak, Christopher. (2008). *Banking on Global Markets: Deutsche Bank and the United States, 1870 - Present*. Cambridge: Cambridge University Press.

Kohn, Meir. (1994). *Financial Institutions and Markets*. New York: McGraw Hill.

Krugman, Paul. (2012). How to End this Depression. *The New York Review of Books* (May).

Krugman, Paul. (1997). *The Age of Diminished Expectations*. Cambridge: MA.: MIT Press)

Lewis, Michael. (2010). *The Big Short: Inside the Doomsday Machine*. New York: W.W. Norton.

McClean, Bethany, and Nocera, Joe. (2010). *All the Devils are Here: The Hidden History of the Financial Crisis*. London: Penguin.

Morgenson, Gretchen, and Rosner, Joshua. (2011). *Reckless Endangerment: How Outsized Ambition, Greed, and Corruption Led to Economic Armageddon*. New York: Time Books.

Morrison, Samuel Eliot. (1965). *The Oxford History of the American People*. Oxford: Oxford University Press.

Moyo, Dambisa. (2011). *How the West was Lost: Fifty Years of Economic Folly – and the Stark Choices Ahead*. New York: Farrar, Strauss and Giroux.

Neal, Larry. (2011). A Reading List for Economic Historians on the Great Recession of 2007-2009: Its Causes and Consequences. *The Journal of Economic History*, *71*(4) 1095-1102.

Nietzsche, Friedrich. (1996, first published under a different title in 1873). *Vom Nutzen und Nachteil der Historie für das Leben*. Munich: Die Taschenbibliothek.

North, Douglass C. (1990). *Institutions, Institutional Change and Economic Performance*. Cambridge: Cambridge University Press.

Overy, Richard. (2009). *The Morbid Age: Britain Between the Wars*. London: Allen Lane.

Rajan, Raghuram. (2010). *Fault Lines: How Hidden Fractures Still Threaten the World Economy*. Princeton, Princeton University Press.

Reinhart, Carmen M. and Rogoff, Kenneth S. (2009). *This Time is Different: Eight Centuries of Financial Folly*. Princeton: Princeton University Press.

Reinhart, M. Carmen. (2012). A Series of Unfortunate Events: Common Sequencing Patterns in Financial Crises. NBER Working Paper No. 17941.

Romer, Christiana D. (2011). A Financial Crisis Needn't Be a Noose. *New York Times Economic Review*, December 17.

Rose, Mary Toner. (2012). An Overlooked Central Bank Rescue: How the Bank of France Ended the American Panic of 1907. Working Paper, Infiniti Conference, Dublin, 2012.

Roubini, Nouriel and Mihm, Stephen. (2010). *Crisis Economics: A Crash Couse in the Future of Finance*. New York: Penguin Press.

Roubini, Nouriel. (2006). Why Central Banks Should Burst Bubbles. *International Finance*, *9*, 87-107.

Shiller, Robert J. (2003). *The New Financial Order Risk in the 21st Century.* Princeton: Princeton University Press.

Shiller, Robert J. (2008). *The Subprime Solution: How Today's Financial Crisis Happened, and What to Do about it.* Princeton: Princeton University Press.

Sims, Christopher A. (2012). Statistical Modeling of Monetary Policy and its Effects, Working Paper, http://creativeeconomics.org/licenses/by-nc-sa/3.0/

Skidelsky, Robert. (2009). *Keynes: The Return of the Master.* New York: Public Affairs.

Soros, George. (2008). *The New Paradigm for Financial Markets: The Credit Crisis of 2008 and What It Means.* New York: Public Affairs.

Stiglitz, Joseph E. (2010). *Free Fall: America, Free Markets, and the Sinking of the World Economy.* New York: Norton.

Tett, Gillian. (2009). *Fool's Gold: How the Bold Dream of a Small Tribe at J.P. Morgan Was Corrupted by Wall Street Greed and Unleashed a Catastrophe.* New York: Free Press.

The Economist, Lessons of the 1930s. (December 10, 2011).

The Financial Times, May 14, 2012 and through July 2012.

Vinokurova, Natalya. (2012). The 2008 Mortgage Crisis as a Failure of Analogical Reasoning. Working Paper, BHC, Philadelphia, 2012.

Walton, Gary M. and Rockoff, Hugh. (1998). *History of the American Economy.* Fort Worth: Dryden.

Zappia, Carlo. (2012). Re-reading Keynes after the crisis: probability and decision. Working Paper, Università degli Studi Di Siena.

Index

Note: references to Tables appear in bold type

ROUTLEDGE

Other titles from Routledge

The Global Economic Crisis and East Asian Regionalism

Edited by Saori Katada

Regional cooperation in East Asia on various issue areas, such as emergency liquidity mechanisms in finance, the exponential growth of free trade agreements and policy coordination on the environment and public health, developed rapidly after the Asian Financial Crisis. A decade later, the global financial crisis offered a new opportunity for the nascent regional cooperation mechanisms to acquire new depth and meaning - this time, however, in a very different context due to the unfaltering rise of China. How have inter-state cooperation mechanisms, which were devised originally to deal with the problems of the past crisis, fared in the recent global economic turbulence? Can regional integration effectively insulate East Asia from the vagaries of the international market? Should East Asian nations heed the call for *regionalism* or *globalism*?

This volume not only offers one of the first assessments of how the global economic crisis has affected the prospects for regional integration in East Asia, but it also addresses a number of long-standing debates of interest to East Asian specialists, economists and policymakers: Are crises catalysts for revamping developmental models? Do they provide solid foundations for regional solidarity and integration?

This book was originally published as a special issue of *The Pacific Review*.

May 2012: 234x156: 120pp
Hb: 978-0-415-525800
£85 / $140

Studies in the History of Public Economics

Edited by Gilbert Faccarello and Richard Sturn

Many important economic and political debates today refer to the nature and the role of the State: should governments intervene in the economy and interfere with the operation of markets? In which occasions, and how? In order to better understand these questions and the controversies they have raised, this book re-considers the debates crucial for the issues at stake, the most important schools of thought, and the central concepts in an historical perspective. After a tribute to Sir Alan Peacock and the first publication of two hitherto unpublished papers written in the 1950s, the chapters focus on important developments that occurred in Europe during the 19th and early 20th centuries. The final part includes contributions on public economics after World War II, focusing on concepts such as merit goods, externalities and the "Coase theorem".

This book was originally published as a special issue of *The European Journal of the History of Economic Thought*.

December 2011: 234 x 156: 592pp
Hb: 978-0-415-69514-5
£110 / $175

Related titles from Routledge

The Economic and Social Regulation of Public Utilities

An International History

Edited by Judith Clifton, Pierre Lanthier and Harm Schröter Wilkins

Utilities are essential for societies, supplying basic services for nations, organizations and households alike. The proper functioning and regulation of utilities is critical for the economy, society and security. History provides an invaluable insight into important issues of the economic and social regulation of utilities and offers guidance for future debates. However, the history of utility regulation – which speaks of changing, diverse and complex experiences around the world – was sidelined or marginalised when economists and policymakers enthusiastically embraced the question of how to reform the utilities from the 1970s. This book examines the complex regulation and deregulation of energy, communications, transportation and water utilities across Western Europe, the United States, Australia, Brazil, China and India. In each case, attention is drawn to the changing roles of the state, the market and firms in the regulation, organization and delivery of utility services.

This book was originally published as a special issue of *Business History*.

September 2012: 246 x 174: 192pp
Hb: 978-0-415-62298-1
£85 / $135